Ethnicity and the long-term perspective
The African experience

CEAUP Studies on Africa

Volume 1

Series editors:

Alexander Keese
João Carlos Garcia
Maciel Santos

Centro de Estudos Africanos U. P.
Faculdade de Letras da Universidade do Porto
Via Panorâmica s/n
4150-564 Porto

PETER LANG
Bern • Berlin • Bruxelles • Frankfurt am Main • New York • Oxford • Wien

Alexander Keese (ed.)

Ethnicity and the long-term perspective

The African experience

PETER LANG
Bern • Berlin • Bruxelles • Frankfurt am Main • New York • Oxford • Wien

Bibliographic information published by Die Deutsche Nationalbibliothek
Die Deutsche Nationalbibliothek lists this publication in the Deutsche Nationalbibliografie; detailed bibliographic data is available on the Internet at ‹http://dnb.d-nb.de›.

British Library and Library of Congress Cataloguing-in-Publication Data:
A catalogue record for this book is available from The British Library, Great Britain.

Library of Congress Cataloging-in-Publication Data

Ethnicity and the long-term perspective : the African experience / Alexander Keese, ed. -- 1st ed.
p. cm. – (CEAUP studies in Africa ; v. 1)
Includes bibliographical references.
ISBN 978-3-0343-0337-8 (alk. paper)
1. Ethnicity–Zambezi River Valley. 2. Zambezi River Valley–Ethnic relations. 3. Ethnicity–Tanzania. 4. Tanzania–Ethnic relations. 5. Ethnicity–Senegambia. 6. Senegambia–Ethnic relations. 7. Group identity–Zambezi River Valley. 8. Group identity–Senegambia. 9. Group identity–Tanzania.
I. Keese, Alexander.
GN659.M6E86 2010
305.8009678–dc22

2009042675

This project received generous support from Euresearch, Switzerland, and CEAUP, Porto.
All maps appearing are based on original grids being Courtesy of the Perry Castañeda Library, University of Texas, Austin.

ISBN 978-3-0343-0337-8
ISSN 1663-3059

Printed in Switzerland

ALEXANDER KEESE

Preface

This volume is the fruit of a conference held in Porto, Portugal, on 23 and 24 February 2007. Already this conference was characterised by the most fertile of all types of academic exchange: intensive, critical and controversial discussion. If the debate on ethnicity in sub-Saharan Africa has over a long period been characterised by a rather aggressive and sometimes perhaps even dogmatic undertone, it can be hoped that scholarly exchange has now reached a different level. The contributions to this volume, elaborated on the basis of the 2007 conference, can be expected to feed into this new atmosphere – if not of consensus, as Carola Lentz and, in this volume, Paul Nugent have recently claimed – than at least of a more balanced and more empirically oriented debate.

The publication of this volume would not have been possible without the constant support of key members of the Centro de Estudos Africanos da Universidade do Porto (CEAUP). I am particularly grateful to the centre's director, Elvira Mea Azevedo Cunha, for the confidence in my organisational work, and the encouragement she repeatedly gave, and to Maciel Morais Santos, CEAUP's vice-director, for the engagement and assistance in the organisation and realisation of the event. Christian Windler from the University of Berne created the environment in which my engagement as co-ordinator of this conference and book project was possible, while I was still a lecturer at that Swiss university. The publication of the book was possible through financial support by the University of Berne (fund for successful European Research Council Starting Grant applications, from 2007), and by the University of Porto. A part of my own related research activity was financed through a generous grant of the Holcim Foundation, Holderbank, Switzerland.

By far my largest gratitude in the process goes, however, to Raquel Cunha, administrator of CEAUP. She has constantly been of immense help through her untiring and incredibly competent and reliable work. Without the fortunate circumstance of her presence, the successful dynamics of an expanding centre are hardly imaginable.

As far as it personally concerns the editor, I also have to thank a good number of marvellous friends, among whom I will mention those who were particularly helpful conversation partners and company in the process – namely Maria-Lêda Oliveira, Olaf Schlunke, and Marc Althoff. Finally, I am indebted to my mother, Gerda Keese; and Beatriz Valverde Contreras has been at my side during all the months and years of the production process of this volume, and I am grateful for her love and support.

This book – or at least the editor's contribution to it – is dedicated to the wonderful Camille Evrard, for being the good soul of the conference, and as vivid sign of the fact that perseverance in academic work, namely in African studies, can bring with it a most precious gift, which is friendship.

Contents

PART 2: Coastal West Africa

List of Maps

Alexander Keese*

Introduction

If the interested reader had a subject to choose that might be regarded as most discussed whenever the international public focuses on the African continent, ethnic conflict would score very high. Debates on poverty and on development in sub-Saharan Africa have partly lost their attraction, particularly because economic improvement has stagnated for decades in many African countries. Ethnic strife is more recent as a subject of broad discussions. The newly won sad prominence of this topic is easily explained by the fact that mass murder under the cover of ethnic conflict has claimed extreme numbers of victims. Violence between ethnic groups is held responsible for the death of some 3 million persons in the last 15 years, if we combine the (conservative) estimates for Central Africa and Sudan. The brutal results of inter-community bloodshed in those regions are particularly severe even in comparison with the atrocities committed in other inter-state or civil wars, including those in the Balkans and in the Middle East. Concepts of group identities have also played an important role in the explanation of violence in those latter two regions of conflict. However, those struggles were rarely labelled as exclusively 'ethnic' conflicts, although commentators used the concept of 'ethnic cleansing'.[1] The experiences of the region of the Great Lakes and of Darfur have been so extreme that they easily overshadowed all similar developments outside of Africa.[2]

Ethnicity, as a factor of political and group relations in sub-Saharan Africa, is thus omnipresent in contemporary media coverage. Apart from

* CEAUP, University of Porto, Portugal.

1 As discussed in comparative analysis of political scientists, see Harff, Barbara, 'No Lessons Learned from the Holocaust? Assessing Risks of Genocide and Political Mass Murder since 1955', *American Political Science Review* 97(1), pp. 57–73.

2 See, among others, Newbury, David, 'Understanding Genocide', *African Studies Review* 41(1), 1998, pp. 73–97.

the spectacular cases mentioned above, conflict has occurred in many, if not in a majority of post-colonial African states. These conflicts frequently involved groups calling themselves and being called 'ethnic groups'. If we regard the whole of sub-Saharan Africa, the results of group tension in the colonial and post-colonial periods have been divergent but in many circumstances its effects were significant. In some states, this even led to mass murder, and to so-called 'ethnic cleansing', but we also have to consider more sporadic outbreaks of violence, attempts of one group to oust the other from political power, and other similar tendencies.

Rwanda and Burundi were, from 1994, the two cases that absorbed most of the international attention. In relation to the assassination of Rwandan President Juvénal Habyarimana on 6 April 1994, groups of armed Hutu militants killed hundreds of thousands of Tutsi inhabitants of the small but densely populated country of Rwanda.[3] Tutsi-led Rwandan insurgents intervened and took power in Kigali, before attacking the Hutu militiamen and Hutu civilians who fled to neighbouring Congo-Kinshasa, the whole campaign being defined by the media as retaliation on ethnic grounds. Those bloody events were in addition to violence between Tutsi-speaking Banyarmalange and other ethno-cultural groups in Eastern Congo, and were linked to similar conflicts in neighbouring Burundi.[4] In some respects, the struggles of the 1990s followed an ideology that relied on more ancient patterns of legitimisation of violence in the area of the Great Lakes. The justification of group violence through the alleged political marginalisation of involved groups had already been employed from the late 1950s.[5] In that earlier period, a Hutu movement in decolonising Rwanda had profited from the power vacuum left by the

3 Melvern, Linda, *Conspiracy to murder: the Rwandan genocide* (London: Verso, 2004); Reyntjens, Filip, *Rwanda: trois jours qui ont fait basculer l'histoire* (Brussels: Institut africain – CEDAF – Paris: Harmattan, 1995).

4 Willaume, Jean-Claude, *Banyarwanda et Banyamulenge: violence et gestion de l'identitaire au Kivu* (Brussels: Institut africain – CEDAF – Paris: L'Harmattan, 1997); Braeckman, Colette, *Terreur africaine: Burundi, Rwanda, Zaïre, les racines de la violence* (Paris: Fayard, 1996).

5 Nugent, Paul, *Africa since Independence* (Basingstoke: Palgrave Macmillan, 2004), pp. 55–56.

retreat of the Belgian colonial power to overthrow the ruling dynasty, regarded as 'Tutsi' by the rebels.[6]

Or so it seems. As a result of what has been added by historical and political science research, the picture becomes far more complicated.[7] Serious doubts had been formulated already in the 1980s concerning the salience of a Hutu–Tutsi antagonism in Rwanda and Burundi from a historical point of view. At least, one can be sceptical about the existence of a 'traditional' ethnic distinction of 'Tutsiness' and 'Hutuness'.[8] While this question remains subject to academic debate, we have to accept the possibility that, originally, one cannot separate 'Hutu' from 'Tutsi' on grounds of cultural difference. Filip Reyntjens rightly insisted on a second, more contemporary constraint regarding the ethno-cultural dimension of hostilities in Rwanda: during the events of 1994, marauding 'Hutu' militiamen also killed thousands of 'Hutus', including particularly those who had helped their alleged 'Tutsi' neighbours, but also many who would be murdered just in order to pillage their compounds. From that perspective, the genocide was thus not an exclusive genocide against Tutsi, but mass murder of civilians by groups of marauders.[9]

Côte d'Ivoire is another example of the multiple, overlapping, and complex interrelations that appear in recent African conflicts of a type frequently characterised as 'ethnic'. At first glance, the Ivorian frontlines seem to be clearly those of an ethnic group conflict. The opponents are, apparently, southern ethno-cultural groups, particularly the 'Baule', and northern ethnic groups, the latter having organised the army revolt that led to *de facto* secession of the Bouaké region from 2002 to 2007.[10] This being

6 Prunier, Gérard, *The Rwanda Crisis, 1959–1994: History of a Genocide* (London: Hurst, 1997); Chrétien, Jean-Pierre, *Le défi de l'ethnisme: Rwanda et Burundi, 1990–1996* (Paris: Karthala, 1997).

7 Cooper, Frederick, *Africa since 1940: The Past of the Present* (Cambridge: Cambridge University Press, 2002), pp. 1–3.

8 Gahama, Joseph, and Augustin Mvuyekure, 'Jeu ethnique, idéologie missionnaire et politique coloniale. Le cas du Burundi', in Jean-Pierre Chrétien and Gérard Prunier (eds.), *Les ethnies ont une histoire* (Paris: 2nd edn Karthala, 2003), pp. 303–324, 309.

9 Reyntjens, Filip, 'Rwanda, Ten Years on: From Genocide to Dictatorship', *African Affairs* 103(411), 2004, pp. 177–210, 178.

10 Banégas, Richard, 'Côte d'Ivoire: Patriotism, Ethnonationalism and other African Modes of Self-Writing', *African Affairs* 105(421), 2006, pp. 535–552, 541–544.

said, the conflict in Côte d'Ivoire was also over resource allocation, those resources concerning regional more than community disparities. Moreover, the Ivorian northerners were suspected of being devout Muslims attempting to establish Islamic rule in a country that is mixed in its religious composition. Also, the national dimension played a role in the conflict.[11] In many cases, southern groups such as Baule, Agni and Abure identified themselves as 'Ivoiriens' in contrast to Mossi settlers who are (in many cases erroneously) regarded as 'Burkinabè' (nationals of Burkina Faso) and thus still more distant than the average Ivorian northerner.[12]

This role of 'national' criteria as shown for the case of Côte d'Ivoire is, at first glance, an intriguing aspect of the whole complex of ethnic conflict. The occasional and seemingly selective use of 'the nation' as a point of reference in countries where, 'normally', ethnic antagonisms were the most important aspect of internal post-colonial politics is, nonetheless, a typical phenomenon. In the Ivorian case, it appears already at the end of the colonial period. In 1958, shortly before the French government transferred formal autonomy to the territory of Côte d'Ivoire, hundreds of members of different ethno-cultural groups (but now defining themselves as 'Ivoiriens') assembled to start manhunts of immigrants coming from the French territories of Dahomey and Togo, which were also soon to become independent states. While the Ivorian society was highly dispersed in ethnic self-identification already in the 1950s, it was simple and sufficient to formulate a concept of *ivoirité* to oust 'foreign' groups of job rivals (and to harm them physically, if necessary).[13] The same phenomena can be found in West Central Af-

11 Cappell, David A., 'The Nation as Frontier: Ethnicity and Clientelism in Ivorian History', *International Journal of African Historical Studies* 22(4), 1989, pp. 671–696, 682–684.

12 Colin, Jean-Philippe; Georges Kouamé, and Débégnoun Soro, 'Outside the autochthon-migrant configuration: access to land, land conflicts and inter-ethnic relationships in a former pioneer area of lower Côte d'Ivoire', *Journal of Modern African Studies* 45(1), 2007, pp. 33–59, 49.

13 Centre des Archives d'Outre-Mer, Aix-en-Provence (CAOM), FM 1AffPol/2188/6, Cabinet of the French Overseas Ministry, Bureau of Studies, *Note de Renseignements: Incidents de Côte d'Ivoire* (without number), 30 Dec. 1958; CAOM, FM 1AffPol/2188/6, Spénale, French Commissioner of Togo, to Messmer, French High-Commissioner of French West Africa (n° 677/AP.), 7 Nov. 1958.

rica, notably in the neighbouring countries of Congo-Brazzaville and Gabon. Both countries are 'ethnically heterogeneous', as it is called. However, as a result of a 1962 football match, both saw mobs formed to hunt the national 'strangers'. In this near-football-war, national identity became an attractive tool from the perspective of both governments to bring order in highly conflict-ridden societies.[14] The use of national criteria as criteria of group affiliation is of course easier to realise if the victims of exclusion are minorities that have a visible background story. This concerns migrants from Asia, such as the Lebanese in West Africa or 'Indians' in East and Southeast Africa.[15] Moreover, sociological surveys have shown that in some border areas, locals have far more sympathies and feelings of solidarity for national compatriots with a different ethno-cultural identity, than for members of the same ethnic group who are citizens of a different state.[16]

In South Africa, (a part of) 'the Zulu nation' distances itself from central government and from the post-Apartheid state through ethnic propaganda.[17] In this case, ethnicity is not applied as a criterion mutually compatible with statehood, but as an exclusive factor. However, while the South African experience of KwaZulu-Natal is instructive for the power that ethnic affiliation can have as a base of state affiliation, the formulation of 'Zuluness' has to be understood, first of all, as a means of mobilisation in a genuinely political struggle.

14 Ministère des Affaires Etrangères, Paris (MAE), DAM, Gabon, 2081, French Foreign Ministry, Directorate of African and Malagasy Affairs, *Note [sur] les incidents Congo-Gabon (Septembre 1962)* (without number), without date [1962].

15 Akyeampong, Emmanuel K., 'Race, Identity and Citizenship in Black Africa: the Case of the Lebanese in Ghana', *Africa (London)* 76(3), 2006, pp. 297–323, 315–316; Keese, Alexander, 'Colons français, politiciens africains et marchands libanais au Sénégal colonial', *Africa (Roma)* 60(2), 2005, pp. 201–220, 216; Power, Joey, 'Race, Class, Ethnicity, and Anglo-Indian Trade Rivalry in Colonial Malawi, 1910–1945', *International Journal of African Historical Studies* 26(3), 1993, pp. 575–607, 578.

16 Miles, William F.S., and David Rochefort, 'Nationalism versus Ethnic Identity in sub-Saharan Africa', *American Political Science Review* 85(2), 1991, pp. 393–403, 400–401.

17 Coquerel, Paul, 'Les Zulu dans l'Afrique du Sud contemporaine. Le mouvement Inkatha Yenkulelo YeSizwe: Ethnicité et lutte de libération', in Jean-Pierre Chrétien and Gérard Prunier (eds.), *Les ethnies ont une histoire* (Paris: 2nd edn Karthala, 2003), pp. 417–425.

After 'nation', 'race' is a second aspect that has to be discussed in its relation to group identities, and to 'ethnicity', in sub-Saharan Africa. From the point of view of Western observers, situations seem to be dominated by ethnic conflict in an even clearer way if 'racial factors' are involved, the latter being frequently associated with skin colour. This is the case in regions such as Darfur in Sudan or the *Fleuve* regions of Southern Mauritania. In Darfur, the media report on an 'ethnic conflict' between 'Arabs' and 'Dinka'. The underlying idea of this claim is that ethnicity, in the particular case of Sudan, can indeed be defined through 'race', thus describing a scenario in which the 'Arab' Janjaweed, nomad raiders, pillage and plunder in the regions of the 'African' Fur. This scenario seems to lead, in the absence of regulatory efforts of the central government in Khartum, to 'racial' mass murder or even genocide.[18] The corresponding model obtains some support from the fact that during centuries of prosperous slave trade in Sudan, the Black Africans were indeed the more likely target of slave-raiding activities.[19] In Mauritania, the situation seems similar except the comparatively far less violent forms of conflict occurring nowadays. Black Africans in the south of the North-West African country were for long the principal victims of slave-raiding, and they would frequently clash with the 'Arab-dominated' independent central government from the 1970s onwards.

However, even when 'race' is involved, distinctions between groups in situations of conflict are frequently not so easily formulated. In Darfur, ethnological studies have shown that individuals could quite easily traverse the frontier between nomadic 'Arab' and sedentary 'African' identity.[20] It even belonged to the local socio-economic strategies of parts of peasant families to integrate in nomadic warrior groups. Those

18 Mans, Ulrich, 'Briefing: Sudan: The new war in Darfur', *African Affairs* 103(411), 2004, pp. 291–294.

19 Leopold, Mark, 'Slavery in Sudan, Past and Present', *African Affairs* 102(409), 2003, pp. 653–661; Makris, G.P., 'Slavery, Possession and History: The Construction of the Self among Slave Descendants in the Sudan', *Africa* 66(2), 1996, pp. 159–182.

20 Haaland, Gunnar, 'Economic Determinants in Ethnic Processes', in Fredrik Barth (ed.), *Ethnic Groups and Boundaries: the social organization of cultural difference* (Bergen: Univ. Forl, 1969), pp. 58–73, 64.

are thus not homogeneously 'white'. In Mauritania, the same complexities exist as well.[21]

Group violence under ethnic labels and in the context of sub-Saharan African regions is thus a far more complex problem than it seems at first glance. This being said, we have to point out that ethnic conflict that leads to violence is only the most spectacular form in which ethnic affiliations play a role in African countries. Political scientists working on sub-Saharan Africa assume that understanding and respecting ethnic sensibilities is also critical in order to make African governments workable. According to the perspective of Donald Horowitz, only successful ethnic balancing allows for a reduction of the number of unsatisfied politicians and makes local populations less sensitive to propaganda in ethnic terms.[22] The masters of the game are called successful African statesmen: for example the long-time Ivorian president Félix Houphouët-Boigny who is said to have brought into line, in the decades of his presidency before his death in 1993, many potential claimants through his respect for the governmental representation of all the ethno-cultural groups present in the territory.[23]

Those readers who get the impression that the whole story of ethnic antagonisms as presented above is all very simple (and simplified) are probably right. At least most of the examples that are cited as 'classical' have unforeseen complexities. Even worse, those images are not very far removed from the imaginations of colonial administrators, and from so-called early anthropologists: they refer to the same idea of static, irrational 'tribal' behaviour. The historian cannot be content with such simplifications. Moreover, Wyatt MacGaffey has rightly pointed to the danger that such simplified scientific concepts whose implications are not

21 McDougall, E. Ann, 'A topsy-turvy world: slaves and freed slaves in the Mauritanian Adrar, 1910–1950', in Susanne Miers and Richard Roberts (eds.), *The end of slavery in Africa* (Madison: University of Wisconsin Press, 1988), pp. 362–388; Mark, Peter, 'The Evolution of 'Portuguese' Identity: Luso-Africans on the Upper Guinea Coast from Sixteenth to the early Nineteenth Century', *Journal of African History* 40(2), 1999, pp. 173–191, 186.

22 Horowitz, Donald L., *Ethnic Groups in Conflict* (Berkeley – London: University of California Press, 1985), pp. 601–652.

23 Chauveau, Jean-Pierre, and Jean-Pierre Dozon, 'Ethnies et Etat en Côte-d'Ivoire', *Revue Française de Science Politique* 38(5), 1988, pp. 732–747, *passim*.

rectified, are easily employed as 'scientific proof' for the propaganda of interest groups. MacGaffey focused on other myths such as the idea of Bantu migration as founding legend and as argument for local claims. However, ethnicity in itself is an analogous problem.[24]

Ethnicity is, in any way, easily misunderstood as a concept because its definition is so difficult and frequently vague.[25] Groups can be considered different on ethnic terms because of distinct language, but they need not. Ethno-cultural identity can refer to different cultural traits and practices. A common past nearly always plays a role, frequently formulated through common legends of origin and of key group events of more recent historical tradition. However, what is essential is the auto-perception of the group as we-group, in contrast to others that are *defined* as relying on other, distinct features. Those barriers are fluid and open to negotiation, while their constant use makes them become more solidified and established. It is obvious that such a rather vague concept is a challenge to rationalisation, and that attempts to rationalise from inside or from outside are attempts to simplify.

Evidently, Africa's colonial age is a principal source of such attempts at simplification. Colonial administrators trying to understand rural structures in which foreign languages, distant cultural traits and beliefs in sorcery and the supernatural (the latter being not at all uncommon to Europeans, but in contradiction to tendencies of modernisation of the administrator's mind in the late nineteenth century) were a challenge to their capacities of learning. Simplification frequently came in the guise of anthropology, but it was a natural response to very practical problems.[26]

In the period directly after conquest, in which European administrators attempted to establish structures that allowed them effective control without a considerable investment of the resources of the metropole, those perceptions of ethnicity became particularly influential. Such influence depended, of course, on the particular conjunctures of

24 MacGaffey, Wyatt, 'Changing Representations in Central African History', *Journal of African History* 46(2), 2006, pp. 189–207, 202–206.

25 Poutignat, Philippe, and Jocelyne Streiff-Fenart, *Théories de l'Ethnicité* (Paris: Presses Universitaires de France, 1995), pp. 93–95.

26 Bayart, Jean-François, *L'Etat en Afrique. La Politique du Ventre* (Paris: Fayard, 1989), pp. 77–80.

different ideologies of conquest and of legitimisation of conquest. Colonial powers that emphasised the 'mission of civilisation', the battle against African despotism, and the transfer of European cultural institutions and European knowledge to Africans, were less inclined to concede to claims of ethnic rule.[27] However, when it came to installing African chiefs, as a necessary measure of finding auxiliaries for local rule, ethnic homogeneity became nearly always a guiding principle, at least after a certain period. In the late 1920s, at last, a considerable number of so-called chieftaincies was organised according to criteria of ethnic group perception.[28]

The link between identifying ethnic groups and establishing local administration under European rule works in both directions. A number of European administrators became active in carrying out ethnographic studies. Those scholar-administrators delivered first material on group characteristics, a material that was already massively biased because of the administrative necessities that influenced the officials' point of view. From the end of the nineteenth century onwards, and then more intensely from the 1920s, the officials were accompanied in their task of categorisation by an increasingly specialised professional group of anthropologists and ethnologists. Even more, as the education of colonial administrators became in itself more professionalized from the 1900s, the latest results of anthropology also fed back into the repertoire of ideas on which the officials based their forms of governing.[29]

27 Dimier, Véronique, 'Direct or Indirect Rule: Propaganda around a Scientific Controversy', in Tony Chafer and Amanda Sackur (eds.), *Promoting the Colonial Idea. Propaganda and Visions of Empire in France* (Basingstoke: Palgrave, 2002), pp. 168–183.

28 Wooten, Stephen R., 'Colonial Administration and the Ethnography of the Family in the French Soudan', *Cahiers d'Etudes Africaines* 33(3), 1993, pp. 419–446, 431–434; Robinson, David, 'Ethnography and customary law in Senegal', *Cahiers d'Etudes Africaines* 32(126), 1992, pp. 221–237, 232–234; Van Hoven, Ed, 'Representing Social Hierarchy. Administrators-Ethnographers in the French Sudan: Delafosse, Monteil, and Labouret', *Cahiers d'Etudes Africaines* 30(2), 1990, pp. 179–198, 186–189.

29 Ginio, Ruth, 'French Colonial Reading of Ethnographic Research: The Case of the 'Desertion' of the Abron King and its Aftermath', *Cahiers d'Etudes Africaines* 42(166), 2002, pp. 337–357; Conklin, Alice, *A Mission to Civilize: the Republican Idea of Empire in France and West Africa, 1895–1930* (Stanford: Stanford University Press, 1997).

While historical processes of group development were not completely ignored, the anthropologists' perspective on Africans was mostly one of ahistorical, static and clearly distinguishable 'tribes'. Those models of practical anthropology dominated historical analysis and ethnological surveys far into the post-colonial period. In historical studies well into the 1960s, the distinction between 'tribes' was seen as given.

Those images continue to haunt political science as far as it concerns the understanding of contemporary political structures in sub-Saharan Africa. In that context the error is not to be seen in the fact that political scientists regard the political balancing between ethnic groups as a crucial factor of stability in many African countries and regions, and depict conflicts and violence running under ethnic labels as a matter of fact. Indeed, groups that describe themselves as ethnically different (and that are perceived by the international public as ethnically distinct) do obviously matter in regional politics, as we have seen from the examples given above. The problem of those interpretations (in parallel to the problem the mass media have with the understanding of ethnic tensions and ethnic balancing) is that they treat ethnic groups as something that is genuinely stable. Those interpretations do not differentiate between different phases of the existence of a we-group, nor do they take into account that features of identity can be felt or can be employed according to particular circumstances. The attitudes of political analysts and of those political scientists who operate with such a limited idea of ethnicity, are still relatively close to the image of the ahistorical 'tribes' of colonial imagination.[30]

Historians and anthropologists changed their perspective on group identity in sub-Saharan Africa in the 1970s and, particularly, in the 1980s. Most scholars agree now that ethnic groups are something fluid, subject to historical evolutions, in a constant process of renegotiation and change. This turn in historiographical debates started with a stronger focus on the historicity of ethnic group affiliations[31], as expressed in the

30 See, as one example for such schematic sociological classification, Mapp, Roberta E., 'Cross-National Dimensions of Ethnocentrism', *Canadian Journal of African Studies* 6(1), 1972, pp. 73–96.

31 The prototype of an early attempt of such re-interpretation of ethnogenesis, still in some ways relying on a more classical perspective, can be found in Gallagher,

title 'Les ethnies ont une histoire' ('Ethnic groups do have a history') used by Jean-Pierre Chrétien and his colleagues in their paradigmatic collective volume from 1989. The constructivist turn was reinforced by the results of a number of regional or local studies. Most impressive were the conclusions drawn by the contributors of the collective work *Au cœur de l'ethnie* ('At the heart of the ethnic group'), published by Jean-Loup Amselle and Elikia M'Bokolo. Their claim was most far-reaching. Drawing from a number of mostly Central African cases, these contributors identified ethnic identity as a concept imported nearly exclusively by the colonizer, and supported by some African profiteers who employed those ideas to their advantage, such as politicians of ethnic parties in parts of Congo-Kinshasa.[32]

The position of Amselle and M'Bokolo became rapidly the dominant opinion, even in its radical form. It was masterfully elaborated by Amselle who, in another book, underlined the multiple facets of identity African individuals could use. If 'mestizo logics', as the author calls them, are available to and employed by all African individuals, the European conception of 'tribe' was first misleading and second manipulative.[33] The detailed analysis of how the invention of ethnicity was carried out by the colonial state to its advantage was attempted in a third collective work, by Leroy Vail and colleagues, for the larger region of Southern Africa.[34]

The constructivist interpretation of the building of ethnic identity has been facilitated and has, in part, been stimulated by older anthropological studies and by tendencies in other parts of historical research on identity. Among the former we have to consider the observations of

---

Joseph T., 'The Emergence of an African Ethnic Group: the Case of the Ndendeuli', *International Journal of African Historical Studies* 7(1), 1974, pp. 1–26, 5.

32 See, among others, Amselle, Jean-Loup, 'Ethnies et espaces: pour une anthropologie topologique', in Jean-Loup Amselle and Elikia M'Bokolo (eds.), *Au cœur de l'ethnie: ethnies, tribalisme et État en Afrique* (Paris: La Découverte, 1985), pp. 11–48, 38–39; M'Bokolo, Elikia, 'Le 'séparatisme katangais'', in Jean-Loup Amselle and Elikiah M'Bokolo (eds.), *Cœur*, pp. 185–226, 191–193.

33 Amselle, Jean-Loup, *Logiques métisses. Anthropologie de l'identité en Afrique et ailleurs* (Paris: Payot, 1990), p. 88.

34 As is discussed in the various articles in Vail, Leroy (ed.), *The creation of tribalism in Southern Africa* (London: James Currey, 1991 [1989]). See a discussion by the editor in his introduction, pp. 10–13.

Fredrik Barth and others, who emphasised that the members of 'tribes' (in Africa and elsewhere) can rather easily shift their affiliation.[35] The creation of ethnic group identity as a process of construction is also easily brought in line with Eric Hobsbawm's and Terence Ranger's conclusion that societies can be built 'from scratch'.[36] The constructivist elements in the formulation of ethnicity can be described as a process up to some point comparable to the 'imagining of nations' formulated for the nineteenth century, as a Western phenomenon in the first instance, by Benedict Anderson.[37]

However, we have to ask if the constructivists did not go too far. They might be challenged on the grounds that they put their emphasis on the construction of 'ethnicity' because the ethnic factor does not fit at all in the (partly neo-Marxist) theoretical mainstream in research on Africa, as it was dominant in the 1980s and still powerful today.[38] Second, the constructivist explanation for the existence of ethnic identity fits very well with the moralist approach to African history. It is politically correct to claim that it was 'the colonialists', i.e. the colonial regimes, who invented and manipulated 'ethnic groups', as a strategy of divide and rule. This position does not take into account the agency of the African populations themselves, it neglects in a way their history before colonisation, it reduces their political organisation and group cohesion before European conquest to an idyllic Africa of villages and kin groups so frequently imagined by European and American (and some African) scholars.[39] In another contested field, which is the invention of chieftaincy by the colonial authorities, we have indeed passed from the mid-1990s through an important revision.

35 See Barth, Fredrik, 'Introduction', in Fredrik Barth (ed.), *Ethnic Groups and Boundaries: the social organization of cultural difference* (Bergen: Univ. Forl., 1969), pp. 9–38.

36 The collection of articles in Hobsbawm, Eric, and Terence O. Ranger (eds.), *The invention of tradition* (Cambridge: Cambridge University Press, 1984) is still essential as an introduction.

37 Anderson, Benedict, *Imagined Communities: reflections on the origin and spread of nationalism* (London: Verso, 1983), pp. 62–64.

38 Mazenot, Georges, *Evaluer la colonisation* (Paris: L'Harmattan, 1999).

39 Some thoughtful comments about the effects and the African appropriation of European social engineering can be found in Stoler, Ann Laura, and Frederick Cooper, 'Between Metropole and Colony. Rethinking a Research Agenda', in Frederick Cooper and Ann Laura Stoler (eds.), *Tensions of empire: colonial cultures in a bourgeois world* (Berkeley etc: University of California Press, 1997), pp. 1–56, 7–8.

Thomas Spear and others have shown that the participation of African populations in the elaboration of local forms of chieftaincy was immense, despite their being under colonial domination.[40] For the question of ethnogenesis, this aspect has not yet been modified to integrate more strongly the agency of African populations.

The dominance of the constructivist explanation has faded in the past twenty years. In a number of local case studies that have appeared since the publication of M'Bokolo's and Amselle's path-breaking work, researchers identified single aspects of the group identity of local populations as already existent in the pre-colonial period.[41] Nevertheless, many other works take a clear position against 'ethnicity' as a guiding principle of group formation and identify instead village alliances and family links as decisive, as in the case of the large study on the Volta Region carried out by Şaul and Royer.[42] Also, the flexibility of ethnic affiliation and its link to colonial structures and colonial manipulation is clearly held as a main point in the process of ethnogenesis, as is obvious in more recent studies, although the latter are certainly more critical about an exaggeration of the role of the colonial state in ethnic group-building.[43]

It might be optimistic, however, to follow Paul Nugent in his claim that the mainstream in historiography on ethnic group identity has

40 Spear, Thomas, 'Neo-Traditionalism and the Limits of Invention in British Colonial Africa', *Journal of African History* 44(1), 2003, pp. 3–27; Rathbone, *N'Krumah and the Chiefs: The Politics of Chieftaincy in Ghana 1951–60* (Oxford: James Currey – Accra: F. Reimer – Athens: Ohio University Press, 2000), pp. 163–164.

41 Gordon, David, 'History on the Luapula Retold: Landscape, Memory and Identity in the Kazembe Kingdom', *Journal of African History* 47(1), 2006, pp. 21–42, 40; Monson, Jamie, 'Memory, Migration and the Authority of History in Southern Tanzania, 1860–1960', *Journal of African History* 41(2), 2000, pp. 347–372, 355; Ngolet, François, 'Inventing ethnicity and identities in Gabon: the case of the Ongom (Bakele)', *Revue Française de l'Histoire d'Outre-Mer* 321, 1998, pp. 5–26, *passim*.

42 Şaul, Mahir, and Patrick Royer, *West African Challenge to Empire. Culture and History in the Volta-Bani Anticolonial War* (Athens/OH: Athens University Press – Oxford: James Currey, 2001), pp. 15–16.

43 Glassman, Jonathon, 'Sorting out the Tribes: the Creation of Racial Identities in Colonial Zanzibar's Newspaper Wars', *Journal of African History* 41(3), 2000, pp. 395–428, 401, 426.

recently converged in a broad consensus.[44] It would probably be more correct to say that most studies no longer concern themselves with the mechanism behind the creation of group solidarities. What remains is the verdict of Bruce Berman who claimed that none of the dominant or even of the *known* modern ethnic groups of contemporary times existed already as such in the pre-colonial period.[45] As there are few recent studies about the long-term evolution of concepts of identity in sub-Saharan Africa, we are still uninformed about those processes. In many cases, we know from pre-colonial travel reports that a certain ethnic label had already existed in a certain year.[46] Nevertheless, up to now there have been no real attempts to combine information to get a clearer picture of when an ethnic group started to emerge, when its members started to lay more importance on cohesion on ethnic grounds, and, particularly, *why*, that is under the influence of which motivations, this process happened.[47]

A recent book of Daniel N. Posner brought some movement in the debate about ethnic solidarity. Posner claimed, from the example of elections in Zambia, that ethnicity is defined according to circumstances, and that individuals attempt to modify their perspective if, in that way, they get increasing chances to win in the political struggle for power. Posner's focus is on a repertoire of factors that can define ethnicity, not on ethnicity as part of a repertoire of factors that are constituent for identity.[48] While his model for ethnic voting behaviour in Zambia is based on assumptions taken from decision theory that are still more difficult to prove outside the field of elections, his book has contributed enormously in stimulating the debate on identity repertoires from which

44 On Nugent's position see 'The Historicity of Ethnicity: Mandinka/Jola and Ewe/Agotime Identities in the Nineteenth and Twentieth Centuries', in this book.

45 Berman, Bruce, 'Ethnicity, Patronage and the African State: the Politics of Uncivil Nationalism', *African Affairs* 97(388), 1998, pp. 305–341, 311.

46 Horta, José da Silva, 'La Perception du Mande et de l'Identité Mandingue dans les Textes Européens, 1453–1508', *History in Africa* 23, 1996, pp. 75–86.

47 This has been carried out very rarely, with some notable exceptions, see particularly the recent publication on the Chikunda by Isaacman, Allan, and Derek Peterson, 'Making the Chikunda: Military Slavery and Ethnicity in Southern Africa, 1750–1900', *International Journal of African Historical Studies* 36(2), 2003, pp. 257–281.

48 Posner, Daniel N., *Institutions and Ethnic Politics in Africa* (Cambridge – New York – Melbourne: Cambridge University Press, 2005), pp. 21–22.

individuals and groups can choose and apply different categories, according to circumstances.

Researchers might have to take into account more profoundly the parallel existence of different categories that can co-exist with ethnic solidarities, or that might form part of ethnic identity. Already René Lemarchand had pointed to the existence of those principles, and had emphasised the fact that they do in no way constitute a 'zero-sum game', excluding one another.[49] It is promising to follow a path of analysis in which the varying employment of the different factors of group identity is regarded over a longer time period.

However, those parallel solidarities can respond as guiding principles to fundamentally distinct situations of group experience. This is particularly the case for religion, but is also valid for kinship, clan solidarities, and lineage policy. In some areas of sub-Saharan Africa, religion as a major defining principle of group cohesion is far more openly used in conflicts than ethnic affiliation. During some constellations of conflict, particularly during protracted intergenerational conflicts, ethnicity is not an appropriate principle to legitimise claims, while religious practice can obviously be such a successful guiding principle, as Felicitas Becker shows for the case of rural Islamism in Tanzania.[50] Nevertheless, religion can also be equated to ethnic group identity, as we can see for nineteenth-century Senegal. Here, in some of the central provinces of the pre-colonial state of Kajoor, villages were divided, from the perspective of both the future French coloniser and his informants, into 'Lebu' (an ethno-cultural definition) and 'Marabout' (a religious definition referring to allegiance to Muslim spiritual leaders) communities.[51]

Clan orientation is also an alternative concept to ethno-cultural solidarity. In that context, some Central and East African regions are particularly interesting, as they are subject to prolonged group migration and a

49 Lemarchand, René, 'Political Clientelism and Ethnicity in Tropical Africa: Competing Solidarities in Nation-Building', *American Political Science Review* 66(1), 1972, pp. 68–90, 83, 87.

50 Becker, Felicitas, 'Rural Islamism during the 'War on Terror': A Tanzanian Case Study', *African Affairs* 105(421), 2006, pp. 583–603, 588–589.

51 Archives Nationales Sénégalaises (ANS), GGAOF Fonds Ancien 1D17, Vincens, Chef de Génie, *Rapport sur la reconnaissance militaire exécutée dans le Diander du 24 au 27 8bre 1860* (n° 1), 15 Sept. 1860, p. 4.

sort of relatively mobile warlordism, in which bandit leaders managed to control large parts of territory and of its populations for a limited period. This is a fact for the Luapula River region in present-day Zambia, where 'the Kisabambas' remained a loose unit faced with the self-defined 'Lunda invaders', only becoming established as an ethno-cultural group under British colonial rule.[52] The scenario is similar in the Zambesi River region.[53] In both areas, ethno-cultural solidarity was, in pre-colonial times, too broad a concept to be successful, particularly as the ensemble of the populations in the area was due to permanent shifts. Ethnic labels in such regions seem to be the exclusive result of colonial attempts at classification, attempts that were not based on anything else than ad hoc collection of local names and group identifications.

Finally, we have the state as a category. Although in many cases we cannot talk of African 'states' in the sense of the 'modern' state, which means bureaucraticised and rather formalised and effective administrative structures, there are tendencies of loyalty to state institutions. Those appear to have existed already in the pre-colonial period. For an inhabitant of a certain region it could be attractive to identify primarily with the state structures that affectted more directly his everyday life. This idea of group identification with political and administrative structures, which can even be translated into adherence to a 'citizenship', is interesting yet completely under-researched, although first efforts are visible particularly for the case of Ghana.[54] It is remarkable in this context that identification with state structures need not mean that the experiences of groups with those structures are always positive. In the pre-colonial Senegalese state of Kajoor, groups tended to define themselves as

52 Gordon, David, 'Owners of the Land and Lunda Lords: Colonial Chiefs in the Borderlands of Northern Rhodesia and the Belgian Congo', *International Journal of African Historical Studies* 34(2), 2001, pp. 315–338, 324, 327.

53 Isaacman and Peterson, 'Making', p. 275; Capela, José, *Donas, senhores e escravos* (Porto: Afrontamento, 1995); Newitt, Malyn, *Portuguese Settlement on the Zambesi: Exploration, land tenure and colonial rule in East Africa* (London: Longman, 1973).

54 Rathbone, Richard, 'Defining Akyemfo: The Construction of Citizenship in Akyem Abuakwa, Ghana, 1700–1939', *Africa* 66(4), 1996, pp. 506–525, 509–512, 518.

subjects of the state and the *damel* (the 'traditional ruler') despite being regularly plundered by the *damel*'s mobile raiding units, the *ceddos*.[55]

Ethnicity is thus a concept that can coexist or overlap with other markers of group identity. As a conclusion, this brings us back to strategic choice as an essential factor in group mobilisation on ethnic terms. In recent years, several groups have also managed to obtain privileged access to the resources of NGOs by emphasising their long-standing group cohesion, which is occasionally contradicted by research and long-established tradition.[56]

While ethnic solidarities remain in the repertoire of the individual, they are not necessarily expressed in a given situation. It might even be possible to call the ethnic affiliation a 'habitus' useful and used under particular circumstances.[57] It is, however, particularly challenging to analyse under which circumstances ethnicity was used as the principal variable of the individuals' repertoire. Variations among different groups, different regions, and different time periods in sub-Saharan Africa are inevitable. The task remains, nonetheless, to analyse the broader patterns.

55 An introduction to the practices of *ceddo* administration can be found in Diouf, Mamadou, *Le Kajoor au XIXe siècle. Pouvoir ceddo et conquête coloniale* (Paris: Karthala, 1990), p. 67.

56 Igoe, Jim, 'Becoming Indigenous Peoples: Difference, Inequality, and the Globalization of East African Identity Politics', *African Affairs* 105(420), 2006, pp. 399–420, 411–412.

57 Yelvington, Kevin A., 'Ethnicity as Practice? A Comment on Bentley', *Comparative Studies in Society and History* 33(1), 1991, pp. 158–168, 159–160; Bentley, G. Carter, 'Ethnicity and Practice', *Comparative Studies in Society and History* 29(1), 1987, pp. 24–55, 27–29.

Bibliography

Akyeampong, Emmanuel K., 'Race, Identity and Citizenship in Black Africa: the Case of the Lebanese in Ghana', *Africa (London)* 76(3), 2006, pp. 297–323.

Amselle, Jean-Loup, 'Ethnies et espaces: pour une anthropologie topologique', in Jean-Loup Amselle and Elikia M'Bokolo (eds.), *Au cœur de l'ethnie: ethnies, tribalisme et État en Afrique* (Paris: La Découverte, 2006), pp. 11–48.

Amselle, Jean-Loup, *Logiques métisses. Anthropologie de l'identité en Afrique et ailleurs* (Paris: Payot, 1990).

Anderson, Benedict, *Imagined Communities: Reflections on the Origin and Spread of Nationalism* (London: Verso, 1983).

Banégas, Richard, 'Côte d'Ivoire: Patriotism, Ethnonationalism and other African Modes of Self-Writing', *African Affairs* 105(421), 2006, pp. 535–552.

Barth, Fredrik, 'Introduction', in Fredrik Barth (ed.), Ethnic Groups and Boundaries: the social organization of cultural difference (Bergen: Univ. Forl., 1969), pp. 9–38.

Bayart, Jean-François, *L'Etat en Afrique. La Politique du Ventre* (Paris: Fayard, 1989).

Becker, Felicitas, 'Rural Islamism during the 'War on Terror': A Tanzanian Case Study', *African Affairs* 105(421), 2006, pp. 583–603.

Bentley, G. Carter, 'Ethnicity and Practice', *Comparative Studies in Society and History* 29(1), 1987, pp. 24–55.

Berman, Bruce, 'Ethnicity, Patronage and the African State: the Politics of Uncivil Nationalism', *African Affairs* 97(388), 1998, pp. 305–341.

Braeckman, Colette, *Terreur africaine: Burundi, Rwanda, Zaïre, les racines de la violence* (Paris: Fayard, 1996).

Capela, José, *Donas, senhores e escravos* (Porto: Afrontamento, 1995).

Cappell, David A., 'The Nation as Frontier: Ethnicity and Clientelism in Ivorian History', *International Journal of African Historical Studies* 22(4), 1989, pp. 671–696.

Chauveau, Jean-Pierre and Dozon, Jean-Pierre, 'Ethnies et Etat en Côte-d'Ivoire', *Revue Française de Science Politique* 38(5), 1988, pp. 732–747.

Chrétien, Jean-Pierre, *Le défi de l'ethnisme: Rwanda et Burundi, 1990–1996* (Paris: Karthala, 1997).

Colin, Jean-Philippe; Georges Kouamé, and Débégnoun Soro, 'Outside the autochthon-migrant configuration: access to land, land conflicts and inter-ethnic relationships in a former pioneer area of lower Côte d'Ivoire', *Journal of Modern African Studies* 45(1), 2007, pp. 33–59.

Conklin, Alice, *A Mission to Civilize: The Republican Idea of Empire in France and West Africa, 1895–1930* (Stanford: Stanford University Press, 1997).

Cooper, Frederick, *Africa since 1940: The Past of the Present* (Cambridge: Cambridge University Press, 2002).

Coquerel, Paul, 'Les Zulu dans l'Afrique du Sud contemporaine. Le mouvement Inkatha Yenkulelo YeSizwe: Ethnicité et lutte de libération', in Jean-Pierre Chrétien and Gérard Prunier (eds.), *Les ethnies ont une histoire* (Paris: 2nd edn Karthala, 2003), pp. 417–425.

Dimier, Véronique, 'Direct or Indirect Rule: Propaganda around a Scientific Controversy', in Tony Chafer and Amanda Sackur (eds.), *Promoting the Colonial Idea. Propaganda and Visions of Empire in France* (Basingstoke: Palgrave, 2002), pp. 168–183.

Diouf, Mamadou, *Le Kajoor au XIXe siècle. Pouvoir ceddo et conquête coloniale* (Paris: Karthala, 1990).

Gahama, Joseph and Mvuyekure, Augustin, 'Jeu ethnique, idéologie missionnaire et politique coloniale. Le cas du Burundi', in Jean-Pierre Chrétien and Gérard Prunier (eds.), *Les ethnies ont une histoire* (Paris: 2nd edn Karthala, 2003), pp. 303–324.

Gallagher, Joseph T., 'The Emergence of an African Ethnic Group: the Case of the Ndendeuli', *International Journal of African Historical Studies* 7(1), 1974, pp. 1–26.

Ginio, Ruth, 'French Colonial Reading of Ethnographic Research: The Case of the 'Desertion' of the Abron King and its Aftermath', *Cahiers d'Etudes Africaines* 42(166), 2002, pp. 337–357.

Glassman, Jonathon, 'Sorting out the Tribes: the Creation of Racial Identities in Colonial Zanzibar's Newspaper Wars', *Journal of African History* 41(3), 2000, pp. 395–428.

Gordon, David, 'Owners of the Land and Lunda Lords: Colonial Chiefs in the Borderlands of Northern Rhodesia and the Belgian Congo', *International Journal of African Historical Studies* 34(2), 2001, pp. 315–338.

Gordon, David, 'History on the Luapula Retold: Landscape, Memory and Identity in the Kazembe Kingdom', *Journal of African History* 47(1), 2006, pp. 21–42.

Haaland, Gunnar, 'Economic Determinants in Ethnic Processes', in Fredrik Barth (ed.), *Ethnic Groups and Boundaries: The Social Organization of Cultural Difference* (Bergen: Univ. Forl., 1969), pp. 58–73.

Harff, Barbara, 'No Lessons Learned from the Holocaust? Assessing Risks of Genocide and Political Mass Murder since 1955', *American Political Science Review* 97(1), 2003, pp. 57–73.

Hobsbawm, Eric and Ranger, Terence (eds.), *The Invention of Tradition* (Cambridge: Cambridge University Press, 1984).

Horowitz, Donald L., *Ethnic Groups in Conflict* (Berkeley – London: University of California Press, 1985).

Horta, José da Silva, 'La Perception du Mande et de l'Identité Mandingue dans les Textes Européens, 1453–1508', *History in Africa* 23, 1996, pp. 75–86.

Igoe, Jim, 'Becoming Indigenous Peoples: Difference, Inequality, and the Globalization of East African Identity Politics', *African Affairs* 105(420), 2006, pp. 399–420.

Isaacman, Allan and Peterson, Derek, 'Making the Chikunda: Military Slavery and Ethnicity in Southern Africa, 1750–1900', *International Journal of African Historical Studies* 36(2), 2003, pp. 257–281.

Keese, Alexander, 'Colons français, politiciens africains et marchands libanais au Sénégal colonial', *Africa (Roma)* 60(2), 2005, pp. 201–220.

Lemarchand, René, 'Political Clientelism and Ethnicity in Tropical Africa: Competing Solidarities in Nation-Building', *American Political Science Review* 66(1), 1972, pp. 68–90.

Leopold, Mark, 'Slavery in Sudan, Past and Present', *African Affairs* 102(409), 2003, pp. 653–661.

MacGaffey, Wyatt, 'Changing Representations in Central African History', *Journal of African History* 46(2), 2006, pp. 189–207.

Makris, G.P., 'Slavery, Possession and History: The Construction of the Self among Slave Descendants in the Sudan', *Africa* 66(2), 1996, pp. 159–182.

Mans, Ulrich,'Briefing: Sudan: The new war in Darfur', *African Affairs* 103(411), 2004, pp. 291–294.

Mapp, Roberta E.,'Cross-National Dimensions of Ethnocentrism', *Canadian Journal of African Studies* 6(1), 1972, pp. 73–96.

Mark, Peter, 'The Evolution of 'Portuguese' Identity: Luso-Africans on the Upper Guinea Coast from Sixteenth to the Early Nineteenth Century', *Journal of African History* 40(2), 1999, pp. 173–191.

Mazenot, Georges, *Evaluer la colonisation* (Paris: L'Harmattan, 1999).

M'Bokolo, Elikia, 'Le 'séparatisme katangais'', in Jean-Loup Amselle and Elikiah M'Bokolo (eds.), *Au cœur de l'ethnie: ethnies, tribalisme et État en Afrique* (Paris: La Découverte, 1985), pp. 185–226.

McDougall, E. Ann, 'A topsy-turvy world: slaves and freed slaves in the Mauritanian Adrar, 1910–1950', in Susanne Miers and Richard Roberts (eds.), *The End of Slavery in Africa* (Madison: University of Wisconsin Press, 1988), pp. 362–388.

Melvern, Linda, *Conspiracy to Murder: The Rwandan Genocide* (London: Verso, 2004).

Miles, William F.S. and Rochefort, David A., 'Nationalism versus Ethnic Identity in sub-Saharan Africa', *American Political Science Review* 85(2), 1991, pp. 393–403.

Monson, Jamie, 'Memory, Migration and the Authority of History in Southern Tanzania, 1860–1960', *Journal of African History* 41(2), 2000, pp. 347–372.

Newbury, David, 'Understanding Genocide', *African Studies Review* 41(1), 1998, pp. 73–97.

Newitt, Malyn, *Portuguese Settlement on the Zambesi: Exploration, Land Tenure and Colonial Rule in East Africa* (London: Longman, 1973).

Ngolet, François, 'Inventing ethnicity and identities in Gabon: the case of the Ongom (Bakele)', *Revue Française de l'Histoire d'Outre-Mer* 321, 1998, pp. 5–26.

Nugent, Paul, *Africa since Independence* (Basingstoke: Palgrave Macmillan, 2004).

Posner, Daniel N., *Institutions and Ethnic Politics in Africa* (Cambridge – New York – Melbourne: Cambridge University Press, 2005).

Poutignat, Philippe, and Jocelyne Streiff-Fenart, *Théories de l'Ethnicité* (Paris: Presses Universitaires de France, 1995).

Power, Joey, 'Race, Class, Ethnicity, and Anglo-Indian Trade Rivalry in Colonial Malawi, 1910–1945', *International Journal of African Historical Studies* 26(3), 1993, pp. 575–607.

Prunier, Gérard, *The Rwanda Crisis, 1959–1994: History of a Genocide* (London: Hurst, 1997).

Rathbone, Richard, 'Defining Akyemfo: The Construction of Citizenship in Akyem Abuakwa, Ghana, 1700–1939', *Africa* 66(4), 1996, pp. 506–525.

Rathbone, Richard, *N'Krumah and the Chiefs. The Politics of Chieftaincy in Ghana 1951–60* (Oxford: James Currey – Accra: F. Reimer – Athens/OH: Ohio University Press, 2000).

Reyntjens, Filip, *Rwanda: trois jours qui ont fait basculer l'histoire* (Brussels: Institut africain – CEDAF – Paris: Harmattan, 1995).

Reyntjens, Filip, 'Rwanda, Ten Years on: From Genocide to Dictatorship', *African Affairs* 103(411), 2004, pp. 177–210.

Robinson, David, 'Ethnography and customary law in Senegal', *Cahiers d'Etudes Africaines* 32(126), 1992, pp. 221–237.

Şaul, Mahir, and Patrick Royer, *West African Challenge to Empire. Culture and History in the Volta-Bani Anticolonial War* (Athens/OH: Ohio University Press – Oxford: James Currey, 2001).

Spear, Thomas, 'Neo-Traditionalism and the Limits of Invention in British Colonial Africa', *Journal of African History* 44(1), 2003, pp. 3–27.

Stoler, Ann Laura, and Frederick Cooper, 'Between Metropole and Colony. Rethinking a Research Agenda', in Frederick Cooper and Ann Laura Stoler (eds.), *Tensions of Empire: Colonial Cultures in a Bourgeois World* (Berkeley etc.: University of California Press, 1997), pp. 1–56.

Vail, Leroy (ed.), *The creation of tribalism in Southern Africa* (London: James Currey, 1991 [1989]).

Van Hoven, Ed, 'Representing Social Hierarchy. Administrators-Ethnographers in the French Sudan: Delafosse, Monteil, and Labouret', *Cahiers d'Etudes Africaines* 30(2), 1990, pp. 179–198.

Willaume, Jean-Claude, *Banyarwanda et Banyamulenge: violence et gestion de l'identitaire au Kivu* (Brussels: Institut africain – CEDAF – Paris: L'Harmattan, 1997).

Wooten, Stephen R., 'Colonial Administration and the Ethnography of the Family in the French Soudan', *Cahiers d'Etudes Africaines* 33(3), 1993, pp. 419–446.

Yelvington, Kevin A., 'Ethnicity as Practice? A Comment on Bentley', *Comparative Studies in Society and History* 33(1), 1991, pp. 158–168.

PART 1:

East and South-East Africa

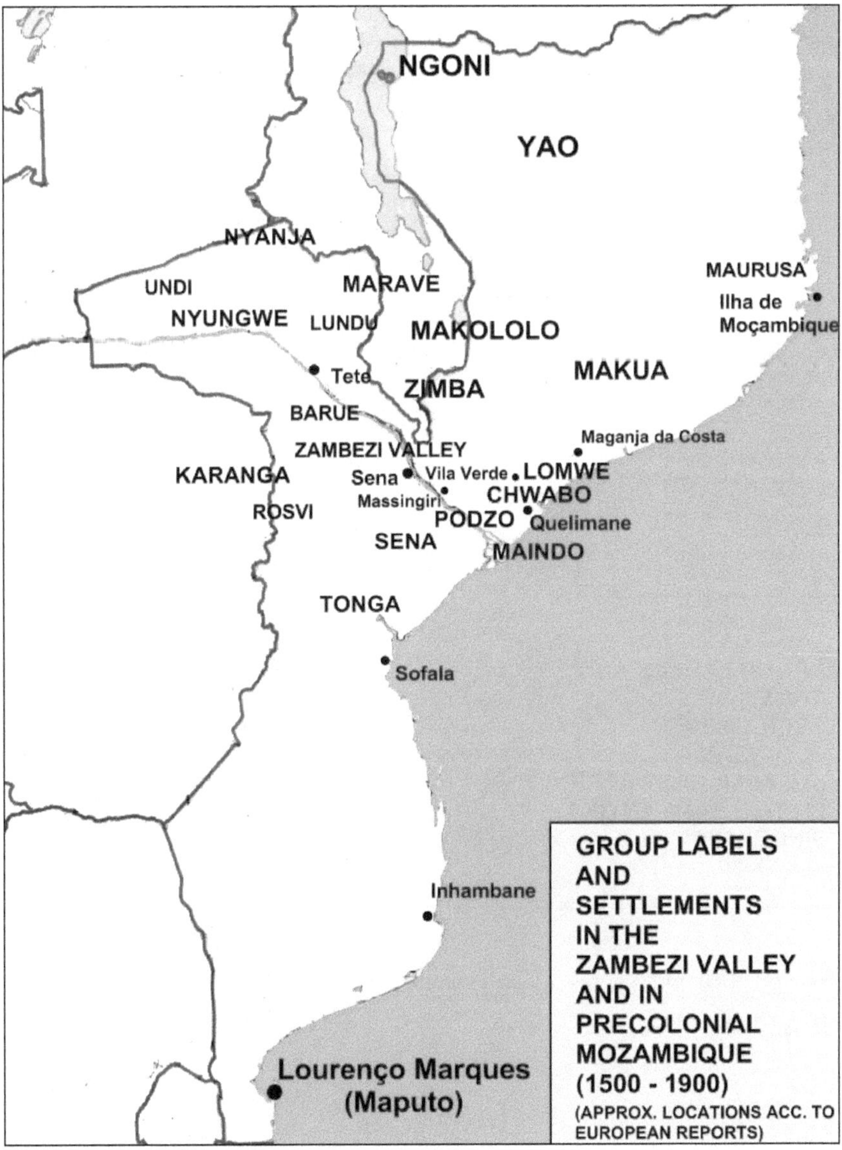

Group Labels and Settlements in the Zambezi Valley and in Pre-colonial Mozambique (1500–1900)

Group Labels and Names of Settlements in Tanzania (German East Africa, British Tanganyika), since 1890

EDUARDO MEDEIROS* AND JOSÉ CAPELA**

Processes of Identity-Building in the Zambesi Valley: Ethnic Solidarity and the Zambesian Ethos

Introduction: the Ethnic Panorama of Zambesia

The space called 'Zambesia' whose populations we will characterise in the following pages, was far greater than what this geographic name implies today. It had, as its central geographic axis, the vast river and the basin irrigated by it.[1] For a long time, this river had been a frontier, certainly not an impenetrable one, but at least a natural border between regions. This border guaranteed separation, but without clear-cut lines.[2] Mixture and

* University of Evora, Portugal.

** CEAUP, University of Porto, Portugal.

1 About the Zambesi Valley, an immense selection of literature exists, of which we will here discuss two texts that reflect very different historical contexts, see Dos Santos, Frei João, *Ethiópia Oriental* (Lisbon: Typographia do Commércio de Portugal, 1891); *idem.*, *Etiópia Oriental e Vária História de Cousas Notáveis do Oriente.* Introduction by Manuel Lobato, notes by Manuel Lobato and Eduardo Medeiros (Lisbon: CNCDP, 1999 [1609]), and Maugham, Reginald C.F., *Zambezia: A General Description of the Valley of the Zambezi River from its Delta to the River Aroangwa, with its History, Agriculture, Flora, Fauna and Ethnography* (London: John Murray, 1910).

2 On 'limits' and symbolic boundaries of social identities see Cohen, Anthony P. (ed.), *Symbolising Boundaries: Identity and Diversity in British Cultures* (Manchester: Manchester University Press, 1986); and Cohen, Anthony P., 'Boundaries of Consciousness, Consciousness of Boundaries: Critical Questions for Anthropology', in Hans Vermeulen and Cora Govers (eds.), *The Anthropology of Ethnicity: Beyond 'Ethnic Groups and Boundaries'* (Amsterdam: Het Spinhuis, 1994), pp. 59–78.

métissage were normal in the regional context.[3] The geography of the river also shaped routes of migration, of trade, and of warfare. Moreover, through the medium of its arteries circulate vital fluids that, in the stream of cultural and genetic memory, arrive in our hands.[4]

The valley, and the neighbouring, scarcely settled regions on both sides of the river, had been occupied by Bantu peasants during the earlier Iron Age, between the second century BC and the eleventh century AD. Subsequent centuries, forming the later Iron Age, saw the arrival of new groups of inhabitants, also Bantu, making a living from agriculture. The settlement processes took place in the context of wars or during periods of peace, until the end of the fifteenth century. They would continue throughout the following centuries, although with a lesser impact: the last one occurring on the southern bank of the river, with the arrival of the Ngunis.[5] All these settlements would repeatedly bring about strong exchange processes, including influxes and outfluxes of cultural material. They were the cause of constant socio-cultural reorganisation that shaped an immense territory of plural cultural entities. The whole local history is marked by plurality and by a permanent reprocessing of borders between identities at religious, linguistic, lineage, and political levels.[6]

3 See Amselle, Jean-Loup, *Logiques métisses. Anthropologie et identité en Afrique et ailleurs* (Paris: Payot, 1990); Hannerz, Ulf, 'Fluxos, fronteiras, híbridos: palavras-chave da Antropologia transnacional', *Mana (Rio de Janeiro)* 3(1), 1997, pp. 7–39. For a critical analysis of the notion of mestizo identity see Alva, J. Jorge Klor de, 'The Postcolonization of the (Latin) American Experience: A reconsideration of 'Colonialism', 'Postcolonialism', and 'Mestizaje'', in Gyan Prakash (ed.), *After Colonialism: Imperial Histories and Postcolonial Displacements* (Princeton: Princeton University Press, 1995), pp. 241–275. Compare as well the admirable novel by Coelho, João Paulo Borges, *As Duas Sombras do Rio* (Lisbon: Caminho, 2003), about the two banks of the Zambesi in Zumbo territory.

4 This phrase is inspired by the work of Carvalho, Ruy Duarte de, *Desmedida: crónicas do Brasil* (Lisbon: Edições Cotovia, 2008), p. 69.

5 On the Nguni of the Zambesi Valley, in particular on the Gaza-Nguni, see Newitt, Malyn, *A History of Mozambique* (London: Hurst, 1995); and Pélissier, René, *La Naissance du Mozambique. Résistance et révoltes anticoloniales (1854–1921)* (Orgeval: Author's edition, 1984), 2 vols. (Portuguese edition: *História de Moçambique – Formação e oposição (1854–1918)* (Lisbon: Editorial Estampa, 1987–1988), 2 vols.).

6 Cf. Birnbaum, Pierre (ed.), *Sociologie des nationalismes* (Paris: Presses Universitaires de France, 1997), p. 40.

We have little concrete information about the people during the earlier stages of occupation.[7] Some archaeological and linguistic traces refer to larger political territories, such as the so-called Maravis in the north, or the Muene-Matapas in the south.[8] Those political units constitute territorial macro-entities about which we know few details. We are still less informed concerning their more refined internal borders: we only know that those micro-borders allowed groups of people from different lineages to create their own identities in a space formed by identical socio-cultural features. For example, matrilinearity was typical north of the river, while patrilinear arrangements dominated on the southern bank. Some of those smaller groups were to be found in both territories referred to above, but were culturally entirely distinct, as would be the case with the Makololos, or with the group defined through the 'Zambesian Ethos'.

Within those agricultural settlements, and subsequently in hunting territories and in others rich in iron ore and gold, through peaceful or violent contact, various mixtures of populations occurred. These led to the formation of ethnic groups, several of which have not left us any trace. The latter is easily explained by the fact that ethnic identity has its basis in the concept of culture. In a way similar to racial concepts, ethnicity presupposes distinctions of species among individuals; in this sense, culture was defined as an inventory of remnants, habits, techniques, material objects, all these making it possible to classify different groups of populations.[9] Therefore, one has to ask which type of culture (past or modern) is referred to in the observations we have received.

7 See the observations of Mary Tew on the region of Lake Nyassa in Tew, Mary, *Ethnographic Survey of Africa: East Central Africa, Part I: Peoples of the Lake Nyassa Region* (London: International African Institute, 1950), and Ishemo, Shubi Lugemalila, *The Lower Zambezi Basin: A Study in Economy and Society, 1850–1920* (Aldershot: Avebury, 1995).

8 Beach, David N., *The Shona and Zimbabwe, 900–1850* (Gwelo (Zimbabwe): Mambo Press, 1980); Rita-Ferreira, António, *African Kingdoms and Alien Settlements in Central Mozambique (c.15th–17th Cent.)* (Coimbra: Departamento de Antropologia, Universidade de Coimbra, 1999).

9 Cunha, Maria Manuela Carneiro da, 'A identidade como memória', in *Dinâmicas multiculturais, novas faces, outros olhares. Actas das sessões plenárias do III° Congresso Luso-Afro-Brasileiro de Ciências Sociais* (Lisbon: ICS-UL, 1994), pp. 193–223.

Moreover, we have to ask which definition of ethnicity was employed from the past.[10] The Portuguese written *coevos* from the seventeenth and eighteenth century, to mention only the oldest European sources, are useful for cultural references. Unfortunately, however, they do not permit the analysis of the cultural micro-spaces and of their borders.

Asian conquerors had arrived in the region before the Portuguese. They influenced, above all, through their forms of commerce, the formation of political units in the territory, since the latter appear to have been created in order to control trade. Moreover, on both river banks, and in the Zambesi Delta, Asian residents converted, in a religious and cultural sense, a part of the local elites. The same was true for the African merchants coming to the coast, the *ajauas* (Yao). Finally, there was also some biological mixture. However, it was mainly the European intrusion and the creation of the *prazos* – which will be discussed below in detail – in connection with the slave trade, and slave raiding, that would alter the region through immense cultural and social changes.

The contact with Europeans either destroyed the pre-existing political structures, or reconstituted them in the service of the traffic. This traffic would shape new local identities: individuals would define themselves as slave-catchers (as in the case of the Yao of Nyassa) or as refugees from those predations. Various historians have already investigated this particular chapter in Zambesian history.[11] The ethnic space in the valley was partially transformed in the period of the trade, but the majority of ethnic groups remained stable into the colonial period. Local

10 About the Hodierna ethnicity in Mozambique, compare Serra, Carlos, *Combates pela mentalidade sociológica* (Maputo: Livraria Universitária, 1997), and *idem* (ed.), *Identidade e Moçambicanização* (Maputo: Livraria Universitária, 1998).

11 See, among others, Figueiredo Morais, João M., 'O princípio e o presente: a Arqueologia na redescoberta do passado em Moçambique', *ICALP-Revista do Instituto de Cultura e Língua Portuguesa* 18, 1989, pp. 74–92; Sinclair, Paul J., *Space, Time and Social Formation: A Territorial Approach to the Archaeology and Anthropology of Zimbabwe and Mozambique, c. 0–1700 AD* (Uppsala: Societas Archaeologica Upsaliensis, 1987); Rita-Ferreira, António, 'Grupos Étnicos e História Pré-colonial de Moçambique', *Moçambique – Aspectos da Cultura Material* 6, 1986, pp. 15–31; Rita-Ferreira, António, *Fixação Portuguesa e História Pré-Colonial de Moçambique* (Lisbon: JICU, 1982); Bannerman, James, *Notes and Questions Regarding the Archaeology, Language and Ethnohistory of Central Mozambique between the Zambezi and Save Rivers* (Harare: Panafrican Congress, 1995).

languages were subject to some changes and innovations. Some attributes of identity became less prominent, or even disappeared, for example tattoo practices. Most important, however, was the fact that ethnic groups would not assume an administrative function in the structures of the modern Portuguese colonial system. On the other hand, the *prazos* would have in the Chikundas (Atxikunda) their base of both war organisation and long-distance commerce.[12]

The Chikundas were captives transformed into soldiers, who came from various social and political formations. They had parted from their regions of origin for very different reasons, including kidnapping, flight, war captivity, asylum-seeking, beside others. In the *butacas*, the camps where those individuals were integrated in regiments, mixture of different cultures was inevitable. This laid the ground for new situations of individual identity, which outweighed the older patterns of affiliation. Creation of new identity led as well to the 'Africanisation' of exogenous institutions as it has been called by Isaacman: elements from different contexts converged in new, innovative forms.[13] The same process would in fact happen in the countless *quilombos*, settlements of refugee slaves emerging over the whole of the period of the slave trade, and, even more strongly, after the abolition of the official commerce.[14]

In the surroundings of Tete, Sena, Quelimane, and other localities and river markets of the Zambesi, new identities also emerged, becoming known as Nyungwes (Nhungwè), Senas (Asena) and Chuabos (Atxuabo).[15] Again, in those cases, individuals of very different origins

12 About the Chikundas we have a rich scholarly literature at our disposition, among which we find a useful introduction in Isaacman, Allen F., 'The origin, formation and early history of Chikunda', *Journal of African History* 13(3), 1972, pp. 443–461.

13 Isaacman, Allen F., and Barbara S. Isaacman, *Mozambique. The Africanization of a European Institution: The Zambezi Prazos, 1750–1902* (Madison: University of Wisconsin Press – London: North Central Publishing, 1972); Isaacman, Allen F., and Barbara S. Isaacman, *Slavery and Beyond: The Making of Men and Chikunda Ethnic Identities in the Unstable World of South-Central Africa, 1750–1920* (Portsmouth/NH: Heinemann, 2004).

14 Capela, José, 'Como as Aringas de Moçambique se transformaram em Quilombos', *Tempo (Departamento de História da Universidade Federal Fluminense)* 20, 2006, pp. 83–108.

15 The populations of the Tete and Quelimane regions would identify themselves with those centres. Foreign visitors, however, would not employ the expressions

converged through mixtures and creolisations, thus forming the 'peoples of the Lower Zambesi'. The populations of the northern interior of the current Province of Zambézia would belatedly be labelled, during the twentieth century, as Lomwe (Lómuè), and usually be associated with the Makuas.

It is safe to affirm that the majority of the populations that would contribute to the 'Zambesian Ethos', were inscribed in this space of syncretisms, including fusions between different African cultural groups, enlarged by exogenous cultural and religious elements. In other regions of Zambesia, similar processes would happen, as in Maganja da Costa, or in the 'land' of the Makololos.[16] Frequently, the particular relation to the territory or the locality was a source of finding appropriate group labels.[17] Group names like Nyanja (meaning river or lake), Yao (related to the Yao or Chau mountain), Chwabo (for the populations of Quelimane), Nyungwe (for the populations of Tete), Sena (for the populations living at the foot of Sena, referring to the ancient small fortress of Sena rebuilt in the eighteenth century) and Makua (populations of the Namuli mountains) are all ethnonyms that contain historical and symbolic meanings.

We can, therefore, refer to a complex ethnic history in the space of Zambesia before the Portuguese imperial and capitalist occupation at the end of the nineteenth century. The 'fixation' of ethnic groups, with the names given to them over the twentieth century – and frequently in fact on erroneous grounds – are a 'montage' (which could well be called 'in-

---

'Nyungwe', 'Sena', and 'Chwabo' during the seventeenth and eighteenth centuries. Still in 1886, Father Courtois translated what we would today describe as Xinyungwe language, as *chisendzi cha ku Nyungue* (*kafir* of Tete), see Courtois, Victor José, *Dicionário Portuguez-Cafre-Tetense – ou Idioma falado no Districto de Tete e na vasta região do Zambeze Inferior* (Coimbra: Imprensa da Universidade, 1899). These ethnographic expressions appear in the documents only during the twentieth century.

16 Isaacman, Allen, and Elias Mandala, 'From Porters to Labor Extractors: The Chikunda and Kololo in the Lake Malawi and Tchiri River Area, 1885–1891', in Catherine Coquery-Vidrovitch and Paul Lovejoy (eds.), *The Workers of African Trade* (Beverly Hills: SAGE Publications, 1985), pp. 209–243.

17 Cf. Liesegang, Gerhard, 'Territorialidades sociais e identidades com referência a Moçambique', in Carlos Serra (ed.), *Identidade/Moçambicanidade/Moçambicanização* (Maputo: Livraria Universitária – Universidade Eduardo Mondlane, 1998), pp. 99–159.

vention') created during the high and late colonial periods. António Rita-Ferreira has given us a synthesis of these colonial classifications.[18] Concerning the later periods, already in the post-colonial phase, Eduardo Medeiros[19] and others, such as Carlos Serra,[20] have initiated attempts at deconstructing those classifications for the Mozambican case. They affirmed – the former as a provocation – that the so-called Makuas do not exist as an ethnic group, and that the Makondes have their origins in the *quilombos*, while both groups have lived with fluid ethnic boundaries. The label 'Makua' [Mkhuwa], like a short period later the label 'Maravi', appeared as a foreign ethnicist concept, which did not have any relation to the self-identification of the respective populations. Paraphrasing Pierre Bourdieu, those ethnic classifications rose as a possible way in which to perceive, describe, and construct the local social environment, within a certain principle of vision and division.[21] The use of the expression 'Makua', for example, was maintained over the long-term period with this relation to alterity, although the territorial meaning which 'Makua' once had was altered with new classifications. It was only during the last fifty years of Portuguese colonialism, with the general designation of the Mozambican people as 'indígenas', that the label became more universal and part of the everyday life of at least some of the locals. Nevertheless, this process was slow, and not based on a real ethnic conscience.

However, side by side with those social and cultural constructions and reconstructions that shaped the different Bantu groups, there emerged in the long term a second, more explicitly Zambesian process that will be described as follows. At variance with the processes of ethnic differentiation described for different parts of sub-Saharan Africa in the nineteenth

18 Rita-Ferreira, António, *Agrupamento e caracterização étnica dos indígenas de Moçambique* (Lisbon: Ministério do Ultramar, Junta de Investigações do Ultramar, 1958); Rita-Ferreira, António, *Povos de Moçambique – História e Cultura* (Porto: Afrontamento, 1975).

19 Medeiros, Eduardo, 'Etnias e etnicidade em Moçambique. O advento do Mundo Sena. Das origens a 1918', in José Carlos Venâncio (ed.), *O Desafio Africano* (Lisbon: Veja – Universidade da Beira Interior, 1997), pp. 59–82.

20 Serra, *Combates*; Serra, *Identidade.*

21 Bourdieu, Pierre, *O Poder Simbólico* (fourth edition, Lisbon: Difel, 1994 [1989]), pp. 137–138.

and twentieth century, creolisation[22] and biological and cultural intermixture, based on both Bantu culture with European and Asian influences, and the religious and cultural impact of the Portuguese presence, led to an overarching type of identity. In particular geographic zones, determined through missionary activity and *luanes* (large residences) of the lords of the *prazos*, would emerge mixed, assimilated individuals, *donas* (ladies), 'línguas',[23] *sipaios* (guards) and so on. These different groups formed what will be defined here as the 'Zambesian Ethos'. The individuals adhering to this overarching identity would still be interrelated with the 'new' local ethnic groups (like the above-mentioned Nyungwes, Senas, Chwabos, or the Podzos, Maindos, etc.), but they lived in a border situation as described by Hannerz, in a permanent process of trans-ethnic acculturation. The latter was linked to symbolic demarcation of the present African social identities, understood by some of the anthropologists analysing those acculturations as participation of the 'wilderness' in modern civilisation, or, more accurate, in the processes of globalisation going on during this epoch.[24]

22 About the concept of cultural creolisation, see Fabian, Johannes, 'Popular culture in Africa: Findings and Conjectures', *Africa* 48(4), 1978, pp. 315–334; Drummond, Lee, 'The cultural continuum: A theory of intersystems', *Man* 15(2), 1980, pp. 352–374; Jackson, Jean, 'Is there a way of talking about culture without making enemies?', *Dialectical Anthropology* 14, 1989, pp. 127–143; and Hannerz, Ulf, 'The World in Creolisation', *Africa* 57(4), 1987, pp. 546–559; Hannerz, Ulf, 'Scenarios for Peripheral Cultures', in A. D. King (ed.), *Culture, Globalization and the World-System* (London: Macmillan, 1991), pp. 107–128.

23 This label was given to the translators working for the Portuguese administration and the colonial services.

24 Cf. the definitions given by Victor W. Turner (*Dramas, Fields, and Metaphors: Symbolic Action in Human Society* (Ithaca: Cornell University Press, 1974)) reflecting on the interpretation of flux, bringing this flux into the concepts of *communitas* and *liminality* (a term borrowed from Arnold van Gennep's formulation of *Rites de Passage* – 'transition rites' – which accompany every change of state or social position, or certain points in age. These are marked by three phases: separation, margin, and *limen* (the Latin for threshold). For a Portuguese version, see Turner, Victor W., *O processo ritual* (Petropolis: Ed. Vozes, 1974), pp. 116–159.

The 'Zambesian Ethos' – Ethos or a Question of Identity?

In José Capela's *Donas, Senhores e Escravos*, we find an attempt to characterise the particular nature of colonisation in Mozambique. In this characterisation, cultural factors clearly overshadow material aspects. The chosen criterion of analysis is the behaviour of local protagonists, without however omitting social and economic structures. In what follows, we will emphasise the same aspects for a more concrete and circumscribed case, focusing on what will be described as the 'Zambesian Ethos'. We will regard under this label the peculiar aspects of a particular group situation under colonial rule. Furthermore, we will also link the concept of 'ethos' to the 'beginning of a specific construction of reality, based on a pre-reflexive belief in the indubitable value of the tools of the construction and of the objects in this manner constructed'.[25]

Years after Mozambican independence, one of the authors of this article – José Capela – was invited to a marriage in Maputo. The act of civil registration was performed in the so-called Palácio da Familia, which is a beautiful building inspired by classical Greek art. A crowd of celebrating people accompanied the couple, singing and dancing. When the author stepped into the atrium of the palace he noticed that there were various assessors referring to the numerous weddings to be held. As the author knew only the husband, who had not yet appeared, he asked himself which ceremony was the right one. The husband was originally from Zambesia, and the author could thus turn to a group that projected Zambesianess: the forms of behaviour were impressive, modest, aristocratic, and clearly showing mixed descent. A single glance allowed him to grasp a morphology of identity that was very strongly emphasised, and, on the other hand, a homogeneity that was evident.

A short time before, the author had been visited by a person known for his efforts concerning local history in Quelimane, from where this individual originated. He was also recognised for the ways in which he commemorated (and during this period such behaviour clearly was politically incorrect!) some ancient colonial contacts of his. During this

25 Pierre Bourdieu, *Meditações Pascalianas* (Oeiras: Celta Editora, 1998), p. 85.

encounter, the author saw reappearing before him the Zambesian *muzungo* (literally to be translated as 'master' or 'lord'), disconnected from space and time. Being of mixed descent (*misto*), of good appearance, in modest but appropriate clothes, he did not come as a beggar, but he simply represented, in combination with his role as cultural agent of the old colonial state, a cultural heritage from the past. He continually invoked this past, which was probably more mythical than real (however, recounted by him, it appeared more real than mythical). In his speeches he showed a level of literacy that was considerably higher than the Mozambican average. The author provoked a small flash of anger when, maladroitly, he asked his interlocutor if his maternal language was Chisena … (This happens more often, as in Zambesia, the visitor is surprised by the Atticism of the Portuguese spoken by local conversation partners!)

Among the author's contacts also was the state agent José Roldão (1900–1979). A founder in Quelimane of the *Associação Africana da Zambézia*, contributor to the local press, correspondent of Beira and Lourenço Marques newspapers, he was distinguished by his outstanding Portuguese, both in written and spoken form. He was also devoted to the memory of the most emblematic signs of Lusitan patriotism in Zambesian territory.[26] In a short text he commemorates how in Quelimane, during his childhood, locals felt about the assassination of the Portuguese Dom Luís, Prince of Beira. The text, being an anthology from the formal point of view, displays patriotism along Metropolitan lines. It shows an emotional bond with the monarchical and aristocratic canon:

> When I arrived at our place, my mother, black, illiterate, but speaking nevertheless in Portuguese, called me to attend to her and fixed a black ribbon at the sleeve of my shirt. Astonished, I asked her why she attached to me such a band. I wanted to know what the meaning of that all was. She explained to me: 'You, child, are Portuguese. The King of Portugal and his son were murdered, the latter being the Prince Dom Luís, whom you know, and your schoolmates as well, as he disembarked at the docks of the Capitania and you accompanied him to the church

26 Angius, Matteo, *A figura e obra do jornalista José Júlio Roldão (1900–1979) – Contribuição para a história da imprensa em Moçambique* (Diss. de Licenciatura, Universidade Eduardo Mondlane, Maputo, 1997).

> where the Te-Deum was intonated. For those reasons we are all fighting.' I am not ashamed to confess publicly that I cried.[27]

Practices of name-giving are also an important expression of this particular identity. In the area where colonisation was effective, namely in those regions where the presence of colonial agents was stable, the latter being *reinois* (i.e. born in the Kingdom of Portugal) and, above all, Goans, we can still today find traces of this presence in the local family names. This is particularly the case with those family names indicating noble origins, such as Lacerda, Alves da Silva, Arouca, Carrilho, Cirne, Costa Xavier, Coutinho, Frichaut, Garção, Lobo, Xavier Botelho, Bragança, Castelo Branco, Colaço, Ferrão, Ferro, Pinto de Magalhães, Mascarenhas, Menezes, Nazareth, Noronha, Quadros, Sá, Saldanha, Sant'Ana Afonso, Xavier Velasco, Vaz dos Anjos, Melo Virgolino, Pedroso Gamito and Portugal da Graça. Side by side with those whose ancestors are linked to the Order of Christ (the most popular of the religious orders) or some other order, and with those who were decorated with militia posts, we find others who have their origins in a more down-to-earth plebs. The latter are still at the present time unembarrassed to remember a family tradition that refers to the title of the lord of a *prazo*; in this function their family had owned slaves and controlled rent-paying peasants as if they were on the same level as their more aristocratic neighbours.[28]

The 'Ethos' in Literature

The analysis of literary testimony is an important way of obtaining more tangible evidence for the existence of the 'Zambesian Ethos': we can find traces if not the direct expression of this type of society, through concrete and obvious descriptions of lordly sumptuousness. The first one we have to mention is A. de Portugal Durão, a navy official, and one of the conquerors of Zambesia. He was an administrator of the com-

27 *Diário de Moçambique*, 6 May 1966.

28 Personal observation of the author from his presence in the field.

pany of the same name, and in this function he contributed to the demolition of the Old Regime in Mozambique. His testimony from 1914 is of the greatest importance: he was at the same time the official charged with the military conquest of the central parts of Mozambique and, consecutively, founding-father of the local version of plantation capitalism, and the Director of the *Companhia de Zambézia*. Moreover, he was an attentive savant of the history, the structures and internal processes of local communities. The latter fact enabled him to give a lucid analysis of the process of social change happening around him:

> Great merchant houses disappeared, and in their place, occupying even their ancient facilities, others were founded, equipped with even more capital; some small traders also disappeared because of either not having the education to show an effort or of lacking the professional skills. The Zambesia of the *donas* (mistresses of the luanes), of the *batuques* (hand-played drums, and the respective dances), of the *muzungos* (lords), of pantagruelia's lunches, of the white and black nabobs, served by legions of *nhenhas* (native young maids) and moleques (native young servants), the old Zambesia, which was without any doubt a picturesque place but little productive, was substituted by another one that, perhaps brutally, brushed away the old one, and the former was victorious because it was strong and because it mercilessly obeyed the law of progress.[29]

We might say that this author was someone who took a sort of 'class struggle' to be the motor of history. Durão was also conscious that, in his function, he himself contributed to the final destruction of the Old Regime.

In the unpublished novel *Luane*, by the author Sant'Ana Afonso, the narrator describes how the grandfather Gonçalves prepares his speech and the national anthem in the local language in order to receive Portuguese President Carmona. In that context, Afonso gives an impression of everyday life of *Mazungo* families in the suburbs of Quelimane. Presenting the following story, the author emphasises the peculiarity of the 'creole' protagonist of the fictive story:

29 Durão, A. de Portugal, *O Distrito de Quelimane – Agricultura e Mão D'Obra*, Conferência realizada na Sociedade de Geografia de Lisboa em 21 de Março de 1914, p. 52.

> The history of a very remote childhood that after so many and so many more alterations to its form and to its way of speaking, was recorded here in the style of a chronicle, in the direct language of the syntax of a Black great-great-great-grandmother, but already landlady through her regal status, before being *assimilada* (person with Portuguese citizen status), by a definitive and radical cut of the umbilical cord attaching her (the great-great-great-grandmother) circumnavigating (clearly with her heart) the Cape of Good Hope and Cape Bojador – and the Adamastor incessantly searching him, and the Gulf of Guinea already allowing an idea of the Restelo [in Lisbon] – to Lusitania.[30]

At an early point, the narrative invokes the role of the Lady (*dona*) – royal nobility – and 'creolism', in which this aristocracy defines itself locally.

In the following, the moment of the arrival of the Portuguese President comes closer:

> The *luaneiros* (owners of the *luanes*, the central houses of the *prazos*) members of the great Zambesian families were also in a state of ecstasy and showed strong emotions. The visit had an important historical significance, as it was a major step bringing them closer to the mother-nation.

The next scene describes the crowd already gathered at the airport waiting for the landing of the President's airplane:

> ...there, we also found the representatives of the *Clube Africano* where the *luaneiros* of the land were associated, mulattoes and still ascendant *assimilados*. And those representatives also came in form of a defile, showing in their midst the most beautiful female mulattoes …

After the reception at the airport, the local nobility attended a lunch in the Governor's palace, and no one had remembered to invite Gonçalves:

> They left him aside, just so, as if he was a bad type of a negro, like a *nhaquinze*, or even like a *macambuzi* [an outcast].
> He felt deep sadness, coming from the bottom of his heart, and rising, rising until it even made him show watery tears. But this was not possible. It was even a shame.
> But why?!
> Was it not true that his father had been a real White man?

30 Afonso, Sant'Ana, *Luane* (unpublished text, in the author's possession). The President General Carmona visited Moçambique in 1939.

> And his mother was she not a Lady with a certain royal patent and so on and so on? Not mentioning that his grandfather had been a *caneco* [a Catholic Indo-Portuguese] who had attended classes of Gregorian music when being in Goa, and he was informed about the laws because he had been a judge!

The illustrious guest left and the Chwabo – here meaning the Quelimane land of the above-mentioned group of the same name – returned to its monotonous life:

> Everyone in his given place, but already with some exception to the rule, following the ancient rules of the game earned from the *aringas* [the traditional fields of local peasants] and the immense *prazos* according to the convenience of everyone. But, doubtlessly, it was the Whites who commanded and disposed of local resources.
> This does not mean, nevertheless, that there was no mulatto with a distinguished lineage in this or that post of influence, a *mestiço* or even an Indian, as those had always been the eminent persons of the bureaucratic elite of the land. They held the cards in their hands, the stamps and the seals.
> […]
> Under the great roof one could only find the owners of the *luanes*, the *muzungos* that demand particular respect, being well installed in the airiest parts …
> This *muzungo* Natividade knew how to organise good lunches. Even a bored mixed-race who seemed to be a White person according to his skin colour, but was regarded by the people as a jealous native, was present to eat, drink and amuse himself, and this was not even the truth because they gossiped there that when his father made his mother pregnant, the father soon fled and no one knew his name. For this background story he was left with his skin of a disguised white, but his hair was nearly frizzy like a native and his nose – *chiça* [please!] – was a nose that only a Black man could have. But with that he was impressively ugly. Because being Black with a Black man's nose is normally beautiful. But not being White with a Black man's nose!
> He registered himself autonomously – this was what even the *muzungos* said.
> Being Rodrigues Pimentel! I never knew a Rodrigues Pimentel in this region!
> […]
> But the bored mixed-race did not lend any importance to those things. He only wanted to eat and to drink.
> Afterwards, he already wanted to be accepted as *muzungo*. Indeed, he had some small parcel of land and he liked to claim it was even a *luane*. How could it be a *luane*? Having twenty coconut-trees?! Perhaps, it only had eighteen.

Those are examples of the author's technique, a technique he employs during the whole of the narration, utilising a style that is strong enough to draw us into the 'exoticism' of the social milieu described. He constantly, nearly obsessively, appeals to markers we could call racial. Also, he invokes in a quite nostalgic way the erratic identity of a problematic status.

The novel *Zambeziana*, written by Emílio de San Bruno, a navy official passing his military service in Quelimane, reveals a certain moment and a certain social group during the transition from nineteenth to twentieth century. Fátima Mendonça, in her critical comment to the 1999 edition, describes San Bruno's style as 'exotic discourse'. This 'exotic' component is clearly present for the reader who 'discovers' those structures, but the author also portrays the forms of behaviour typical of a certain 'civilisation', that had not ceased to exist because its dimensions had shrunk. The depiction is not limited to exoticism and stereotypes of the sexuality of African women. In our eyes, although in a less incisive form than the one found in *Luane*, San Bruno's work also represents 'Zambesianess'. The lack of incisiveness explains itself by the fact that the author does not have a clear objective in writing. While *Luane* is meant to demonstrate a certain identity, *Zambeziana* constitutes a report of exoticism and of an attack on the older 'civilisation' through the new colonisation by 'foreign' companies. However, San Bruno transmits to us the exoticism of that world through striking observations that, rather than being mere folkloric anecdotes, voice vaguely what later on would be labelled 'Lusotropicalism'. In *Zambeziana*, the ladies and the *muzungos* are not only a category of description, they represent, although in a rather diffuse way, a localised and well-defined universe of 'civilisation'.[31] All these fictional accounts, including also Maria Sorensen's *Dona Theodora e os Seus Muzungos*, invoke the protagonists of the same universe. They transmit to the reader what supposedly were the typical images associated with the Zambesian culture.[32]

31 San Bruno, Emílio de, *Zambeziana, Cenas da Vida Colonial* (Maputo: Arquivo Histórico de Moçambique, 1999).

32 Sorensen, Maria, *Dona Theodora e os seus Mozungos* (Maputo: Ndjira, 1998).

Historical Reasons

The 'Crown Prazos' constituted in Mozambique the material and structural base of the formation of a system and of a patriarchical society. They are also a quasi-mythical factor that remains prevalent. Only a few years ago, while the author visited the plantations of the Company of Madal, in the vicinity of Quelimane, at a certain moment the agronomist in his company, called attention to 'the *prazo* of the Conde de Vila Verde'. The locals continue to call the land in the region *prazos*, and those *prazos* are designated by the names of landowning dynasties that had disappeared during the nineteenth century!

The distribution of the land by title through signature of the emphyteutic lease contract was introduced to Mozambique in the seventeenth century. Indeed, the practice was the most viable form of granting land titles and it was perfectly adequate to local tradition. It is thus justified for Allen Isaacman to classify this form as 'the Africanization of a European Institution'.[33] Effectively, following the 1916 account of Vilhena,

> the first Portuguese who disembarked in Zambesia exercised the *prazo* regime and, even more, it existed in fact before, in the political and social organisation of the native populations already living there. The *mambo*, or highest Kaffir chief of earlier times is now the state, represented, in that case, by the district governor; the subchiefs depending on him are the landlords (*arrendatários*); the serf of the earlier epoch is, although living under conditions that are very different, the native settler of today.[34]

While the equation is somewhat forced, a certain parallelism is undeniable. Vilhena continues:

> During his incursion, the Portuguese finds established in the land a social and political organisation that is in all its accents feudal, despite its being in a state of

33 Isaacman/Isaacman, *Mozambique.*

34 Vilhena, Ernesto de, *Regime dos Prazos da Zambézia* (Lisbon: Imprensa Nacional, 1916), p. 16.

> incipient decomposition. ... *The relations between the sub-chiefs and the Mambo are essentially those of the feudal serf to his sovereign.*[35]

They obtain the access to land for a return of service, in 'the same way' as it had been regulated in Medieval Europe.

> Established in the land, without any idea of abandoning this land later on, in an easy and well-appreciated cohabitation with the native woman, speaking the language after a short period, having adopted from the Kaffirs some customary ways of behaviour, and many of the latter's superstitions [...] the Portuguese who at the outset had been the master of small places and of only a few slaves, starts to attack, after some interval, the neighbouring chiefs. They submit to him, and he takes over the control of their land: in short time-span, while his power and resources start to grow with those of the conquered territory, he becomes, in his own heart, in perfect adaptation to the environment, a real Kaffir chief, exercising the same rights that they have.

This happens in the sixteenth century. In the following hundred years, the colonial state becomes slowly established, but without affecting in any way the lordships that had already been created. The lords had already risen to become 'German potentates', as the Jesuit Manuel Barreto called them, knowing them quite well.[36]

This regime continued with remarkable stability until the implantation of liberalism in Portugal. During this interval, Zambesia had seen the appearance of a social stratification perfectly defined in the limits within which the *muzungos* (lords) or ladies (if the master was a woman) situated themselves. The slaves were classified in hierarchical order. Slaves of the *muzungos* owned their own slaves. The inhabitants of the land were the *colonos* (dependent settlers). As the emphyteuts were obliged to pay the *foro* [rent] to the Portuguese Crown and to make their contribution to offensive or defensive wars through militias constituted by slaves and *forros* [freedmen] of their land, the system could be called 'typically feudal'. The settlers paid an annual rent to the landlords, this rent consisting of part of their harvests. The designation of *colono* is evidently derived from Portuguese medieval terminology.

35 Vilhena, Ernesto de, *Regime dos Prazos da Zambézia* (Lisbon: Imprensa Nacional, 1916), p. 16.
36 *ibid.*

The system had its obvious roots in the particular environment of Mozambique. Since we claim that it was the basis of a particular idea of 'civilisation', it becomes still more important to analyse the projections of its existence on to a time period when it had already ceased to exist. The memory of the system is fundamental to nineteenth-century images of identity in the Zambesian context.

While the Metropole saw numerous changes, the Crown Prazos of Mozambique and the whole system of which they were an essential part resisted Mousinho da Silveira's legislation. The decree of 13 August 1832 that in theory extinguished the Crown Prazos remained a dead letter in Mozambique. It was the same with Sá de Bandeira's decree of 1st June 1838, which required that the Governor-General did not renew the patents of *prazos* that had expired. Finally, there was also no attempt to incorporate the land in a new administrative organisation via the argument that those *prazos* were unused. The system thus remained in place. Successive attempts at legislation were futile, including even the 1854 decree that abolished the institution of the *prazos* for the whole of the territories of Mozambique. Even with the latter attempt, there were no practical changes. On the contrary, the legislation that was defined as innovative strengthened in the end the old system. A provincial *portaria* of 12 December 1867 that was finally to regulate the application of the 1854 decree, auctioned the payment of the *imposto de palhota* (hut tax) created by the same decree. Following the law, this tax replaced 'whatever obligations, personal services or tributes of any given type, by taxation for the settlers and the free inhabitants'. This adjustment would be organised through the *prazos* and the native tax through labour obligations continued to be calculated by family head. Continuing to follow Vilhena, we can claim that the ancient lordships or the emphyteutic lease contracts were well maintained, and that the only thing that changed was their name. The ancient division of the land was also preserved. The system remained in place and 1867 was not at all a date of change. This fact was confirmed by the decree of 27 October 1880 which officially stopped the execution of the 1854 decree. In the decree of 1880, the Portuguese state maintained the principle that the land concessions given to the emphyteuts as a compensation for the formal abolition of the *prazos* were to be transferred as *prazo* for five years. The Governor-General Augusto Castilho (1885–1889), who was an ardent defender of the reservation of administrative tasks to the state, saw himself obliged, grudgingly, to auction the farming of the *mussoco* (native tax). However, in that context he introduced an innovation in the region that was the concession of lands to the first real plantation company to be established in Mozambique: the Companhia da Cultura e do Comércio do Ópio. This innovation was not due to the activity of the governor but was the fruit of the commercial successes of former ivory and slave traders having their base in Mozambique, who obtained an investment of capital from Europe.[37] It is a curious fact in that context, that the governor gave to this venture and to the Companhia do Mahindo, the right to farm taxes for thirty years! The *prazo* of Maganja-Aquém-Chire was conceded to this first company, and the Companhia do Mahindo received a *prazo* of the same name. Thus, *prazos* were rented out even with the respective secular designations! The ancient order continued to live on in those lands, both in regard to the demarcation of those territories and to their denomination. The exercise of lordly power, frequently transferred to an *arrematante da cobrança do imposto* (bidder of the tax), the settlers' obligation to do unpaid work, the exclusive role of commerce, the seemingly permissive right of the settlers to 'be able to go to complain in the city', all show that the system of land rent continued to exist, in parallel with the continuation of the landlord having the role of local judge. The fresh attempt at reform brought forward by the decree of 18 November 1890, by António Enes, configured the legal frame in which the *prazos* were to exist well into the twentieth century.[38]

While it cannot be ignored that at the same time the social structure of Mozambique went through great transformations, particularly after the installation of plantation companies on the land, there is no doubt that the representation of power, but also the form of power, and the pattern of local social relations, remained intact and continued thus to refer to the Old Regime. This becomes evident from the following testimony:

37 Capela, José, 'Conflitos Sociais na Zambézia, 1878–1892 – A transição do Senhorio para a Plantação', *Africana Studia* 1, 1999, pp. 143–173.

38 Enes, António, *Moçambique* (Lisbon: Agência Geral das Colónias, 1946), p. 333.

> Regarding the aspects related to the institution of the *prazos* in the province of Mozambique, it is obvious that in this part of Portuguese territory, we find in fact a certain type of feudal lord whose powers are greater than those of the more eminent authority of the monarchy. It is also clearly apparent that an institution that causes such abuses as those presented by the Council to Your Excellence and to which others might be added, is an anti-political and anti-economic institution, and is in open opposition to the interest and the development of this vast and most prosperous possession.
>
> [...]
>
> Now appears the decree of 18 November 1890, by which the *prazos* are currently governed. For that reason, this decree merits a more profound analysis. The report preceding the decree commences with a presentation that explains the particular tradition of the *prazos* as the main cause for their continuing existence. It also claims: But the African *prazos* are resistant to the laws and regulations, condemning the former through the tenacity of tradition and, above all, through the energy of historical laws that direct the evolutions of societies and that continue to play a role, not only this one ... Given these circumstances, it seems to me to conform with best scientific approaches to legislate instead of violently extirpating those elements which are such deeply rooted institutions in order to substitute them with forms of organisation modelled on theories that are not adapted to the social state of the indigenous races of Mozambique, managing them according to civilised prescriptions and to the necessities and the objectives of Portuguese rule in Africa.[39]

In a subsequent report, the same governor, arguing against what he classified as the 'retrograde and anti-political regime', repeatedly called the readers' attention to the fact that the landlords of the *prazos* held 'the commercial monopoly, controlled the industry, the lands, and even the natives themselves'. The governor proposed the abolition of trade monopolies, of the landlord's role as agent of the authority, of his preferential rights, of the guarantee given to him that he can refuse any person to make his residence in the *prazos*. Literally taken, those proposals would have led to the abolition of real feudal power. Nevertheless, the governor congratulated himself on the fact that Maganja da Costa already held many *aforamentos* (cases of letting *prazos* by lease), and would have even more in the future![40]

39 Carvalho, F., *Distrito de Quelimane: Relatório do Governador 1911–1912* (Lourenço Marques: Imprensa Nacional, 1912), p. 24.

40 Carvalho, F., *Distrito de Quelimante, Relatório do Governador 1914–1915* (Lourenço Marques: Imprensa Nacional, 1916), p. 5.

In 1913, the Governor of Tete reflected upon 'modernisation' of the General Regulations of the *Prazos*. He elaborated on that issue as follows:

> The only positive result of regulating the *prazos* was to create, or, rather, to re-establish, a caste of feudal lords that could have been useful in another epoch – I would not contest that particular point – but who currently have no further right of existence.[41]

He recurred to the comment of the Conselho Ultramarino, pointing out the ongoing existence of a 'certain type of feudal lord'[42] By way of a conclusion, he analysed as follows:

> The regime of the *prazos* in Zambesia is a relic of periods that have ended and that are missed by no one. To speak of *prazos* means recording an order of things that expressed itself only through oppression and obscurantism; it includes evoking a painful reminiscence of *doações em fateosim*, *emphyteusis*, *laudémios*, *morgadios*: *coutos e resgates*, *fidalgos e vilões* [all medieval Portuguese terms], lords and slaves, all in all a system of obsolete arrangements, which are entirely incompatible with a democratic regime.[43]

In concordance with the testimony given by those governors of Tete and Quelimane, already in the twentieth century, we might be led to believe that the system of lordships was simply maintained without giving weight to the fact that the proper existence of an administrative apparatus of a modern colonial state contradicts those institutions. Nevertheless, although there was a slow transformation in progress, the projections of the old system continued to be felt in an all-dominating form. Furthermore, this was a fact because the plantation system installed was too unstable (particularly regarding questions of capital investment) to supersede the more ancient structure without having recourse to means that were not appropriate. This was the case with obligatory labour services and the hut tax. The maintenance of the traditional notions of status was not possible in the face of the relations of production where we can point to a violent rupture. This being said, in most fields of social relations there was not only preserved the traditional sumptuous lifestyle of the lordships, but all

41 Carrilho, João Luís, *Relatório do governador do Distrito de Tete, 1911–1912* (Lourenço Marques: Imprensa Nacional, 1913), pp. 6–8.

42 *ibid.*, p. 9.

43 *ibid.*, p. 24.

the imagery and representations of power and of feudal relations. The designation given to the feudal type of obligations was retained in the expression 'imposto de palhota' well until the end of the colonial period. The 'native' (*indígena*) of 1960 living in Zambézia paid to the colonial state the *mussuco* in the same manner the 'colono' had paid the *mussoco* to the lord of the seventeenth century.

Cultural Reasons

In the first quarter of the nineteenth century, regarding Moçambique Island and Queimante, the Bishop Brother Bartolomeu refers to 'the education of those *reinóis* [settlers born in Portugal] that are sons of the land'. By including the 'sons of the land' ('filhos do país') in the group of the *reinóis* he puts all the descendents of Portuguese settlers in the same cultural category, whatever their background, and even despite the fact that in their great majority, if not nearly in their totality, those settlers born in Mozambique were the children of African mothers. Today, we could indeed call them Luso-Africans. As the 'peopling' of the province was the primary colonial objective, however, the more evident cultural reference would be of religious affiliation. At this point, 'the cross and the sword' were joined. It is obvious that in the absence of a type of family that had an entirely European configuration, and at the heart of a social environment that had nothing to do either with European religious practice or with European culture, the education of these Portuguese descendants 'clearly shows their necessary contact with indigenous Kaffirs, Moors and Indian mixed-race'.

After a short interval, the practices and beliefs of these Luso-Africans adjusted to locally prevalent customs. They were fluent in local languages and spoke a truncated Portuguese, as exemplified by Brother Bartolomeu. This was the subsequent evolution on the Ilha de Moçambique, but it happened in all parts of Mozambique where a colonising process was underway. From the point of view of the colonizer, this was a sort of cultural subversion. Not only had the descendant integrated himself in the prevailing social environment, even for the authentic *reinol*, he would not have any alternative than to come to terms with his environment whose support was essential for survival. Thus, they 'went native' (*'cafrealizavam'*). These effects were still more sustained as formal education was limited to the few cases of missionary activity. Moreover, the latter, in a way that was rather paradoxical from the perspective of the colonizer (although logical from the missionnaries' point of view), catechised in local Bantu languages. This was in particular the case for the Jesuits. We can generalise that the message of Christianity, in the particular form in which it appeared in Mozambique, contributed little or nothing to a process of cultural colonisation. In Mozambique, if the Christians of European origin had not already adapted to the local environment, at least their descendants blended completely with local cultural customs, given the above-mentioned 'necessary contact with indigenous Kaffirs, Moors and Indian mixed-race, of whose barbarous customs the settlers would be great followers ...'[44]

Understanding cultural activity in a broad sense, we can claim that the aspect in which Zambesian peculiarity becomes evident is the aristocratic lifestyle. It is most visible in the way of life of the ladies. They appeal, regarding their titles, to a grant of the Queen Dona Maria II. In fact we can verify that our documentation refers systematically to names that follow the title of 'lady' ('Dona'), in full. This taste for aristocratic titles is, in a way, a graphic expression of an unquestionable social hierarchy, which would be perfectly adapted over time. The ladies constitute a homogeneous segment that is clearly significant for the Zambesian aristocracy (in the most etymological sense of the word). This segment had its own profile, without being hereditary or a consequence of matrimony. The ladies are the owners of the land and they are, in the majority of the cases, the persons exercising the lordly powers. In cases in which the husband administers the lordship, he acts on land owned by the ladies. In sum 'the ladies show a clear notion of personality, they exhibit their eminence, they act as landlords and exert violence if they deem it necessary to resort to those means'.[45] With such forms of behaviour, the ladies underlined their aristocratic status. The hierarchy

44 Rau, Virgínia, 'Aspectos Étnico-Culturais da Ilha de Moçambique em 1822', *Studia* 11, p. 136.

45 Capela, José, *Donas, Senhores e Escravos* (Porto: Afrontamento, 1995).

that formed the respective stratification was well delineated: on a lower level than the ladies one could find the *sinharas* and the *nhanhas*. There is some debate about the exact meaning of those designations, but the primacy of the lady is beyond doubt. In the course of the nineteenth century, the hierarchy became adapted to a morphology of racial character (straight or curled hair, skin colour, etc.), but if we look at this process through the perspective of preceding centuries, it is easy to perceive that the hierarchy works through social stratification, through a hierarchy of power.

The aristocratic notion of local behaviour was connected to the presence of persons of knightly origins, who were *reinóis* or Goans. Public posts were regularly taken by members of the nobility and the successful leadership in colonial missions was normally rewarded with a noble title. At the beginnings of the definitive conquest of the East African coast, a considerable part of the armed forces involved were members of the Portuguese aristocracy, which was particularly the case in the War Navy. After the proclamation of liberalism in Portugal, we find the careers of many nobles involving emigration to the African colonies either in the service of the large royal or plantation companies, or on their own account. One example is the tenth Count of Vila Verde, Pedro de Almeida e Noronha Portugal Camões Albuquerque Moniz e Sousa, who possessed his own *prazo* before integrating in the Company of Madal. It was probably his career that inspired Eça de Queiroz when the latter in *A Ilustre Casa de Ramires* refers to a certain Gonçalo, departing from Lisbon to Zambesia, where he obtained the concession of the *prazo* of Macheque.[46]

The sumptuous behaviour of this aristocratic caste became legendary. This was also due to the weakness of missionary efforts: missionaries were largely unable to proceed with the conversion of local populations, and did not even control the Portuguese settlers when it came to the fulfilment of their religious obligations. Consequently, the implantation of 'occidental culture' was frustrated from the outset. Moreover, part of traditional local culture was regarded in some way as picturesque. The missionaries, and Portuguese arrivals in general, were not insensible

46 Queiroz, Eça de, *A Ilustre Casa de Ramires* (fifteenth edition, Lisbon: Edição Livros do Brasil, 1970), p. 346.

to the inventiveness of skilled craftsmen to be found all along the course of the Zambesi River, which found visible expression in ivory sculpture and silver artefacts. Traditional manufacture also had its value in the eyes of the Portuguese. If some elements of Portuguese intrusion resulted, from an economic perspective, in the benefits of increased commercial profit, they also provoked a progressive reduction in the variety of those arts, which became evident in a standardisation of wooden sculpture and in the production of greater quantities of domestic utensils.[47]

Formal education played a role only from the end of the nineteenth century. The literate inhabitants of Mozambique were normally of Goanese origin. The seminary, the creation of which had been intended by Marquês de Pombal, never functioned properly, and the sons of merchants in Mozambique who grew rich through the slave trade were sent to study in Goa, Mauritius, Europe, Brazil, or Montevideo. The latter frequently did not return, or in the few cases in which they reappeared in Mozambique, they integrated in the local societies without being the agents of any visible change.[48] We can ascertain that the 'Zambesian Ethos' did not incorporate any attributes imported from modern formal schooling.

Conclusion

The phenomenon of Portuguese colonisation in South-east Africa left in the Zambesi Valley the most profound and lasting marks of its presence. Above other reasons, this was due to a certain symbiotic accommodation between colonisers and colonised populations with regard to cultural encounter and interest. The Portuguese impact in Zambesia shows a unique type of evolution of identity over the centuries: the populations concerned developed their notion of 'Zambesianess', which would eclipse all forms of ethno-cultural community.

47 Author's local observation along the Zambesi missionary stations.

48 Capela, José, *O Tráfico de Escravos nos Portos de Moçambique, 1733–1904* (Porto: Edições Afrontamento, 2002), p. 156.

When from the beginning of the sixteenth century the colonisers slowly penetrated the hinterland of Mozambique and established themselves in those regions, they did not have the material means or supporters enough to conquer the area, nor even the resources to guarantee their proper subsistence. Moreover, the first European incursions were individual initiatives. After a short interval, entering the areas of local rulerships, they would have established relations with local structures. Those relations, being normally of commercial nature, concerned the 'traditional rulers', but also trade networks which for some period already facilitated long-distance trade. The new intruders obtained their own lordships from those sovereigns, which meant rule over physical space and over persons. Those lordships welcomed refugees wishing to escape from lineage justice. The *alienígena* (foreigner) professional traders, acquired through the grace of the indigenous sovereign, through marriage in the royal house, but sometimes also through military action, the status of *muzungo*. In this way, they were able to find themselves at the same level as the heir of the chieftaincy of the lineage. This occurred repeatedly with the descendants of those Europeans, or of Goans, with African women. The process led to the formation of great lordships that would finally dominate the geographic area extending to the interior from the Indian Ocean in a belt between the left side of the Zambesi River to the north, and the Save River, to the south. As this lordly or masterly institution had been formally sanctioned by the Portuguese Crown in the sixteenth century, it created in this part of Africa a particular community status. This status combined experiences of traditional political and social organisation with elements imported by the intruders, leading to a symbiosis of values that allowed the system to exist until the end of the nineteenth century. Some aspects of its pertinent elements are even projected onto current local culture in Zambesia. The system did not become dominant without conflicts, those conflicts including military violence. However, it was not because of such internal violence that the system of lordships or dominions vulgarly called *Prazos da Coroa* finally ended.

Within this system, the social groups were perfectly delimited one from the other, and the aristocratic self-assertion derives from the nature of the implanted social relations, in which the proper values of the lordship accommodated themselves nearly perfectly in introducing on the one hand elements from European systems of rule, and preserving, on the other hand, parts of traditional lineage rule. The continuing presence of European 'gentlemen farmers' contributed well to the installation in the Zambesi Valley of these aristocratic aspirations and practices.

These aristocratic assumptions manifest themselves in the morphology both of language and of social representation. They appear in local literature. The most impressive exponents of the system are the ladies of Zambesia whose social position has no parallel in other geographic areas of Portuguese colonisation. They took the lordship of the lands by title, they ruled over slaves and African settlers, they armed ships active in the slave trade, they commanded war campaigns, and they were always addressed as 'ladies' (*donas*) being at the same level as the *muzungos*.

Even today, the Mozambican coming from Zambesia proudly exhibits the name that identifies him, and congratulates himself if his interlocutor responds to the true or pretended aristocratic claims of such an announcement. The continuities of this regional identity precluded ethnic mobilisation in Zambesia.

Bibliography

Afonso, Sant'Ana, *Luane* (unpublished text).

Alva, J. Jorge Klor de, 'The Postcolonization of the (Latin) American Experience: A reconsideration of 'Colonialism', 'Postcolonialism', and 'Mestizaje'', in Gyan Prakash (ed.), *After Colonialism: Imperial Histories and Postcolonial Displacements* (Princeton: Princeton University Press, 1995), pp. 241–275.

Amselle, Jean-Loup, *Logiques métisses. Anthropologie et identité en Afrique et ailleurs* (Paris: Payot, 1990).

Angius, Matteo, *A figura e obra do jornalista José Júlio Roldão (1900–1979) – Contribuição para a história da imprensa em Moçambique* (Diss. de Licenciatura, Universidade Eduardo Mondlane, Maputo, 1997).

Bannerman, James, *Notes and Questions Regarding the Archaeology, Language and Ethnohistory of Central Mozambique between the Zambezi and Save Rivers* (Harare: Panafrican Congress, 1995).

Beach, David N., *The Shona and Zimbabwe, 900–1850* (Gwelo (Zimbabwe): Mambo Press, 1980).

Birnbaum, Pierre (ed.), *Sociologie des nationalismes* (Paris: Presses Universitaires de France, 1997).

Bourdieu, Pierre, *O Poder Simbólico* (Lisbon, Difel, fourth edition 1994 [1989]).

Bourdieu, Pierre, *Meditações Pascalianas* (Oeiras: Celta Editora, 1998).

Capela, José, *Donas, Senhores e Escravos* (Porto: Afrontamento, 1995).

Capela, José, 'Conflitos Sociais na Zambézia, 1878–1892 – A transição do Senhorio para a Plantação', *Africana Studia* 1, 1999, pp. 143–173.

Capela, José, *O Tráfico de Escravos nos Portos de Moçambique, 1733–1904* (Porto: Edições Afrontamento, 2002).

Capela, José, 'Como as Aringas de Moçambique se transformaram em Quilombos', *Tempo (Departamento de História da Universidade Federal Fluminense)* 20, 2006, pp. 83–108.

Carrilho, João Luís, *Relatório do governador do Distrito de Tete, 1911–1912* (Lourenço Marques: Imprensa Nacional, 1913).

Carvalho, F., *Distrito de Quelimane: Relatório do Governador 1911–1912* (Lourenço Marques: Imprensa Nacional, 1912).

Carvalho, F., *Distrito de Quelimante, Relatório do Governador 1914–1915* (Lourenço Marques: Imprensa Nacional, 1916).

Carvalho, Ruy Duarte de, *Desmedida: crónicas do Brasil* (Lisbon: Edições Cotovia, 2008).

Coelho, João Paulo Borges, *As Duas Sombras do Rio* (Lisbon: Caminho, 2003).

Cohen, Anthony P. (ed.), *Symbolising Boundaries: Identity and Diversity in British Cultures* (Manchester: Manchester University Press, 1986).

Cohen, Anthony P., 'Boundaries of Consciousness, Consciousness of Boundaries: Critical Questions for Anthropology', in Hans Vermeulen and Cora Govers (eds.), *The Anthropology of Ethnicity: Beyond 'Ethnic Groups and Boundaries'* (Amsterdam: Het Spinhuis, 1994), pp. 59–78.

Courtois, Victor José, *Dicionário Portuguez-Cafre-Tetense – ou Idioma falado no Districto de Tete e na vasta região do Zambeze Inferior* (Coimbra: Imprensa da Universidade, 1899).

Cunha, Maria Manuela Carneiro da, 'A identidade como memória', in *Dinâmicas multiculturais, novas faces, outros olhares. Actas das sessões plenárias do III° Congresso Luso-Afro-Brasileiro de Ciências Sociais* (Lisbon: ICS-UL, 1994), pp. 193–223.

Dos Santos, Frei João, *Ethiópia Oriental* (Lisbon: Typographia do Commércio de Portugal, 1891).

Dos Santos, Frei João, *Etiópia Oriental e Vária História de Cousas Notáveis do Oriente*. Introduction by Manuel Lobato, notes by Manuel Lobato and Eduardo Medeiros (Lisbon: Comissão Nacional para as Comemorações dos Descobrimentos Portugueses, 1999 [1609]).

Drummond, Lee, 'The cultural continuum: A theory of intersystems', *Man* 15(2), 1980, pp. 352–374.

Durão, A. de Portugal, *O distrito de Quelimane – Agricultura e Mão D'Obra*, Conferência realizada na Sociedade de Geografia de Lisboa em 21 de Março de 1914.

Enes, António, *Moçambique* (Lisbon: Agência Geral das Colónias, 1946).

Fabian, Johannes, 'Popular culture in Africa: Findings and Conjectures', *Africa* 48(4), 1978, pp. 315–334.

Figueiredo Morais, João M., 'O princípio e o presente: a Arqueologia na redescoberta do passado em Moçambique', *ICALP-Revista do Instituto de Cultura e Língua Portuguesa* 18, 1989, pp. 74–92.

Hannerz, Ulf, 'The World in Creolisation', *Africa* 57(4), 1987, pp. 546–559.

Hannerz, Ulf, 'Scenarios for Peripheral Cultures', in A. D. King (ed.), *Culture, Globalization and the World-System* (London: Macmillan, 1991), pp. 107–128.

Hannerz, Ulf, 'Fluxos, fronteiras, híbridos: palavras-chave da Antropologia transnacional', *Mana* (Rio de Janeiro) 3(1), 1997, pp. 7–39.

Isaacman, Allen F., 'The origin, formation and early history of the Chikunda of south-central Africa', *Journal of African History* 13 (3), 1972, pp. 443–461.

Isaacman, Allen F., and Barbara S. Isaacman, *Slavery and Beyond: The Making of Men and Chikunda Ethnic Identities in the Unstable World of South-Central Africa, 1750–1920* (Portsmouth/NH: Heinemann, 2004).

Isaacman, Allen F., and Barbara S. Isaacman, *Mozambique. The Africanization of a European Institution: The Zambezi Prazos, 1750–1902* (Madison: University of Wisconsin Press – London: North Central Publishing, 1972).

Isaacman, Allen, and Elias Mandala, 'From Porters to Labor Extractors: The Chikunda and Kololo in the Lake Malawi and Tchiri River Area, 1885–1891', in Catherine Coquery-Vidrovitch and Paul Lovejoy (eds.), *The Workers of African Trade* (Beverly Hills: SAGE Publications, 1985), pp. 209–243.

Ishemo, Shubi Lugemalila, *The Lower Zambezi Basin: A Study in Economy and Society, 1850–1920* (Aldershot: Avebury, 1995).

Jackson, Jean, 'Is there a way of talking about culture without making enemies?', *Dialectical Anthropology* 14, 1989, pp. 127–143.

Liesegang, Gerhard, 'Territorialidades sociais e identidades com referência a Moçambique', in Carlos Serra (ed.), *Identidade/ Moçambicanidade/ Moçambicanização* (Maputo: Livraria Universitária – Universidade Eduardo Mondlane, 1998), pp. 99–159.

Maugham, Reginald C.F., *Zambezia: A General Description of the Valley of the Zambezi River from its Delta to the River Aroangwa, with its History, Agriculture, Flora, Fauna and Ethnography* (London: John Murray, 1910).

Medeiros, Eduardo, 'Etnias e etnicidade em Moçambique. O advento do Mundo Sena. Das origens a 1918', in José Carlos Venâncio (ed.), *O Desafio Africano* (Lisbon: Veja – Universidade da Beira Interior, 1997), pp. 59–82.

Newitt, Malyn, *A History of Mozambique* (London: Hurst, 1995).

Pélissier, René, *La Naissance du Mozambique. Résistance et révoltes anticoloniales (1854–1921)* (Orgeval: Author's edn, 1984), 2 vols. (Portuguese edn: *História de Moçambique – Formação e oposição (1854–1918)* (Lisbon: Editorial Estampa, 1987–1988), 2 vols.).

Queiroz, Eça de, *A Ilustre Casa de Ramires* (thirteenth edition Lisbon: Edição Livros do Brasil, 1970).

Rau, Virgínia, 'Aspectos Étnico-Culturais da Ilha de Moçambique em 1822', *Separata of Studia* 11, pp. 123–162.

Rita-Ferreira, António, *Agrupamento e caracterização étnica dos indígenas de Moçambique* (Lisbon: Ministério do Ultramar, Junta de Investigações do Ultramar, 1958).

Rita-Ferreira, António, *Povos de Moçambique – História e Cultura* (Porto: Afrontamento, 1975).

Rita-Ferreira, António, *Fixação Portuguesa e História Pré-Colonial de Moçambique* (Lisbon: JICU, 1982).

Rita-Ferreira, António, 'Grupos Étnicos e História Pré-colonial de Moçambique', *Moçambique – Aspectos da Cultura Material* 6, 1986, pp. 15–31.

Rita-Ferreira, António, *African Kingdoms and Alien Settlements in Central Mozambique (c.15th–17th Cent.)* (Coimbra: Departamento de Antropologia, Universidade de Coimbra, 1999).

San Bruno, Emílio de, *Zambeziana, Cenas da Vida Colonial* (Maputo: Arquivo Histórico de Moçambique, 1999).

Serra, Carlos, *Combates pela mentalidade sociológica* (Maputo: Livraria Universitária, 1997).

Serra, Carlos (ed.), *Identidade e Moçambicanização* (Maputo: Livraria Universitária, 1998).

Sinclair, Paul J., *Space, Time and Social Formation: A Territorial Approach to the Archaeology and Anthropology of Zimbabwe and Mozambique, c. 0–1700 AD* (Uppsala: Societas Archaeologica Upsaliensis, 1987).

Sorensen, Maria, *Dona Theodora e os seus Mozungos* (Maputo: Ndjira, 1998).

Tew, Mary, *Ethnographic Survey of Africa: East Central Africa, Part I: Peoples of the Lake Nyassa Region* (London: International African Institute, 1950).

Turner, Victor W., *Dramas, Fields, and Metaphors: Symbolic Action in Human Society* (Ithaca, Cornell University Press, 1974).

Turner, Victor W., *O processo ritual* (Petropolis: Ed. Vozes, 1974).

Vilhena, Ernesto de, *Regime dos Prazos da Zambézia* (Lisbon: Imprensa Nacional, 1916).

Malyn Newitt*

Kinship, Religion, Language and Political Control: Ethnic Identity among the Peoples of the Zambesi Valley

Introduction: the Problem of Ethnicity

Ethnic identity is, to say the least, an elusive concept. Take, for example, this extract from Harry Langworthy's thesis on the Cewa.

> This work could either be called a history of the Chewa and Undi's kingdom or a history of Undi's Malawi empire. However, it is probably more accurate to speak of the Chewa people and kingdoms...Malawi can also be used to refer to the various rulers of such peoples as the Chewa, Chipeta, Zimba, Nyanja, Mang'anja, Ntumba and Mbo. Linguistically and culturally these people are much the same, and might be called after their rulers as Malawi peoples. Non-Malawi peoples, such as the Nsenga and the Lomwe, were at various times ruled by the Malawi rulers... The name Chewa appears to be of relatively recent origin, at least for some of the peoples to whom it refers. It might be more historically accurate to say that this study concerns the western Malawi peoples, or the western Nyanja-speaking peoples.[1]

The contortions that the author, a distinguished Africanist, has got himself into merely reflect the confusion that surrounds the whole issue of ethnicity, its origin and development, and its meaning to different people at different times.

When the Portuguese first attempted to describe the peoples of East Central Africa they were doing so at a time when, in the European world, it was as important to establish what religion people practised and whom they recognised as their sovereign as it was to describe their nationality.

* King's College, London.

1 Langworthy, Harry, *A History of Undi's Kingdom to 1890: Aspects of Chewa History in East Central Africa* (PhD thesis, Boston University, 1969), pp. v–vi.

First and foremost, therefore, the Portuguese tried to establish what religion people practised, what states existed and who the rulers were with whom they had to deal. Kings and emperors were more important than tribes or nations (the Portuguese used the word *'nação'* in describing the African people with whom they had contact) and ethnic descriptions were of a broad and generic kind. Indeed the Portuguese often assumed that to designate the name of a state or the name of a chief or king was sufficient description for the inhabitants.

It was in the eighteenth century that attitudes began to change and attempts were made to distinguish between different peoples using other criteria. This was linked to the rise of the natural sciences. Botanists and zoologists became immersed in the task of classifying and describing species and sub-species and it was natural to assume that the human race could also be described and classified in the same way. So physical anthropology was born as well as ethnography and the cruder classifications based on 'race'. In the nineteenth century it was common for writers to claim that moral and cultural qualities could be, and were, inherited as part of an individual's genetic make up. The inhabitants of India or Africa were separated into numerous distinct castes and tribes to which were assigned innate physical, moral and cultural characteristics.

With the founding of the colonial empires, ethnic classification became of great importance for governments. It was used as a means for wielding power – a device for grouping people so that they could be allocated to some chieftaincy for the purposes of government. In post-colonial Africa ethnicity has frequently been emphasised by rulers or aspirants for power in order to secure political support and it is in this socio-political arena that ethnicity still retains a crucial importance.[2]

Ethnic or national identity is not, however, something imposed or manipulated by ruling elites. Self-identification is equally important. This exists at a number of levels and takes a variety of forms; the recognition of immediate blood kinship (lineage) and the acknowledgment of belonging to a wider clan; the acceptance of cultural affinity with those speaking the same language, practising the same religion and following

2 See, for example, Vail, Leroy, and Landeg White, 'Tribalism and the Political History of Malawi', in Leroy Vail (ed.), *The Creation of Tribalism in Southern Africa* (Berkeley – Los Angeles: University of California Press, 1991 [1989]), pp. 151–192.

the same social customs; the description of oneself in terms of occupation or geographical location; and, of course, the recognition of the political authority to whom one is subject. Self-identification is primarily functional and is concerned with the protection and support that can be derived from group membership.[3] By implication it involves the identification and naming of those to be excluded from the group.

Separate and distinct ethnic identities often seem to have been adopted as a device for establishing or asserting the autonomy or independence of a particular society. When a group broke away from whoever exercised overrule, it was important to adopt a new name, even though such a distinction did not necessarily imply a different language or different social customs, or even a different origin from neighbouring groups. António Gamitto, writing of the situation in 1831, lists the different 'tribal' names of the people in Zambesia from Quelimane to west of the Luangwa and explains that:

> all these people today are totally independent of each other, and each is known by its own name. Nevertheless, it is beyond dispute, that all are of the same Maravi race, having the same habits, customs and language.[4]

Livingstone, twenty-five years later, says exactly the same thing:

> The country north of the mountains here in sight of the Zambesi is called Senga, and its inhabitants Asenga, or Basenga, but all appear to be of the same family as the rest of the Manganja and Maravi.[5]

The problem of ethnicity is complicated still further by the way in which names have been used. Many names, which are still employed to describe

3 Robert Papstein makes the point that ethnic rivalry between the Luvale and the Lunda intensified during the period of the slave trade as people sought protection against being enslaved. See Papstein, Robert, 'From Ethnic Identity to Tribalism: the Upper Zambezi Region of Zambia, 1839–1981', in Leroy Vail (ed.), *The Creation of Tribalism in Southern Africa* (Berkeley – Los Angeles: University of California Press, 1991 [1989]), pp. 372–394.

4 Gamitto, A.C.P., *King Kazembe,* translated by Ian Cunnison (Lisbon: Junta da Investigações do Ultramar, 1960 [1854]), vol. 1., p. 64.

5 Livingstone, David, and Charles Livingstone, *Narrative of an Expedition to the Zambesi and its Tributaries* (London: Duckworth, 2001 [London: Murray, 1865]), p. 150.

ethnic groups or subgroups, can be shown to be very ancient. Obvious examples would be Karanga or Zimba or Maravi – all labels recorded in the sixteenth or early seventeenth centuries. However, the survival of these names over five hundred years disguises the different ways in which they have been used. The Karanga are today a small sub-group of the northern Shona and the name is no longer utilised, as it was in the seventeenth century, to describe all Shona-speakers and their chiefly dynasties. The name Maravi, first used to describe the invaders who established chieftaincies at the end of the sixteenth century, then became attached to the capital of one of these chiefs, and finally to whole populations between the Shire and Luangwa before largely disappearing as an indicator of specific ethnic identity and surviving only as a geographical term (for example Malawi, Lake Malawi, Maravia in Tete province).

This paper argues that, although there are permanent poles of identification like common languages, chiefly titles, and spirit cults, which can be shown to have existed for many centuries, the East Central African region, and Zambesia in particular, was always a kaleidoscope of shifting political formations giving rise to a constantly changing pattern of identification – both self-identification and identification by others. Moreover the ethnic names which were used at different times never became a stable form of scientific classification but reflected the changing needs of the populations and of those who tried to establish some form of overrule.

Much of this constant 'rebranding' of peoples can be explained by understanding the nature of African state systems. In her seminal work *Primitive Government*, first published in 1962, Lucy Mair drew attention to the importance of patronage in African state formation:

> In the discussion of the expansion of government, it was shown how significant in this process is the building up of a body of persons who depend upon their leader in such a way that their first loyalty is to him. This relationship of clientage may well be the germ from which state power springs. It is certainly of prime importance in the Interlacustrine Bantu States, where it can sometimes be seen to run through the whole society from top to bottom, everyone except the king being somebody's client and everyone except the lowliest peasant having clients of his own.[6]

6 Mair, Lucy, *Primitive Government* (Harmondsworth: Penguin Books, 1962), p. 166.

If the relation of patron and client can be seen to be fundamental to African polities, big and small, it is also fundamental to the creation of groups, which subsequently identify themselves as distinct from their neighbours.

Early Portuguese Attempts at Classifying the African Populations

When the Portuguese first settled in the ports of the East African coast at the beginning of the sixteenth century, they made use of descriptive names which were in current use – Tonga to describe the inhabitants of the Zambesi valley and coastal lowlands; Karanga for the peoples of the high veldt; Bororo and Makua for the populations north of the river and the all-purpose term 'Mouros' for the coastal Muslim populations. It is likely that these generic terms, referred broadly to perceived linguistic and cultural differences but did not pretend to any more specific identification. João dos Santos, writing in 1609, is quite clear about this:

> All these Cafres are called Mocarangas, as all speak the Mocaranga language, and for this reason all these lands are also called Mocaranga, except parts of the kingdoms along the seacoast, where other languages are spoken, particularly the Botonga tongue, for which reason these lands are called Botonga and their inhabitants Botongas.[7]

And Manuel Barretto writes in 1667 that in 'our lands are all Botonga of the same language and nation'.[8]

7 Dos Santos, João, *Etiópia Oriental e Vária História de Cousas Notáveis do Oriente* (Lisbon: Comissão Nacional para as Comemorações dos Descobrimentos Portugueses, 1999 [Évora, 1609]), pp. 204–205. Santos (p. 247) calls the Makua a *'nação'* distinguished by cultural traits like the filing of teeth.

8 Barretto, Manuel, 'Informação do Estado e Conquista dos Rios de Cuama', in G.M. Theal (ed.), *Records of South Eastern Africa*, 9 vols (Cape Town, 1898–1903; reprinted Cape Town: C. Struik, 1964), vol. 3, pp. 436–508, 481.

Indeed, although the term Karanga probably covered all the people who were specifically Shona-speakers, the term Tonga meant simply 'slave' or 'subject' and was a general term used by the Karanga and Maravi, to describe the subject populations of the Zambesi valley and the coastal lowlands who had little in common with each other – speaking different dialects, recognising different political authorities and venerating different spirit cults. As late as the 1830s Gamitto used the name 'Butonga' to describe the Tumbuka and defined the term, not as an ethnic group but as 'immigrant cultivator'.[9] Up to the present, the term 'Tonga' has been used as an ethnic descriptive term for peoples as varied as the 'Valley Tonga' of Zambia, the 'Lakeside Tonga' of Malawi and the inhabitants of the hinterland of Inhambane. The term, which exists in one form or another in all Bantu languages, turns up in the most unexpected places – and is even used for the descendants of contract workers resident in the island of São Tomé in the Gulf of Guinea.

The term Ndau, used today to describe a section of the Shona-speaking population of Zimbabwe and Mozambique also originated as a pejorative term used by the Nguni to describe people they had conquered.[10]

These broad linguistic classifications, on which the Portuguese relied for at least three centuries after their arrival in eastern Africa, were supplemented, after the European practice, by dividing the land and the population into identifiable polities or states. The African population was perceived as belonging to kingdoms and the Portuguese decided to order these by assuming the existence of an original 'empire of Monomotapa' from which the kingdoms had broken away but to which they were still loosely connected through tradition, the payment of tribute and the recognition of titles. Later they were to imagine the existence north of the Zambesi of an 'empire of Maravi… governed by its emperor, named Caronga' and an 'empire of Moenemugi' – though this

9 Gamitto, *King Kazembe*, vol. 1, p. 147.

10 Ranger, Terence, 'Missionaries, Migrants and the Manyika: the Invention of Ethnicity in Zimbabwe', in Leroy Vail (ed.), *The Creation of Tribalism in Southern Africa* (Berkeley – Los Angeles: University of California Press, 1991 [1989]), pp. 118–150, especially 121. See also MacGonagle, Elisabeth, *Crafting Identity in Zimbabwe and Mozambique* (Rochester: University of Rochester Press, 2007), p. 16.

name, as Gamitto pointed out, was simply the honorific title born by many minor chiefs of the region.[11]

Subordinate to these imagined 'empires' were kingdoms. Writing in the 1630s António Bocarro, in an often quoted passage, described how Mokaranga 'is divided among petty kings and other lords with fewer vassals…who are all vassals of Monomotapa'. He then lists twenty-two kingdoms, each with its own name and a royal title. In many instances the name of the kingdom is used to describe the people who live in it – very much after the fashion of contemporary Europe.[12]

The logic of allocating populations to kingdoms is that they can be classified as rebels and coerced if they do not accept such an allocation. The same logic can also lead to claims being made to control land and resources, and in the seventeenth century the Portuguese made generous use of this attribution of sovereignty, asserting that African kings, by signing various treaties, had transferred population, land and mineral resources to Portugal.[13]

Once the existence of defined states had been decided on, it then became important to establish who was the legitimate ruler of these states. Disputed succession provided opportunities for intervention, for patronage and for the further extension of power relations. Moreover the Portuguese tried to impose their own notions of primogeniture on kingdoms whose rules of succession were adelphic or obeyed systems even more complex. Missionaries took the lead in this as they sought to make converted kings monogamous and recognised only the eldest son of the first wife as the true heir. As in the Congo, primogeniture became a way of imposing authority and reordering social and political hierarchies. What started as system of scientific classification had become an instrument of power and conquest.

11 For a discussion of the concept of an 'empire of Monomotapa' see Newitt, Malyn, *A History of Mozambique* (London: Hurst, 1995), p. 40; Gamitto, *King Kazembe* vol. 1, p. 92; Barretto, 'Informação', p. 480.

12 Bocarro, António, 'Livro do Estado da Índia', in George M. Theal (ed.), *Records of South Eastern Africa collected in various libraries and archive departments in Europe*, 9 vols. (Cape Town, 1898–1903; reprinted Cape Town: Struik, 1964), vol. 3, pp. 254–435, 357–358.

13 Newitt, *History*, pp. 83, 90.

Expansion of the Karanga Chieftaincies

In constructing their image of the ethno-politics of East Central Africa the Portuguese were trying to establish a permanent system of empires and kingdoms in a world where the locus of power constantly changed, where polities appeared and disappeared and populations were highly mobile.

As the Portuguese built their factory and fort at Sofala in the early years of the sixteenth century, they witnessed and reported on the conquest of the coastal regions inland from Sofala and Inhambane by chiefs who were probably originally associated with Great Zimbabwe. The Portuguese used the term Karanga for these ruling dynasties, which all shared a coherent body of political custom, belief and ritual.[14]

As the Portuguese soon came to realise, Karanga kingship, like that of so many other African monarchies, was far removed from contemporary European ideas of monarchy. It was a complex system balancing the interests of rival clans with different traditions of origin and different relations to the land. Moreover, the influence of these clans extended into the spirit world where the dead as well as the living wielded power and influence. The spirit cults of the ancestors and the rain-callers constituted a focus of loyalty and a system of authority every bit as important as that of the chiefs who had established their overrule.[15]

What, of course, the Portuguese were trying to come to terms with was a world where dynasties of chiefs were often held to be distinct from the people over whom they ruled. These dynasties were frequently distinguished by a separate narrative of origins and remained strongly identified with a particular clan or lineage. The Karanga were originally dynasties of chiefs who shared common traditions of origin and a common language but the description 'Karanga' did not necessarily extend to all the people over whom they ruled. By the end of the sixteenth century, however, the Portuguese were using the name almost exclusively for the territory and

14 For a detailed discussion of Shona origins see Beach, David N., *The Shona and Zimbabwe 900–1850* (London: Heinemann, 1980).

15 Mudenge, S.I.G., *A Political History of Munhumutapa c. 1400–1902* (Harare: Zimbabwe Publishing House, 1988), pp. 119–134.

population ruled over by the Monomotapa[16], the other Karanga chieftaincies having acquired distinctive names and dynastic titles that clearly differentiated them from each other. According to Santos,

> Monomotapa and the Mocaranga his vassals wear a white shell on the forehead, hanging from the hair as an ornament, and Monomotapa wears another large shell on his breast. These shells they call *andoros*, and they are looked upon with hatred by Quiteve, as they are insignia of his enemy Monomotapa, and therefore neither Quiteve nor his vassals wear *andoros*, although they are all of them Mocrangas.[17]

The so-called Rosvi are another example of a ruling elite maintaining an identity distinct from the populations over whom they ruled and from the rulers who had gone before them. When in the 1680s Changamira Dombo, a man of relatively humble origin, conquered the lands of the long-established Karanga chieftaincy of Butua, he not only founded a new ruling dynasty but established his kin and followers as a new aristocracy who called themselves Rosvi. In the eighteenth century the Portuguese came to use the term Rosvi (which they rendered Borobzes) for all the inhabitants of the kingdom of Butua.[18]

What the Portuguese had witnessed south of the Zambesi was repeated in the north. In the second half of the sixteenth century, after a prolonged period of drought, the region north of the Zambesi was invaded by armed groups organised, like the Imbangala of Angola, in war camps and practising cannibalism. These war bands ranged further north still to Cape Delgado, Kilwa and even as far as Mombasa and Melinde. The Portuguese referred to these invaders as Zimba and Mumbos (possibly Mbo), names which have continued to be used to describe specific ethnic groups to the present. These migrants eventually established new chieftaincies stretching from the Luangwa to the Shire and the Mozambique lowlands, the most famous of which were Lundu, Kalonga (or

16 In 1667 Manuel Barretto could write 'Mokaranga is the name of the famous kingdom of Monomotapa, and the natives are called Mokarangas'. See Barretto, 'Informação', p. 482.

17 Santos, *Etiópia*, p. 222.

18 Mudenge, S.I.G., *The Rozvi Empire and the Feira of Zumbo* (PhD thesis, London University, 1972); Caetano Xavier, Inácio, 'Notícias dos Domínios Portugueses de África Oriental 1758', in António Alberto de Andrade (ed.), *Relações de Moçambique Setecentista* (Lisbon: Agência Geral do Ultramar, 1955), pp. 139–188, 145.

Caronga) and Undi, and to which the Portuguese gave the name Maravi (from which the modern Malawi is derived).[19]

As a ruling elite the Maravi remained distinct from the bulk of the population. According to Langworthy, 'Undi's tributary kings and chiefs were originally either close junior kinsmen of Undi or his companions on the migration into the area'.[20] Belonging to one or other of the chiefly clans (the Banda and the Phiri) was more important for the Maravi elites than any wider ethnic identity. Most chiefs came from the Phiri clan, which possibly descended from the original Maravi invaders, while the Banda clan, which also provided some chiefs, may have originated with the conquered, pre-Maravi population. Belonging to these clans conferred both status and legitimacy.[21]

The authority of the Maravi chiefs was dependent on their ability to distribute wealth in various forms among their followers. Tribute received from the population was used to support the ruler and, in theory at least, was redistributed among the principal sub-chiefs on whom his authority depended. Goods obtained through trade were also dispensed as patronage and this explains why the chiefs in this region tried to control itinerant traders and to insist that trade was either conducted directly with themselves or at centrally controlled markets.[22] Although the Maravi chiefs established complex relationships with the spirit cults and clans of the conquered peoples, theirs was a state system that, like that of their Karanga contemporaries, rested ultimately on patronage.

The kingdoms that were ruled by Maravi dynasties were not composed of homogeneous populations, but over time the name 'Maravi', originally referring to dynasties of chiefs, eventually became attached to their kingdoms and then became a generic name used to describe the populations of those kingdoms. However, as soon as the Maravi kingdoms began to fragment in the nineteenth century, the groups that

19 Newitt, Malyn, 'The Early History of the Maravi', *Journal of African History* 23(1), 1982, pp. 145–162.

20 Langworthy, *History*, p. 28.

21 *ibid.*, pp. 14, 28. The Luvale provide another example of chieftaincy being confined exclusively to a single clan, the NamaKungu, all of whose members are deemed to be chiefs. See Papstein, 'Identity', p. 376.

22 Langworthy, *History*, pp. 38–39.

broke away and established their independence assumed new names and new identities.

The Ngoni invasions of the nineteenth century provide further examples of invading war bands, developing more or less stable states. The Ngoni war parties that invaded Central Africa in the period 1820 to 1840 were probably quite small and were led by chiefs linked to the ruling clan of the Ndwandwe. Eventually, these Ngoni chiefs and their immediate followers established a series of powerful chieftaincies in southern Mozambique, Malawi, northern Mozambique, Zambia and Tanzania, absorbing the local populations who then assumed an 'Ngoni' identity.[23]

In these conquests (of the Karanga, the Maravi and the Ngoni) two processes of assimilation can be seen. The conquerors themselves would build up their personal followings through the capture and incorporation of young men of fighting age, and the acquisition of booty in the form of women, children and slaves with which to reward their clients and followers. However, they would also establish relations with the conquered populations who would be reduced to paying tribute and would be required to recognise sovereignty and overlordship by attendance at periodic ceremonies. In some cases assimilated and subject populations alike adopted the customs, languages and rituals of the conquerors and so became, in effect, part of their ethnic group, but in others the rulers and the ruled remained separate and distinct.

In the construction of a new identity for conquered populations, the acceptance of a common narrative of origins was of particular importance. Langworthy has described the role of oral history in creating this new ethnicity. The traditional histories of the ruling elite are remembered not only to buttress their legitimacy but to provide a sort of cultural cement binding together the disparate elements in the population. 'History explains who the people are, why they are in the area and justifies their existence… the remote period of history further serves to unify the people and their rulers… commoners may have had diverse origins…yet, in general they have come to accept their rulers' remote pe-

23 Liesegang, Gerhard, *Beiträge zur Geschichte des Reiches der Gaza Nguni im südlichen Moçambique 1820–1895* (doctoral dissertation, University of Cologne, 1967); Liesegang, Gerhard, 'Nguni Migrations between Delagoa Bay and the Zambesi, 1821–1839', *African Historical Studies* 3(2), 1970, pp. 317–337.

riod of history as a type of tribal history' – a good example of the 'invention of tradition' as a way of creating a kind of ethnic solidarity.[24]

However, cultural assimilation did not always work this way and there are examples of the conquerors being themselves absorbed into the ethnic culture of the conquered. This happened in Barue where the conquering Karanga dynasty gradually adopted the language and culture of the 'Tonga' population, so that Manuel Barretto, writing in 1667, says specifically that 'the natives of this kingdom are Botongas'.[25] A key factor would often be the power and importance of local spirit cults. All conquerors had to come to terms with these cults which in some cases retained as great an influence over the lives of the people as the chiefs themselves. These cults, providing a kind of 'shadow' authority, might survive when the secular authority of chiefs was on the wane or had disappeared altogether, and veneration of the spirit mediums of these cults could prove a stronger cultural cement than identification with a state, a chieftaincy or a supposed ethnicity.

The importance of the Mbona rain shrine on the Shire is a case in point. The influence of this shrine probably prevented the Lundu chieftaincy imposing an unchallenged political hegemony and a distinct ethnicity on the population of region. When the Lundu chieftaincy collapsed in the face of attacks by Yao and Makololo in the nineteenth century, the Mbona shrine continued to provide the focus for a distinctive Manganja identity.[26] Another case is provided by the Makewana spirit medium and rain-caller who was closely linked with the Undi chieftaincy and whose destruction by the Ngoni proved fatal to the survival of Undi's kingdom.[27]

There are also instances of conquered or immigrant populations which for one reason or another did not become assimilated into the language and culture of the majority population. On the high veldt south of the Zambesi there were enclaves of Tonga populations which survived incorporation into the dominant Karanga culture – for exam-

24 Langworthy, *History*, p. 83.

25 Barretto, 'Informação', p. 488.

26 For the Mbona rain shrine see Schoffeleers, Matthew, 'Mbona, the Guardian Spirit of the Manganja' (BLitt thesis, Oxford, 1966).

27 Langworthy, *History*, pp. 73–78.

ple the Tonga of Maramuca and the population of the Inyanga highlands.[28] Among the Cewa, there were people who were known as Tumbuka. In 1831 Gamitto described how 'the Tumbuka are a distinct tribe, and live as peasants (*colonos*) on the Cewa lands, in villages of their own situated among Cewa villages; and in many of the latter there are some Tumbuka inhabitants also'.[29] The Tumbuka, he writes, were not allowed to wear cloth, which was a prerogative of the Cewa 'and any Tumbuka wearing it gets involved in a big case, in which they with their families would be enslaved; in consequence they wear only skins'[30]. In this case dress helped to preserve the notion of a separate ethnic identity which served to keep the Tumbuka in an inferior economic position by defining them as 'different'.

Population Mobility and Social Change in the Zambesi Valley

Chiefly titles, often vested in specific lineages or clans, provide continuity in the history of the region both north and south of the Zambesi. Chiefly titles like Monomotapa, Macombe (of Barue), Makoni (of Maungwe), Chicanga (of Manica) and many others survived over many centuries as did the chiefly titles of Undi, Lundu and Kalonga north of the river. These chieftaincies might experience frequent disputed successions, and their real power might fluctuate a great deal, but the prestige of the titles and of the spirit cults associated with dead title holders remained. However, it might well be asked if the ordinary population shared in this long term stability. Here the evidence is apparently contradictory.

In his book *The Shona and Zimbabwe*, David Beach maintained that what he called 'the little society' – remained relatively unchanged over the centuries. However, he also emphasised the mobility of populations,

28 Abraham, D.P., 'Maramuca: an Exercise in the combined use of Portuguese records and oral tradition', *Journal of African History* 2(2), 1961, pp. 213–235.

29 Gamitto, *Kazembe,* vol. 1, p. 147.

30 *ibid.*, p. 117.

one of the most important causes of which was drought. 'In four years out of five there would be normal rainfall, it was probable that in the fifth there would be *shangwa* in which the community would be forced to look outside agriculture for its survival'.[31] East Central Africa experiences irregular seasonal rainfall, so that settled African populations have had to develop strategies to cope with periodic drought. However, there are also longer dry periods when rains may fail for many years in succession or even for whole decades. Such dry periods are often accompanied by locust swarms and the consequences for settled society can be extreme. People have to abandon marginal land and move to better watered regions where they come into conflict with previously settled groups. Others resort to banditry, robbing traders or attacking settlements, while slavery and the slave trade expand to absorb the growing numbers of the destitute. In such circumstances existing polities can come under severe pressure. Large-scale migratory movements can take place and successful bandit leaders and warlords can attract large followings. This can lead to the establishment of new centres of power, new chieftaincies and new and distinct ethnic identities.[32]

This instability of population, political power and ethnic identity, is especially characteristic of the Zambesi valley where the presence of the Portuguese since the sixteenth century means that it can be documented over a long period of time.

The Zambesi valley has always been a major highway for trade and migration. In times of drought the valley, and in particular the delta area, remain relatively well-watered, attracting migrants and refugees. At the same time it has been an important trade route, linking Central Africa with the Indian Ocean. Indian Ocean merchants (Swahili from the northern coasts of East Africa, Indians, Muslims from Arabia and the Gulf and Portuguese) established trading fairs and river ports, around which settled dependent groups of Africans. These merchants acquired slaves and provided employment for the local free population. Long distance caravans brought ingots from the Copper Belt, ivory from as far

31 Beach, *Shona*, p. 29.

32 Newitt, Malyn, 'Drought in Mozambique 1823–1831', *Journal of Southern African Studies*, 15(1), 1988, pp. 15–35. Similar prolonged periods of drought have been documented for the 1580s and the late eighteenth century.

as lakes Malawi and Tanganyika, and gold from diggings both north and south of the river. There was also important local artisan production of iron hoes, cotton cloth, intricate goldsmith work, canoes and artefacts made of woven straw, all of which contributed to the commerce of the region. The long distance traders, hunters, canoemen, and artisans – people who were largely detached from the primarily agriculture-based societies of the interior – either formed their own communities or became attached to wealthy and powerful patrons. Distinct ethnic identities were acquired by those living in the shadow of such coastal and riverain towns as Sena and Quelimane which provided protection and employment to those who lived in their vicinity. The name Chwabo was given to those living near the fort (or *Chuambo*) of Quelimane; Asena became the name for those near the ancient trading town of Sena, which the Portuguese had originally described generically as Tonga; and wa-Nyungwe described those in the vicinity of Tete (Nyungwe being the local name for Tete). Inhabitants of the Portuguese *prazos* (seigneurial domains) were also often known by the name of the *prazo*.[33] For example, in the later nineteenth century the term a-Mahindo was used to describe inhabitants of the delta *prazo* of Maindo.[34]

While drought and locusts drove agriculturalists from their homelands, and commerce created fluid social relations around the towns and along the trade routes, there were two other factors, which contributed to the instability of political and social relations in the Zambesi valley – the matrilineal lineage systems common north of the river, and the prevalence of disease which prevented the keeping of cattle.

Among the people who inhabit the region north of the Zambesi, extending both sides of Lake Malawi, the dominant social unit of the 'little society' has been the matrilineage. Children belong to the mother's family and descent and inheritance is through her brother's children. One consequence of this has been a tendency for rich and powerful men within matrilineal societies to seek to establish patrilineal families through the acquisition of slave wives whose children would in the future belong to them. This process was particularly important in the nineteenth century when Muslim Yao chiefs extended their control over matrilineal

33 See the article on the 'Zambesian Ethos' by José Capela, in this book.

34 Maugham, R.C.F., *Zambezia* (London: John Murray, 1910), p. 276.

populations in the interior of modern Mozambique and Malawi.[35] The rise of powerful patrilineal lineages in a predominantly matrilineal world can give rise to separate and competitive centres of power, and it was this process which characterised the emergence of warrior-communities, among them the distinct ethnic group of the Chikunda.

The absence of cattle also generated its own political and ethnic dynamic. In the cattle-owning societies of the high veldt the accumulation of cattle, by raiding or by natural increase, was a way of acquiring, storing and increasing wealth. Cattle ownership regulated social relations through the bride price and underpinned political power and patronage through the loaning of cattle. Cattle ownership enabled patriarchal chiefs to maintain their authority over the 'little society' and allowed kings to establish relatively centralised control over large populations and extensive territories. The southern Karanga states of the sixteenth to eighteenth centuries and the Ngoni states of the nineteenth century were examples of such cattle-based state systems. However, in areas where cattle cannot be kept, wealth has to be accumulated and patronage dispensed in other forms. One way of doing this, as has already been described, was through trade and the distribution of imported goods; another was through the acquisition of male and female slaves to increase the productive and reproductive capacity of the community. In many parts of pre-colonial Africa the acquisition of slaves routinely supplemented natural population increase in communities that were fundamentally kin-based and where the agricultural labour of women was the principal source of wealth and economic security. Male slaves could be incorporated as junior kin while women became wives with an important reproductive as well as productive role in the family.

There are numerous references in the Portuguese documents to women being treated as the 'spoils of war'. Three examples will illustrate the point. Santos described the successful campaign of the captain of Tete against the Mumbos in 1592, in which the Portuguese were assisted by fighters recruited from the eleven chieftaincies subject to Tete, after

35 Alpers, Edward A., 'Towards a history of the expansion of Islam in East Africa: the matrilineal peoples of the southern interior', in Terence O. Ranger and I.M. Kimambo (eds.), *The Historical Study of African Religion, with special reference to East and Central Africa* (London: Heinemann, 1972), pp. 172–201.

which 'he returned with his men to Tete, taking with him as captives all the women of the enemy in the place'.[36] Bocarro gives an account of Madeira's attack on Chombe early in the seventeenth century. 'Reaching a village of Chombe's… our Cafres attacked and destroyed it carrying off many black women and much spoil'.[37] Later, he recounts how the judge sent to the Rivers 'attacked the houses and settlement of the slaves of Diogo Simões… and made prisoners of many black, girls and women belonging to Diogo Simoes'.[38]

Where the disease environment prevents the maintenance of large cattle herds, raiding becomes a natural strategy for the survival of the community. Successful communities constantly add to their populations by incorporating captives whose assimilation is achieved by the adoption of various symbols that mark the distinctiveness of the group – dress, body ornamentation, observance of rituals, the narration of oral traditions etc.

In the low veldt regions of the coast and the Zambesi valley, any successful trader, hunter, warlord or bandit leader could quickly build up a following through the purchase or capture of male and female slaves and by rewarding followers with plunder or prestigious imported items. Santos describes with devastating clarity how raiding and warfare supported this system of reward and patronage:

> These Cafre vassals of Tete are very much addicted to war and, if it depended upon them, they would always be fighting, for the sake of the spoil which they obtain; and they say they would rather fight than dig, as those who die in battle end their labour and the survivors become rich with the spoils. For this reason they respond joyfully whenever the captain of Tete summons them to take part in war.[39]

Such societies often began with bands of male warriors or hunters, bound together by rituals that frequently involved cannibalism. Built primarily on the success and charisma of a powerful individual, these groups might prove ephemeral, disappearing with the death or defeat of the original founder. However, once women had been obtained and

36 Santos, *Etiópia*, p. 225.
37 Bocarro, 'Livro', p. 392.
38 *ibid.*, p. 424.
39 Santos, *Etiópia*, p. 226.

families established, they could acquire some permanence, their leaders establishing their legitimacy through adopting practices that in the region designated chiefly authority, winning over the spirit mediums of the local cults, and taking wives from influential local lineages or clans.

Five examples will illustrate this process of state formation.

The Zimba are described by Santos as marauders who were led by 'the chief of a small village who had few subjects but who was most ambitious of human honour'. He had set out to raid his neighbours and eventually attracted fifteen thousand 'Cafres who came to them and wished to accompany them on this expedition, whom they admitted into their army'.[40] The Zimba maintained armed camps and indulged in cannibalism. The armed camps of the Zimba sound very much like the Quilombos of the Imbangala in Angola and their description fits closely the type of warrior society, which is described by Joseph Miller in *Kings and Kinsmen*.[41]

A second case is that of Maurusa, whose chieftaincy lay inland from Mozambique Island, and whose relations with the Portuguese in 1585 were also described by Santos. Maurusa and his followers were invaders

> who made war upon the inhabitants of these lands…and by force of arms took their country from them and kept possession of it. This they did with little difficulty, because of their most cruel custom of eating the flesh of the Cafres…so eager were these Macuas for bloodshed and robbery that they did nothing else but plunder, kill and devour all they came across, and only a few cultivated the lands which they had tyrannically occupied.[42]

The foundation of the Mongas and the career of Matuzianhe provide further examples from the late sixteenth and early seventeenth centuries of leaders of small warrior bands becoming powerful chiefs by conquest, spoils and incorporation.[43]

The third example of state formation is provided by the story of the rise of Musura, who became one of the most powerful chiefs north

40 Santos, *Etiópia*, p. 234.

41 Miller, Joseph, *Kings and Kinsmen: early Mbundu states in Angola* (Oxford: Clarendon Press, 1976).

42 Santos, *Etiópia*, p. 249.

43 Bocarro, 'Livro', p. 365.

of the Zambesi in the mid-seventeenth century and was greatly feared and respected by the Portuguese. According to the Portuguese Jesuit, António Gomes, he began as a slave of the Portuguese,

> [and] as he had great ideas in his mind, he ran away, crossed to the other side of the Zambesi into Bororo land, and came to a village. As he was a strong and brave man he would go into the bush with only his *assegai* and without being noticed come near to the game and kill one or two animals... He did this a few times and some started to gather around him to go with him, and he would divide his catch with the others... the village chief decided to marry him to his daughter... after this, as he was very liberal, he got more followers and each day, at dawn, he struck the neighbouring village, killed the chief and divided everything he found equally... and thus by subjugating some and with others submitting themselves, he gradually gained so much power that he ruled from the banks of the Zambesi to the shores of Mozambique.[44]

His followers also indulged in the ritual cannibalism which characterised initiation into warrior societies of this kind.

An eighteenth-century example is provided by the judge, Francisco Moraes Pereira, who described in 1752 a certain Macambe who had a village near Angoche:

> This rebel was the slave of a Portuguese and had the job of a carpenter but lost his post through being insolent and, fearful of being beaten, fled... There he gathered some fugitive Cafres from Mozambique... For some years he was a vagabond but swelled his following with other fugitive Cafres, fortified himself in the lands I have mentioned and built there a settlement which I was told was very strong and impregnable. From here he makes himself feared by assaults and robberies on the neighbouring settlements.[45]

A final, and this time nineteenth-century, example is provided by the so-called Makololo. Livingstone's porters all adopted the ethnic designation of Makololo to distinguish themselves from the people around them and to maintain their own solidarity as a group, but Livingstone explains that

44 Gomes, António, 'Viagem que fez o Padre António Gomes, da Companhia de Jesus ao Império de Manomotapa; e assistência que fez nas ditas terras de algus annos', *Studia,* 3, 1959 [1648], pp. 155–242. Quotation on page 199.

45 Pereira, Francisco Raymundo Moraes, *Account of a Journey made overland from Quelimane to Angoche in 1752,* edited by Malyn Newitt (Salisbury [Southern Rhodesia]: Central Africa Historical Association, Local Series 14, 1965), p. 27.

'though called Makololo by courtesy, as they were proud of the name, Kanyata, the principal headman, was the only real Makololo of the party... The others belonged to the conquered tribes'.[46] On the departure of Livingstone, this group, having assumed the Makololo identity, established themselves on the Shire River, obtained women and attracted followers, establishing a series of important new chieftaincies in the area that was later to become Nyasaland. Both they and their subjects were subsequently referred to as Makololo.

There was a paradigm for the evolution of such polities – the successful hunter, bandit leader, or warrior attracted followers who were organised as a military elite, often within a fortified war camp (like the Angolan *quilombo*). Women and plunder were acquired through raiding. The children born to these unions formed the basis for new patrilineages, which led in time to the replacement of the war camp by new agricultural, kin-based units. The chiefs meanwhile would seek marriages with local chiefly clans, would establish their own spirit cults and would try to acquire legitimacy from holders of established chiefly titles. If all these stages were successfully completed, a new ethnic group would emerge.

This process of 'state building' was particularly open to those who could draw on outside resources to defeat enemies and reward local followers. Men who had access to the trade networks of the Indian Ocean or to supplies of firearms were particularly well placed and the nineteenth century saw this process repeated again and again.

The Vas dos Anjos family whose base was near the confluence of the Shire and the Zambesi attracted large numbers of clients and founded a chieftaincy that largely replaced the authority wielded in the area by Lundu. To emphasise their independence both of Lundu and the Portuguese the population adopted the name Massingiri, which was that of the *prazo* controlled by the Vas dos Anjos family, and by the end of the nineteenth century this name was being used as an ethnic descriptor.[47] The same was true of the followers of the Caetano Pereira and the da Cruz families. The former called their state Makanga and cemented their chiefly authority by assuming the traditional chiefly title

46 Livingstone, *Narrative*, p. 121.

47 Newitt, Malyn, 'The Massingire Rising of 1884', *Journal of African History* 9(1), 1970, pp. 87–105.

of Chicucuru, the inhabitants also being referred to as Makangas.[48] The latter appear to have taken the Tonga chiefly title of Tontoro which predated the arrival of the first da Cruz in Africa.[49]

The Goanese trader and elephant hunter, Manuel António de Sousa, whose followers constituted the most powerful private army in Zambesia, even married into the ruling clan of Barue. He had himself recognised as the Macombe, and became the holder of the ancient chiefly title. Another case, which evolved in a slightly different way, was provided by the clients of the Alves da Silva brothers who, after the death of the elder brother, João Bonifácio, continued to assert their independence from the Portuguese and from any other chief by establishing in Maganja da Costa what has been described as a military 'republic'. The war bands of Maganja da Costa, like the *Quilombos* of the seventeenth century Imbangala, fit into a recognisable pattern of warrior communities, which initiated recruits through residence in the war camp and through rituals of a more or less violent nature. While the 'republic' of Maganja da Costa existed its inhabitants retained a distinct and separate ethnic identity which was lost when the 'republic' was extinguished.[50]

Another example of the creation of an ethnic identity, that of the Munhai/Vanhai of Chidema, is interesting because it was not directly associated with the Afro-Portuguese. The word Munhai is first heard of being used for the ambassadors of the Monomotapa; by the eighteenth century it is being used to describe the soldiers of the same ruler – in 1758 Inacio Caetano Xavier says they are 'like janissaries, soldiers of the king Monomotapa' and Miranda in 1766 indicates that they have the same ceremonial status as sub-chiefs or visiting ambassadors.[51] The Vanhai, it appears, were a military elite of youths recruited by the Monomotapas who, by the nineteenth century, had acquired an inde-

48 Wiese, Carl, *Expedition in East-Central Africa 1888–1891*, edited by Harry Langworthy (London: Rex Collings, 1983 [1891–1892]), p. 65.

49 Miranda, António Pinto, 'Memória sobre a Costa de África', in António Alberto de Andrade (ed.), *Relações de Moçambique Setecentista* (Lisbon: Agência Geral do Ultramar, 1955 [orig. ca. 1766]), pp. 231–312. Reference to the chieftaincy of Tontoro is made on page 303.

50 Capela, José, *A República Militar da Maganja da Costa 1862–1898* (Maputo: Arquivo Histórico de Moçambique, 1988).

51 Miranda, 'Memória', p. 307; Xavier, 'Notícias', p. 145.

pendent existence and were considered a distinct ethnic group. Livingstone in the early 1860s described 'the natives on the right bank, in the country called Shidema, who are Banyai, and even at this short distance from Tette, independent, and accustomed to lord it over the Portuguese traders'.[52] By the end of the nineteenth century the term is being used to describe an independent population who lived by banditry and by exacting tolls on trade on the middle Zambesi.

A footnote can be added to this story which shows how embedded this pattern of ethnic formation is in the history of Zambesia. In the late 1970s Renamo was formed as a guerrilla army to oppose the Frelimo government of Mozambique. Once again the forcible recruitment of youths and their initiation into the ethos of the band through residence in war camps and the committing acts of murder and mutilation seems well attested. The Renamo fighters even acquired a distinct ethnic identity being known as Matsangas after the name of their original leader, Matsangaissa.[53]

Zambesi Slavery and the Chikunda

The rise of the Chikunda as a proud and clearly differentiated ethnic group has long been recognised as a special case in Zambesian history. They are usually described as being the descendants of the slaves of the Portuguese and, in a sense, this is true as the term 'Chikunda' was employed by the Portuguese in the eighteenth century to describe their personal slaves. However, this has led to profound misunderstanding – not least by the principal historian of the Chikunda, Allen Isaacman. Isaacman has some fine passages on the oppressive nature of Zambesi slavery and on the way in which the Chikunda subsequently reinvented themselves as elephant hunters but he saw Portuguese slavery in Zambesia as an institution similar in many respects to the military slavery found in North Africa, India or the Middle East and even South Amer-

52 Livingstone, *Narrative*, p. 46.

53 Vines, Alex, *Renamo Terrorism in Mozambique* (London: James Currey, 1991), p. 74.

ica.[54] However, the implication that the Chikunda are exceptional in the history of East Central Africa and that parallels have to be found in slave societies outside Africa is fundamentally wrong. The Chikunda have to be seen as similar to other Zambesian military/hunter communities and understood in the context of the relations of patronage that form the basis of all African polities.

The nineteenth century Chikunda formed war and hunting camps, recruited women and children to swell their numbers and performed war rituals to initiate recruits. Like other war bands, they adopted distinctive dress and body marks to distinguish them from surrounding peoples. The process by which the Portuguese acquired Chikunda slaves was little different from the slavery and clientship common in all African societies. Portuguese or Afro-Portuguese traders or warlords, themselves known by an ethnic name as *muzungos*, recruited soldiers, carriers, canoemen, traders and hunters by the well established method of offering rewards and patronage. The reward frequently took the form of women captured in warfare, or firearms or privileged access to imported goods. Recruitment was never a problem. There were always large numbers of available men, only loosely attached to matrilineages or who had been displaced by war or famine. Santos records that during the famine of the late 1580s 'so great was the scarcity of provisions that the Cafres came to sell themselves as slaves merely to obtain food and exchanged their children for an *alqueire* of millet'.[55] Under the protection of powerful Afro-Portuguese patrons, these Chikunda became a privileged group cultivating their own customs, living separately from the peasantry, and acquiring their own slaves and clients. Livingstone records 'a rather singular case of voluntary slavery: a free black, an intelligent active young fellow… told us he had sold himself into slavery'… 'And how much did you get for yourself?' we asked. 'Three thirty-yard pieces of cotton cloth', he replied 'and I forthwith bought a man, a woman, and child, who cost me two of the pieces".[56] He then bought more slaves and set up in business as a canoe operator. This, of

54 Isaacman, Allen E., and Barbara F. Isaacman, *Slavery and Beyond. The making of men and Chikunda Ethnic Identities in the unstable world of South-Central Africa, 1750–1920* (Portsmouth/NH: Heinemann, 2004), p. 6.

55 Santos, *Etiópia*, p. 278.

56 Livingstone, *Narrative*, p. 41.

course, is the sort of clientship, which Lucy Mair described as the basic building block of all African political systems.

Conclusion

Ethnicity is not a fiction, and cannot be dismissed as merely something invented by missionaries or colonial administrators. Society in East Central Africa showed strong elements of continuity which help to create identities – languages, spirit cults, chiefly titles – which can be shown to have existed for centuries. However, drought and famine as well as the influence of long distance trade made populations mobile and very unstable, particularly in the Zambesi valley. New centres of power could be created by warrior or hunter communities through slavery and patronage and these could sometimes establish permanent chieftaincies adopting the symbols of legitimacy and gaining the endorsement of the spirit cults. Ethnic identities evolved to distinguish these new societies from the old, and to mark the newly asserted independence of communities that had thrown off the overrule of others. In the turbulent world of Zambesia a strong ethnic identity might also afford some protection.

Ethnic distinctions, in the sense the identification of groups larger than those of clan and lineage, always existed and were very relevant to the needs of communities but ethnicity was a fluid commodity and the communities that formed and reformed over a period of five centuries were far removed from the permanent 'tribes' which the 'scientific' anthropology that arose from the European Enlightenment tried to conjure into existence.

Bibliography

Abraham, D.P., 'Maramuca: an Exercise in the combined use of Portuguese records and oral tradition', *Journal of African History,* 2(2), 1961, pp. 213–235.

Alpers, Edward A., 'Towards a history of the expansion of Islam in East Africa: the matrilineal peoples of the southern interior', in Terence O. Ranger and I.M. Kimambo (eds.), *The Historical Study of African Religion, with special reference to East and Central Africa* (London: Heinemann, 1972), pp. 172–201.

Barretto, Manuel, 'Informação do Estado e Conquista dos Rios de Cuama', in G.M. Theal (ed.), *Records of South Eastern Africa,* 9 vols. (Cape Town, 1898–1903; reprinted Cape Town: C. Struik, 1964), pp. 436–508.

Beach, David N., *The Shona and Zimbabwe 900–1850* (London: Heinemann, 1980).

Bocarro, António, 'Livro do Estado da Índia', in George M. Theal (ed.), *Records of South Eastern Africa collected in various libraries and archive departments in Europe*, 9 vols. (Cape Town, 1898-1903; reprinted Cape Town: Struik, 1964), vol. 3, pp. 254–435.

Caetano Xavier, Inácio, 'Notícias dos Domínios Portugueses de África Oriental 1758', in António Alberto de Andrade (ed.), *Relações de Moçambique Setecentista* (Lisbon: Agência Geral do Ultramar, 1955), pp. 139–188.

Capela, José, *A República Militar da Maganja da Costa 1862–1898* (Maputo: Arquivo Histórico de Moçambique, 1988).

Dos Santos, João, *Ethiópia Oriental e Vária História de Cousas Notáveis do Oriente* (Lisbon: Comissão Nacional para as Comemorações dos Descobrimentos Portugueses, 1999 [Évora, 1609]).

Gamitto, A.C.P., *King Kazembe,* translated by Ian Cunnison (Lisbon: Junta da Investigações do Ultramar, 1960 [1854]).

Gomes, António, 'Viagem que fez o Padre António Gomes, da Companhia de Jesus ao Império de Manomotapa; e assistência que fez nas ditas terras de algus annos, *Studia,* 3, 1959 [orig. from 1648], pp. 155–242.

Isaacman, Allen F., and Barbara S. Isaacman, *Slavery and Beyond. The making of men and Chikunda Ethnic Identities in the unstable world of South-Central Africa, 1750–1920* (Portsmouth/NH: Heinemann, 2004).

Langworthy, Harry, *A History of Undi's Kingdom to 1890: Aspects of Chewa History in East Central Africa* (unpublished PhD thesis, Boston University, 1969).

Liesegang, Gerhard, *Beiträge zur Geschichte des Reiches der Gaza Nguni im südlichen Moçambique 1820–1895* (doctoral dissertation, University of Cologne, 1967).

Liesegang, Gerhard, 'Nguni Migrations between Delagoa Bay and the Zambesi, 1821–1839', *African Historical Studies* 3, 1970, pp. 317–337.

Livingstone, David, and Charles Livingstone, *Narrative of an Expedition to the Zambesi and its Tributaries* (London: Duckworth, 2001 [London: Murray, 1865]).

MacGonagle, Elisabeth, *Crafting Identity in Zimbabwe and Mozambique* (Rochester: University of Rochester Press, 2007).

Mair, Lucy, *Primitive Government* (Harmondsworth: Penguin Books, 1962).

Maugham, R.C.F., *Zambezia* (London: John Murray, 1910).

Miller, Joseph, *Kings and Kinsmen: early Mbundu states in Angola* (Oxford: Clarendon Press, 1976).

Miranda, António Pinto, 'Memória sobre a Costa de África', in António Alberto de Andrade (ed.), *Relações de Moçambique Setecentista* (Lisbon: Agência Geral do Ultramar, 1955 [orig. ca. 1766]), pp. 231–312.

Mudenge, S.I.G., The Rozvi Empire and the Feira of Zumbo (PhD thesis, London University, 1972).

Mudenge, S.I.G., *A Political History of Munhumutapa c. 1400–1902* (Harare: Zimbabwe Publishing House, 1988).

Newitt, Malyn, 'The Massingire Rising of 1884', *Journal of African History* 9(1), 1970, pp. 87–105.

Newitt, Malyn, 'The Early History of the Maravi', *Journal of African History* 23(1), 1982, pp. 145–162.

Newitt, Malyn, 'Drought in Mozambique 1823–1831', *Journal of Southern African Studies,* 15(1), 1988, pp. 15–35.

Newitt, Malyn, *A History of Mozambique* (London: Hurst, 1995).

Papstein, Robert, 'From Ethnic Identity to Tribalism: the Upper Zambezi Region of Zambia, 1839–1981', in Leroy Vail (ed.), *The Creation of Tribalism in Southern Africa* (Berkeley – Los Angeles: University of California Press, 1991 [1989]), pp. 372–394.

Pereira, Francisco Raymundo Moraes, *Account of a Journey made overland from Quelimane to Angoche in 1752,* edited by Malyn Newitt (Salisbury [Southern Rhodesia]: Central Africa Historical Association, Local Series 14, 1965).

Ranger, Terence, 'Missionaries, Migrants and the Manyika: the Invention of Ethnicity in Zimbabwe', in Leroy Vail (ed.), *The Creation of Tribalism in Southern Africa* (Berkeley – Los Angeles: University of California Press, 1991 [1989]), pp. 118–150.

Schoffeleers, Matthew, 'Mbona, the Guardian Spirit of the Manganja' (BLitt thesis; Oxford, 1966).

Vail, Leroy, and Landeg White, 'Tribalism and the Political History of Malawi' in Leroy Vail (ed.), *The Creation of Tribalism in Southern Africa* (Berkeley – Los Angeles: University of California Press, 1991 [1989]), pp. 151–192.

Vines, Alex, *Renamo Terrorism in Mozambique* (London: James Currey, 1991).

Wiese, Carl, *Expedition in East-Central Africa 1888–1891: a report,* edited by Harry Langworthy, translated by Donald Ramos (London: Rex Collings, 1983 [orig. from 1891–1892]).

FELICITAS BECKER*

Vernacular Ethnic Stereotypes: Their Persistence and Change in Southeast Tanzania, ca. 1890–2003

It has been one of the largest and most important tasks of African historiography after colonialism to dismantle colonial constructions of 'tribal', ethnic identity. The main means to do so was the reconstruction of the 'invention of tribalism' in colonial Africa. The contemporary importance of this project lay in indicting colonial constructions of ethnicity as politically expedient and authoritarian.[1] Whatever they might have been beforehand, under colonialism 'chiefs' and 'tribes' became instruments of manipulation and domination, whose practices and rights were defined according to the political requirements of the state rather than an organic understanding of social and political relations.[2]

Since the foundational 'invention of tribalism' literature has been written, other authors have added nuance to and questioned some of the original assertions. Bill Bravman, for instance, has described the making of Taita ethnic identity as a collective project rather than a colonial imposition.[3] Similarly, John Lonsdale' 'moral economy' approach to Kikuyu history hinges on an acknowledgment of values shared within an ethnic social collective, and Thomas Spear has asserted the limits of

* Simon Fraser University, Vancouver, Canada.

1 See especially Vail, Leroy (ed.), *The creation of tribalism in Southern Africa* (London: James Currey, 1989).

2 For an influential recent restatement of these insights, with a divergent explanation for its authoritarian character, see Mamdani, Mahmood, *Citizen and subject. Contemporary Africa and the legacy of late colonialism* (Princeton: Princeton University Press, 1996).

3 Bravman, Bill, *Making ethnic ways: communities and their transformations in Taita, Kenya, 1800–1950* (Oxford: James Currey, 1998).

colonial invention with regard to social hierarchies in African societies.[4] In fact, even strong proponents of the 'invention of tribalism' approach acknowledged that tracing these colonial manipulations did not of itself lead to an understanding of the social and historical relevance of ethnic categories. The question remains: if ethnic categories as we know them were manipulated, does it follow that without such colonial manipulations there would have been no such thing as ethnicity? Even if differences in language, way of life or settlement history are undeniable, is it any more useful to speak of the units thus defined as 'ethnic' ones, rather than in discredited colonial parlance as 'tribes'?

The continuing salience, and increasing viciousness, of ethnic divisions in the post-colonial era, of which Rwanda is only the most notorious example, also points to problems with an 'invention of tribalism' approach. The attempt to explain such events as the outcome of state-centered, elite politics for which the people doing the actual fighting on the streets are simply puppets, presupposes an improbable amount of manipulation and indoctrination.[5] Ordinary African citizens, after all, are not merely dupes. We are left wondering how certain social categories become charged with significances that move people to act in such dramatic ways.

The following pages seek to trace understandings of ethnic categories beyond the apparatus of colonial and post-colonial regimes, by considering a region where crucial elements of the classical 'invention of tribalism' narrative are conspicuous by their absence. The codification of ethnic identities, where we know of it, typically depended heavily on the combination of colonial ascriptions of authority to 'tribal' political intermediaries on one hand and mission education on the other. The former provided the incentive for the invention of 'tribal' tradition, the latter provided local scribes and intellectuals for the entrenchment of such narratives. Where mission education was scant and the colonial regime based on clans rather than tribes, decentralized and weak, we

4 Berman, Bruce, and John Lonsdale, *Unhappy valley: conflict in Kenya and Africa* (Oxford: James Currey, 1992); Spear, Thomas, 'Neo-Traditionalism and the Limits of Invention in British colonial Africa', *Journal of African History* 44(1), 2003, pp. 3–27.

5 See, for example, Prunier, Gérard, *The Rwanda crisis: history of a genocide* (New York: Columbia University Press, 1995).

would have to expect discourses on 'tribe' and ethnic mobilization to be faint. Such was the case in Southeast Tanzania, where the present author has conducted her fieldwork.

The findings in this region at first sight correspond with the prediction. Local writing on ethnic identities and histories is scant and there is barely any record of ethnic tension or ethnically-based political claims. Yet this does not mean that ethnic appurtenance was not talked about. The ways in which it was and is, their implicit points of reference and practical significance, are the material of this essay. The following considerations cannot aim to 'prove' that ethnicity has some reality in the minds and actions of the Africans discussed. Rather, it takes the recognition that ethnic terms are and were salient in local discourse as its starting point, accepting that they must have meant something to their users. Their examination yields the observation that ethnic terms functioned within larger geographic and social frames of reference, which however were not those of the colonial state. They changed over time, and in some ways at the present time are more similar to their pre-colonial precedent than to those of the colonial interlude.

Early Colonial Views on Ethnicity and their Pre-Colonial Roots

Like East Africa at large, the Southeast of Tanzania entered the colonial era after a period of intensifying commercial exchange, both locally and along the networks that linked the region with the wider Indian Ocean, Europe and the Americas.[6] That access to the resources for and from this trade became a mainstay of social and political competition in East

6 Alpers, Edward A., *Ivory and slaves in East Central Africa. Changing patterns of trade to the later nineteenth century* (London: Heinemann, 1975); Sheriff, Abdul, *Slaves, Spices and Ivory in Zanzibar. The Integration of an East African commercial empire into the world economy, 1770–1873* (Oxford: James Currey, 1987).

Africa is by now well documented.[7] Guns for coercion and cloth for patronage were the politically crucial import goods from the trade. Concerning the wares supplied in return, there was greater variety: while slaves and ivory made up most of the value of the export trade, porterage and grains with which to feed the caravans were no less essential, and a more local exchange in arrowheads, salt, hides and other goods took place in the shadow of long-distance trade.[8]

The ensuing scramble for opportunity took place at every level. Established chiefs used the new resources to expand and intensify their rule.[9] Ambitious upstarts exploited the scope for coercion, protection and patronage to establish control over expanding fiefs. In coastal towns, rich Omani and poor African immigrants, local oligarchs; slaves and ex-slaves struggled over access to trade and their roles in the public sphere.[10] Social identity was a central site of these urban contestations: establishing yourself in town meant establishing yourself as a *muungwana,* a 'free-born citizen'. Yet up country, too, it was not only rulers who struggled for their advantage: Steve Rockel tells us that as the so-called Central Route became the mainstay of long-distance trade between Zanzibar and the Great Lakes region, diverse people asserted themselves as Nyamwezi and hence as professional porters and small-scale traders along this route.[11] When the Zanzibari trader Tippu Tip established his fiefdom at its western end, in the Eastern Congo, some of his armed followers called themselves *waungwana,* transposing a category of descent and social distinction from the coast into the East African interior.

7 Glassman, Jonathon, *Feasts and riot: revelry, rebellion, and popular consciousness on the Swahili coast, 1856–1888* (Oxford: James Currey, 1995); Becker, Felicitas, *Becoming Muslim in Mainland Tanzania, 1890–2000* (Oxford and London: Oxford University Press for the British Academy, 2008), chapter 1, and *idem*, 'Traders, 'big men' and prophets: political continuity and crisis in the Maji Maji rebellion, 1905–07', *Journal of African History* 45(1), 2004, pp. 1–22.

8 Rockel, Stephen, *Carriers of culture: labor on the road in nineteenth-century East Africa* (Portsmouth/NH: Heinemann, 2006); Becker, *Becoming Muslim*, chapter 1.

9 Bennett, Norman Robert, *Mirambo of Tanzania, ca. 1840–1894* (New York: Oxford University Press, 1971); Iliffe, John, *A modern history of Tanganyika* (Cambridge: Cambridge University Press, 1979), chapter 1.

10 Glassman, *Feasts, passim.*

11 Rockel, *Carriers.*

European travelers of the day, and pioneering historians of the region, treated this as a quasi-ethnic designation.[12]

In this last case, people thrown together by war, disorder and the desire for loot created a quasi-ethnic identity for themselves out of a language of social distinction which, as part of their Swahili vernacular, was one of the few things they actually had in common. The Nyamwezi, though, are to this day spoken of as one of Tanzania's peoples, and they were perceived as such already by nineteenth-century explorers. Yet they became visible to outsiders as an ethnic group because of their profession: their role as porters on the Central Route. The affiliations that came down to us as ethnic ones were elided into social identity framed by the long-distance trade regime.

When discussing the mixture of immigrants into Tanzania's Southeast, Terence Ranger observed the equivalent process: 'Makua', he concluded, meant above all 'elephant hunter', 'Mwera' meant 'indigenous agriculturalist'.[13] Yet while agriculture, ivory hunting and local produce trades took place in the Southeast, a number of factors combined to make participation in the slave trade the most prominent feature of this region's role in the pre-colonial order. It lay between areas near Lake Malawi that supplied slaves in large numbers, and the coastal town of Kilwa, the largest slave-exporting harbour of the period. From the 1850s, incursions by Ngoni and Mbunga migrants from the west heightened insecurity in the region and produced a local supply of slaves.[14] Among the people living through this situation, social relations easily acquired an exploitative edge, and the large-scale incursions from the west ramified into a myriad of local confrontations.[15] On-going

12 Page, Melvin, 'The Manyema hordes of Tippu Tip', *International Journal of African Historical Studies* 7(1), 1974, pp. 69–84.

13 Ranger, Terence O., 'European attitudes and African realities: the rise and fall of the Matola chiefs of South-East Tanzania', *Journal of African History* 20(1), 1979, pp. 63–82.

14 Redmond, Patrick, *The politics of power in Songea Ngoni society 1860–1962* (Chicago: Adams, 1985); Larson, Lorne E., *A history of the Mahenge (Ulanga) district, ca. 1860–1957* (PhD thesis, University of Dar es Salaam, 1976).

15 Becker, *Becoming Muslim,* chapter 1; see particularly the career of the Yao 'big man' Machemba on the Makonde plateau, documented in Schmid, Rochus, *Aus kolonialer Fruehzeit* (Berlin: Safari Verlag, 1922); Maples, Chauncy, 'Results of the

immigration by several language groups present also, or mostly, in Portuguese territory south of the Ruvuma River created further scope for contestation. This immigration by Makonde, Yao, and Makua people was slow and small-scale, but nevertheless resulted in confrontations with and displacement of Ngindo- and Mwera-speakers already present north of the Ruvuma.[16]

Against this background, we can observe a number of stereotypes and valuations that were attached to different ethnic groups in the region, and marked them out no less than, or possibly even more than, the diversity of their different languages. They survive in written sources, and in some cases the writers' characterizations are self-interested. For instance when missionaries at the Masasi station described their Makua dependants as homely, guileless, agricultural fellows, it is fair to assume they were seeking to reassure their British audience that they had come upon people amenable to and deserving of Christianization.[17] Yet we also find such points of view in contexts where the writer's interests are less clear and the context suggests that they are parroting local perceptions, as well as in Swahili-language sources.

It is worth dwelling for a moment on the relationship between these stereotypes and distinctions by language. The reality of language diversity is attested to in the present time by both linguists and local people. Derek Nurse identifies Mwera, Yao, Makua and Ngindo as distinct, but related languages, with Makua standing out as belonging to a more distant branch.[18] People in the Southeast, in their turn, sometimes remark on the fact that Makua is 'harder to learn' for a speaker of any of the other regional languages than the others. Nevertheless, multilingualism is, and by all accounts has been, so much a fact of life that a separate language only tenuously delineates a separate group. On the road, among

---

exploration of the country lying between Lake Nyasa and the Indian Ocean, 1880–88', *Journal of the Manchester Geographic Society* 1, 1885, pp. 69–85; and *idem*, 'Masasi and the Rovuma District in East Africa', *Proceedings of the Royal Geographic Society* 2, 1880, pp. 338–353.

16 Ranger, 'Attitudes'.

17 Maples, 'Masasi'.

18 Nurse, Derek, ''Historical' classification of the Bantu languages', in John Sutton (ed.), *The growth of farming communities in Africa from the equator southwards* (Nairobi: BIEA, 1996), pp. 65–81.

multilingual strangers, it is conceivable that the marks of a distinctive way of life were more important for a person's ethnic identification than their language. Thus while the existence and distribution of these languages highlights the great age and intricacy of the process of migration, it does not give reason to assume the existence of distinct societies to correspond to the different language groups.

Rather whether language or way of life was paramount in identifying an ethnic group depended on context. Different people inhabited different niches in the webs of economic and political relations that spanned the region. Moreover, these niches could take on different aspects for different observers. Ranger concluded that Yao immigrants in the interior district of Masasi treated local Mwera people as the indigenous owners of ritual and agricultural knowledge. Yet an official of the German colonial government in the coastal town of Lindi around 1900 reported that the Mwera people living in the town's hinterland were 'a nation of thieves', where parents trained their children to swipe possessions from the town's residents.[19] This assertion clearly reflects strained relations between the townspeople and their neighbours, and the views of African residents of the town rather than of the administrator himself – there is no record of any visitor having stolen from the European residents. Moreover, nothing followed from this characterization; steps to intensify control over the Mwera were only taken in response to their participation in the anti-colonial Maji Maji War of 1905–07.[20]

Further north around this time, German missionaries described the Matumbi people, inhabitants of the eponymous hills, as 'knorrig', literary 'gnarled'; as reticent, earthly, and proud to be so.[21] Like the Mwera near Lindi, these hill dwellers had strained relations with the nearby town, in their case Kilwa. Some of them showed active contempt for the Islamic identity of the town dwellers. Both during the Maji Maji War and during

19 Bundesarchiv, Berlin, Germany (BArch), R 1001/288, Ewerbeck, German Administrator (Bezirksamtmann) of Lindi, to Gouvernement, Dar es Salaam, 14 April 1897, p. 104; also, BArch, R 1001/1040, Leader of Military Column (*Kompagnieführer*) Fromm, *Report on journey to the Mbemkuru*, 18 Aug. 1896, p. 2.

20 Iliffe, *History*, chapter on the Maji Maji war.

21 Mayer, Pater Ambrosius, 'Aus den Matumbibergen', *Missionsblaetter von St Ottilien* 14, 1910, pp. 115–118; Krumm, Bernhard, 'Grundriss einer Grammatik des Kimatumbi', *Mitteilungen des Seminars fuer Orientalische Sprachen* 15(3), 1912, pp. 1–63.

earlier local confrontations over the use of local resources such as salt gardens, they swooped down on plantations near the town and devastated them.[22] They were the first to take arms in the Maji Maji War, making careful use of their rugged terrain, and especially caves, to limit the impact of German punitive expeditions.[23] To some extent, then, the missionaries' characterization in fact reflects the place of the Matumbi in the political economy of the region: they interacted with the trading towns from a position of relative independence, thanks to their strategic position.

The group on which European observers expended the most ink, though, were the Yao: they were wily, well-travelled (hence a contrast to the Makua to the mind of Masasi's missionaries), and, in the words of one passing German traveler in 1902, both Arabized and 'exemplary'.[24] These stereotypes, again, implicitly refer to several decades' worth of social and political change. From at least 1850, Yao people had become the most important intermediaries in long-distance trade between the Lake Malawi region and the Kilwan coast. Exploiting connections with the older trade with the Portuguese on the Mozambican coast, a handful of Yao leaders had set themselves up as 'sultans' in the Mozambique/Malawi region and fitted out large-scale caravans.[25] During the following decades, these caravans successfully negotiated the dangers of Ngoni intrusion, and their individual Yao participants developed a shrewd understanding of trade practices on the coast. Early German administrators in Lindi compared these expert porters favourably with the ragtag porters on the route to Kilwa.

22 On conflicts between Matumbi and coastal people, Tanzania National Archive G 8/19, Bezirksamtmann von Eberstein to Gouvernement, Dar es Salaam, 7 Sept. 1893, pp. 41–46. On the devastation of coastal plantations during the Maji Maji War, see 'Schadensprotokolle' (damage reports) in Tanzania National Archive G 3/76; Krumm, 'Grundriss'.

23 Gwassa, Gilbert, *The outbreak and development of the Maji maji war, 1905–07* (PhD thesis, University of Dar es Salaam, 1973); *idem*, 'African Methods of Warfare in the Maji Maji rising', in Bethwell A. Ogot (ed.), *War and Society in Africa* (London – Nairobi: Heinemann, 1972), pp. 123–149.

24 Busse, Walter, 'Forschungsreisen durch den südlichen Teil von Deutsch-Ostafrika', *Beihefte zum Tropenpflanzer* 3, 1902, pp. 93–119.

25 Alpers, *Ivory*; Tanzania National Archive, G 1/35, Bezirksamt, Kilwa, to Gouvernement, Dar es Salaam, 19 Nov. 1899, p. 169.

Yet the notion of the wily, well-travelled Yao did not exist only among the Europeans who reported it. The German traveler who reported their 'Arabization' was himself only passing through and dependent for information on his local fellow travelers. Some vernacular sources repeat the cliché: A tale in the Mwera language, collected around 1930, describes relations between a Swahili and a Yao man who try to outwit each other in competition for access to up-country trade: as in the reality of ca. 1900, the Yao wins.[26] Reporting a dramatic incident in Lindi involving a python, a correspondent to the Swahili magazine Mambo Leo in 1926 explained a bystander's ability to resolve the situation partly with the fact that he was a Yao, hence well-informed.[27] The particular attractiveness of Yao identity in the early colonial period is evident also from the fact that one of the strongmen established along the trade route towards Lindi, a certain Nakaam, began to assert a Yao identity over his Makua descent once his position was securely established.[28]

At the opposite end of the scale appear to have been the Ngindo speakers, inhabitants of the open woodland west of the Matumbi hills. Bare of natural defences, this region was frequently under attack from Ngoni invaders as well as from armed caravans passing through. Ngindo were often found among the slaves exported from the region. Although agriculturalists, they dealt with this threat by adopting a semi-nomadic way of life that combined cultivation with extensive hunting and gathering. Meanwhile, they were 'timid' and 'unwarlike' according to early colonial observers.[29] Decades later, at the end of colonial rule, a British

26 Archive of the Mission of the Benedictines, St Ottilien, Joachim Amman, 'Kimwera-folktales'. For another story describing the fractious relationship between a Yao and an Arab, see William Whiteley's papers in the SOAS archive, PP, MS 42 L/45, 'Yao Texts', pp. 1–4.

27 Letter by Hasani Hamis, Lindi, section 'Habari za mikoani', *Mambo Leo* 31, 1925.

28 Weule, Karl, *Native life in East Africa,* translated by Alice Werner (London: Sir Isaac Pitman & Sons, 1909), pp. 115–119. According to Weule, Nakaam told him he was Yao, while Weule's porters took pleasure in deflating this claim. Confronted with the suggestion that he was Makua, Nakaam responded by saying he had been Makua 'long ago'.

29 Adams, Alfons, 'Vom Nyassa-See nach Upogoro und Donde', *Mitteilungen aus den Deutschen Schutzgebieten* 11, 1898, pp. 251–254; *idem*, *Im Dienste des Kreuzes* (Augsburg: Commissionsverlag Michael Seitz, 1899); Rodgers, W.A., 'Past Ngindo

administrator would observe that Ngindo interlocutors used this stereotype as a succinct way to characterize their situation in the late nineteenth century. Here again, a characteristic of this area's place within the regional political economy has been foreshortened into a characteristic of its inhabitants. In different ways, local people, African interlocutors, and European observers all contributed to this process.

Nevertheless, this sort of 'ethnicity' was very different from the colonial image. It was not necessarily an affiliation you were born into, and did not reflect legitimate 'tribal', but rather improvised and predatory forms of authority. Access to long-distance trade and its economic and political resources, rather than cultural or physical characteristics, had secured Yao people a place at the top of the regional pecking order.

Albeit based on manifest differences, above all of language and migration history, ethnicity was a relational category whereby the inhabitants of the region characterized each others' position relative to Zanzibari hegemony and long distance trade.

Colonial Quiescence, Relative Absence of Invention, and the Ghosts of Pre-Colonial Stereotypes

It is clear that this region-wide 'pecking order' and its attendant stereotypes lost their original significance with the introduction of the colonial order. Yet they did not simply disappear: they lingered, and while some eventually faded, others survived transformed. This process occurred even while the colonial notion of 'tribe' remained faint and largely irrelevant.

The crucial factors for the reformulation and hardening of ethnic distinctions under colonialism were the political manipulation of ethnicity under the Indirect Rule regime, and its parallel endorsement and instrumentalization in missionary education. The 'chiefs' who were the most typical indigenous representatives of Indirect Rule in Central, Southern and Eastern Africa were supposed to be legitimized by 'tribal'

Settlement in the Selous Game Reserve'. *Tanzania Notes and Records* 77, 1976, pp. 21–26.

authority, and the people they governed willy-nilly became members of their tribes. Missionaries, in their turn, relied on the notion of tribes and tribal leaders in their own quest for reliable intermediaries, and to formulate collective narratives of salvation. Mission education, in turn, gave local intellectuals the means whereby to develop vernacular versions of 'tribal history' that underpinned their own social roles. While the manipulative character of these evocations of ethnicity is undisputable, the way in which they took effect is less obvious. In spite of many local studies, the politics of Indirect Rule continue to be puzzling. The studies show that colonial regimes were in turns, or even at the same time, overbearing and weak, violent and negotiated.[30]

Southeast Tanzania follows the general pattern of vague, instable, yet nevertheless occasionally highly intrusive political control under Indirect Rule. The legal and organizational form it took in this region, though, differed from the 'tribal chief'-based model widespread in East and Central Africa. Indirect Rule here was organized in 1927–30, ten years after British military administrators had taken the region from German control. Returning from their exploratory searches for African 'manners and customs', officials reported that whatever political cohesion the 'tribes' of the region might have had had crumbled, if not during the slave-trading era, then under the corroding influence of German colonialism between 1890 and 1917.[31] It was not unusual for officials to find the current state of 'tribal' authority falling short of an assumed 'traditional' system, and explanations for these discrepancies could always be found. In this case, though, the architects of Indirect Rule decided against trying to 'reconstruct' the imagined tribal structures. Instead, they devised a system intended to reflect the current decentralized nature of 'traditional' authority, and to accommodate the patchy distribution of the different ethnic groups within the region.

30 Giblin, James, *The politics of environmental control in northeastern Tanzania, 1840–1940* (Philadelphia: University of Pennsylvania Press, 1992); Lumley, Edward K., *Forgotten mandate. A British district officer in Tanganyika* (London: Hurst, 1976); Fields, Karen E., *Revival and rebellion in colonial Central Africa* (Princeton: Princeton University Press, 1985); Mamdani, *Citizen.*

31 For this narrative, see the sections on tribal histories, manners and customs in the District Books of the region, in the Tanzanian National Archive.

Rather than chiefs, Indirect Rule appointees here were called *wakulungwa,* and defined as an awkward cross between lineage and village heads. They were supposed to exert authority over people connected to them by ties of blood, who were assumed also to live in proximity to each other. In fact, spatial and family proximity did not overlap so closely, and villagers played the two categories off against each other to challenge the authority of any one *mkulungwa* over them. Individual *wakulungwa* held authority only over a few villages each, and were supposed to take collective decisions in councils. Ethnic affiliation was considered only at the level of these councils. They were ethnically homogeneous, so that separate, for instance Mwera and Makonde, councils existed for the same area if its population was ethnically mixed.[32]

Unlike many 'Native Authority' chiefs, the *wakulungwa* held no legal control over land. Except on the Makonde Plateau, population densities were low, and competition for land was limited to areas near the coast, where plantations owned by urban dwellers limited access, and to rare patches of particularly good soil in the interior.[33] *Wakulungwa* were in principle responsible for tax collection, but, not being given a share, lacked incentive, and taxes from the region, now called 'Southern Province' fell far below expectations. The only incentive for becoming a *mkulungwa* was the small salary attached to the post, and while a minority among them became skilful local politicians, most sought to limit their interference with their neighbours on behalf of the colonial authorities.[34]

Overall, the stakes for colonial intermediaries were lower than they had been for pre-colonial rulers. Compared to the mosaic of smaller and

32 Tanzania National Archive, files 12800, vols. 1–4, 'Native Administration, Lindi Province'; file 12674 *Lindi Province Native Authority, 1928–35.* For potential problems with the system, Tanzania National Archive 12800, Provincial Commissioner Grierson to Secretariat, Dar es Salaam, 17 May 1929, pp. 13–16.

33 On soil qualities and uses, Tanzania National Archive, J.G. Bennett, L.C. Brown et al., *Mtwara/Lindi regional integrated development programme: The farming systems and development prospects. Report of the zonal survey team in phase 2,* vol. 2. Project report 67 (Surbiton: Land Resources Development Centre, 1979); Becker, *Becoming Muslim,* chapter 3, on rural social stratification.

34 The exasperation of colonial administrators with this strategy is clearly expressed in the modernizing narratives which they imparted to Gus Liebenow. See Liebenow, J. Gus, *Colonial rule and political development in Tanzania: the case of the Makonde* (Nairobi: Heinemann, 1971).

larger 'sultans', warlords, village heads and migration leaders who had controlled people in Southeast Tanzania in the late nineteenth century, the colonial regime lacked both military means of enforcement and the wherewithal for the dramatic public demonstration of power which German observers noted at the onset of colonialism. Moreover, the trade in agricultural commodities remained extremely limited, in size and profits, compared to pre-colonial long-distance trade. Before the rise of cashew in the 1950s, it consisted mostly of sesame, grain, and occasional unpopular attempts at establishing cotton cultivation. Access to trade had earlier been a political issue and was reflected as such in the construction of ethnic identities. Now it was much more widespread, but much less desirable: peasants had to sell crops to obtain money for taxes, schooling and everyday expenses, but they felt vulnerable and gullible while doing so.[35]

The colonial order, then, in fact flattened out earlier hierarchies among ethnic affiliations: in this region, it reduced rather than intensified their political significance. The groups bound to feel this most acutely were the ones who had been near the top of the pre-colonial ethnicized hierarchy: urban *waungwana* and rural Yao. In fact, the economic decline of both groups was dramatic. Colonial sources give a vivid picture of the impoverishment of those patricians who had depended most heavily on the slave trade: the town of Kilwa Kivinje, formerly the slave-trading hub, was likened to a stripped corpse in the 1930s. The fates of the Yao populations who remained in the region after the end of the caravan trade differed: a Catholic missionary in the 1930s described the remainder of Machemba's Yao followers in the Makonde plateau as reticent, but well-entrenched and integrated among their Makonde neighbours.[36] The majority of Tanzanian Yao, though, ended up living in the far western reaches of the Southern Province, and beset by poor market access, administrative neglect and agricultural misfortune.

The history of this Yao population in the district of Tunduru is quite unusual, founded as it is on an incident of organized, large-scale

35 Becker, *Becoming Muslim*, chapter 3, for villagers' experience of trips to town in the inter-war period.

36 'Luagala, 1937–50', *Chronik der Kongregation St Ottilien 1951* (St Ottilien: printed as manuscript, 1951), pp. 137–147.

migration. Small groups of Yao had been settled here around 1900 under local strongmen, but the majority – about 12,000 – arrived in 1912, when Sultan Mataka, as German sources know him, transferred his residence to Tunduru from Mozambique. He was evading increasing harassment by Portuguese troops, but he had also been holding official negotiations with the German colonial government, which was keen to increase the population of the district. An enthusiastic German official had appointed Mataka ruler of 'New Brandenburg' – an appropriate name for Tunduru, considering that Brandenburg was known for poor, sandy soils.[37]

Under the British colonial regime, when long-distance trade was definitely over, this district did particularly badly: dependent on low-value cash crops and far from markets, its producers found it hard to realize any profit from produce trading, and turned to labour migrancy instead. The original large villages under close control of the Sultan broke up into small hamlets as cultivators sought for appropriate soils. Alone among Indirect Rule intermediaries in the province, Mataka and his lieutenants were designated as chiefs, but the administration quickly decided they were ineffectual. When, in the 1930s, the combination of loss of labour through migration, unfamiliar environment and poor rain led to recurring famine, help was slow to arrive and its cost much deplored by administrators.[38]

Yet, as we have seen, the pre-colonial reputation of the Yao is still traceable in vernacular sources from the inter-war period. A missionary ethnographer who lived in Tunduru in the 1920s argued that the Yao mistrusted Christianity not so much because they were so committed to the Islamic teachings that had taken hold among them in the dying years of long-distance trade, but rather because they were keen to distinguish themselves from their non-Yao, increasingly Christian neighbours: 'the

37 On the contacts between the German administration and Mataka, see BArch, R 1001 220, Zache, Bezirksamtmann of Lindi, *Report on a journey to the interior of Lindi region*, 23 January 1900, pp. 14–106, 102 for the 'contract' between Zache and Mataka containing the name Neubrandenburg.

38 Lumley, *Mandate*, pp. 54–59, details the initial failure of famine relief for Tunduru and its uneasy politics; on the cost of relief, see Tanzania National Archive 19365, Provincial Commissioner Grierson to Chief Secretary, 19 Sept. 1932, p. 15.

Yao have always been a 'superior' people'.[39] Current-day Yao informants present controversial views on the meaning of their heritage: while everybody in the region speaks of the Yao as a Muslim people, some Yao interlocutors deplore the quasi-slavery in which the colonial Yao chiefs held their subjects, while others discuss chiefship as part of a distinctive *cultural* tradition.[40] This last view was also in evidence in 1999, when officials at Dar es Salaam's ethnographic museum organized a day to celebrate the Yao and Makua heritage: officials and participants discussed the reverence shown for the current bearer of the name Mataka as a cultural feature, rather than an echo of pre-colonial politics.

On the coast, meanwhile, the former wealth and power of the slave-trading elites has left a very ambiguous imprint. The descendants of Omani immigrants may be credited with a certain sophistication and privileged knowledge, but also suspected of using it destructively, or upheld as protagonists of a morality tale about the fleeting nature of wealth. Thus the living quarter of Lindi's pre-colonial elite, Mikumbi, now a crowded, dilapidated part of town, maintains a certain parochial pride, but is also spoken of as the town's prime hotbed of witchcraft. More generally, townspeople along the coast display ambiguous attitudes towards the group formerly considered most privileged in both wealth and descent: the *masharifu* or descendants of the Prophet. Bearers of esoteric knowledge and deserving of respect, their current generation may also be denigrated as dissolute, given to drink and unworthy of their forebears.[41]

It is worth making clear that there is no reason to assume that the politicization of ethnicity could not have taken very similar forms here to

39 King, Noel Q.; Klaus Fiedler and Gavin White (eds.), *Robin Lamburn – from a missionary's notebook: the Yao of Tunduru and other essays* (Fort Lauderdale: Verlag Breitenbach, 1991), p. 111.

40 Interviews in Mingoyo and Mitwero, 2000.

41 In May 2005, I hired a descendant of a Kilwa Kivinje family to conduct interviews on the history of the *masharifu* of this town. She returned with paltry results, explaining that she had been told the 'real' *masharifu* had died and their current descendants were unreliable informants. This can partly be attributed to reticence towards an outsider, but the topic of the 'decline' of the *masharifu* recurs in informal conversation. Nevertheless, the graveyard where Kilwa Kivinje's *masharifu* have been buried is enough of a landmark to have been included in a recent 'Rapid Rural Appraisal' report. See RIPS library, Mtwara, *Participatory Rural Appraisal report from Kilwa Kivinje*, 1998.

other parts of British Africa. In some regards, it did. This becomes clear when considering the stratagems of the Catholic mission in the region. The mission, the German-speaking Mission Benedictines, was not particularly successful in its efforts, winding up the leaders of a Christian minority in a region that became largely Muslim between ca. 1900 and 1950. The reasons why the mission, and mission education, lost out to Islam are complex and beyond the scope of this study. It is clear, though, that the mission gained considerable importance locally, near its main stations. The situation near Ndanda, the seat of its Abbot-Bishop since the 1930s, is documented in published and unpublished writings by missionaries and traceable in the oral record. Ethnographic writings in the Abbey library show that the missionaries sought to codify the way in which the people nearby chose their *mwenye* or chiefs, and to develop authoritative versions of the history of local dynasties.

It is also clear that a number of nearby notables accepted and tried to work with Mission endorsement, even though it was irrelevant from the point of view of the administration. Where involved, the missionaries added considerable pomp to a *mwenye*'s accession to office, and historical narratives of *mwenye* dynasties became part of their teaching at school. One such narrative that still continues is that of Mchekenje's *mwenye*-ship. A close neighbour of the mission, he had welcomed them on their first appearance at Ndanda. Soon after, though, he participated in the attacks on the mission that were part of the Maji Maji War – under duress, according to the narrative constructed by his successors and the mission. The subsequent reconciliation, and missionaries' assistance during the difficult period after the war, is the material of a redemptive narrative and the origin of an enduring alliance between the Mchekenjes and the mission.

In keeping with the limited influence of the mission, and the small scale of colonial local politics, the reach of these mission-sponsored notables and their historical narratives remained short. Although references to 'tribal' custom are frequent in these accounts, they are focused rather on specific lineages. Nevertheless, the stratagem in action, the construction of legitimating narratives out of the encounter of oral local knowledge and literate mission ethnography, is familiar from missionaries' contribution to the invention of tradition and tribalism in many places. It was the particular structure of Native Authorities in this area, an expedient administrative response to the dispersal of ethnic groups in this region, that limited its impact.

That ethnicity could have become more politicized if there had been more scope and incentive for its manipulation is indicated also by events in the dying days of the colonial order. Presumably due to the existence of a precedent in the councils of *wakulungwa,* the 'district councils' that were colonial Tanganyika's first step towards democratic representation were introduced relatively early in the Southeast, starting in 1952.[42] At the same time, a conjuncture of high world market prices, colonial developpment efforts, and the introduction of cashew nut as a cash crop raised the stakes in the competition for land. At this juncture, we encounter the faint stirrings of organizations based on ethnic affiliation, intended to press the interests of specific ethnic groups within the multiethnic councils or to raise living standards in particular areas.[43] They were, however, soon swept up by enthusiastic commitment to Julius Nyerere and the Tanganyika African National Union (TANU).

Post-Colonial Reformulation: The Return of Distinctions by Wealth and Access

In post-colonial Tanzania, state rhetoric has been careful not to treat ethnicity as a political category. The abolition of 'tribal' chiefs shortly after Independence put an end to any explicit political role of ethnicity. Instead, it has been discussed as a matter of cultural diversity contained within national unity. It forms part of the rhetoric of officials only in a limited, specific way: in connection with local *utamaduni,* 'culture'.[44] The

42 Liebenow, *Political Development.*

43 Tanzania National Archive, accession 16/15/126, File on 'Mwera cooperative society', *passim.* Tanzania National Archive, accession 16/37/8, Letter by Ally Bwamkuu and Jumbe Abderehmani Mohamed, 8 April 1947, file on native complaints, general, 1934–48, p. 155; Liebenow, *Development.*

44 See e.g. Maddox, Gregory, with E.M. Kongola, *Practicing history in Central Tanzania* (Oxford: James Currey, 2006) on Kongola's work as cultural officer and the way he integrated ethnicity into it.

dependence of this notion of culture on recent political history became evident for me for instance when one interviewee, a mistrustful elderly lady, responded to my quasi apologetic explanation that I was interested in things such as *utamaduni* by declaring that 'they did not use to have *utamaduni* in the past': the category of culture as used by the 'cultural officers' in local administrations is a recent creation.

This careful containment of ethnicity in official language notwithstanding, references to ethnicity are salient in everyday conversation in the region. The following discussion does not aim at completion, but seeks to identify some of the subtexts that animate the use of these references. It will be seen that the significance of ethnic terms continues to depend on context, and particularly on the relationship between the speaker and whichever ethnic group he or she is invoking. Nevertheless, there is a certain consistence in the aspects of the context that speakers pay attention to. It could be argued that the concern foremost in the speakers' mind now closely resembles that of the pre-colonial era: it is once again access; now no longer to the commerce in slaves and ivory, but rather to state resources on one hand and commodity markets on the other.

The importance of access is reflected in a stereotype people in Southeast Tanzania share with people in other parts of the country (I first heard it in a Waluguru household in Dar es Salaam): that the Chagga people, from Northern Tanzania's Kilimanjaro region, are particularly keen on money. This assertion occurs in the discussion of Chagga employers, neighbours and traders. In fact, Kilimanjaro has since the colonial era been one of the most prosperous regions of Tanzania.[45] This is attributable partly to the exceptional agricultural potential of the area, but also to the early and widespread uptake of education. The latter allowed Chagga producers relatively far-reaching control over the disposal of their goods, as well as access to high-ranking administrative positions, whose remunerations form an important source of investment.[46] The

45 Iliffe, *History*.

46 On social stratification in the region, see Sender, John, and Sheila Smith, *Poverty, class, and gender in rural Africa: a Tanzanian case study* (London: Routledge, 1990); on the position of the Chagga in the national elite, McGowan, Patrick J., and Patrick Bolland, *The political and social elite of Tanzania: an analysis of social background facts*

characterization of the Chagga as business-minded and stingy, then, sums up the outcomes of natural endowment and historical process in an assumed personal characteristic, not unlike the perception of the Yao as 'wily' summed up their role in long-distance trade a hundred years earlier.

That people in the southeast assume that the Chagga profit from privileged access to the state is evident from a conversation that occurred while waiting to be rescued from a broken-down bus on the notoriously poor road south from Dar es Salaam. Comparing this road to the all-weather roads connecting Dar es Salaam and Kilimanjaro, passengers pondered the question why the roads south had not improved even during the tenure of a president who is himself from Masasi in the Southeast, Benjamin Mkapa. Several passengers agreed that the problem lay not least with the fact that politicians from the south married women from the north – a thinly veiled allusion to the fact that Mkapa's wife Anna is a Chagga. These marriages, it was said, were convenient for southerners, but they turned their attention away from their home regions and ensured that the privileged flow of resources to the north continued.

Here we also encounter the subordination of ethnic peculiarities under the larger issue of regionalism. That place is an important reference point for the formulation of lineage relations as well as ethnicity has been stated in the Tanzanian context. In Dar es Salaam, people from different ethnic groups in the southeast – Makua, Makonde, Yao – may be heard referring to themselves as *watu wa kusini,* people from the south. One telling explication of this notion is found in a painting by Eduardo Tingatinga, the founder of the eponymous style of naïve painting beloved by tourists to Tanzania, who was Makua. In his painting *Wamakua watu wa kusini* (Wamakua, people from the south) he depicts 'typical' Makua activities, among them the heavy reliance on the cultivation of cassava. Cassava reached the south of Tanzania from Mozambique and is an important way to cope with light soils, irregular rain and the scarcity of labour throughout the southeast.

As the discussion on the bus indicated, people from the south conceive of themselves as the inhabitants of a disfavoured region of Tanzania, politically as well as economically and educationally. By and large,

---

(Syracuse University: Program of Eastern African Studies, Maxwell School of Citizenship and Public Affairs, 1971).

the statistics prove them right.[47] There is, however, no local consensus on the causes and implications of this marginal position of the south. In spite of the stereotype of the stingy Chagga, the ethnic diversity of Tanzania as a whole and the Southeast in particular makes it difficult to conceive of this marginality in terms of ethnic division. Nevertheless, the studies in Seppaelae and Koda's account of the marginality of the region, *The making of a periphery,* suggest that some degree of 'othering' of Southeasterners is going on; that people from the north conceive of the 'backwardness' of this region as rooted in ethnic and cultural characteristics: in effect, a mirror image of the myth of the stingy Chagga.

Besides the readiness of Southeasterners to conceive of themselves as a group apart from Northerners or Tanzanians at large, ethnic stereotypes of people within the region are also being discussed. The possibilities for declaring a particular way of cooking or eating, of getting married or making love 'typical' of such and such a group, are of course endless. Sometimes, such claims give the impression of being improvised in the flow of conversation. But there are ascriptions that recur with both persistence and consistency, and that betray something of their historical roots. Such is the case for the association of the Ngindo, the inhabitants of Liwale region, with both witchcraft and witchcraft eradication.

As mentioned, this region had been particularly vulnerable during the nineteenth-century era of slave raiding. Under German colonialism, the Ngindo paid a heavy price for their strong participation in the Maji Maji War, when they endorsed the *maji* medicine that reached them from Matumbi and passed it on to their western neighbours. After this war, they are again, as in the late nineteenth century, described as creatures of the wilderness: mistrustful, evasive, dependent on foraging as well as agriculture. This association with the wilderness was subsequently entrenched by the creation of a large game reserve in the western part of the district, which in 1947 under the name Selous Game Reserve became the world's

47 See Seppaelae, Pekka, and Berta Koda (eds.), *The making of a periphery* (Dar es Salaam: Mkuki na Nyota, 1998), for an extensive discussion of the economic position of the region.

largest. In the present time, too, Ngindo interlocutors assert the closeness of their relationship with the forest, whether as a boon or a burden.[48]

As wilderness and game are deeply implicated in medicine-making, this association is already suggestive also of familiarity with these occult practices, and historical evidence reinforces the suggestion. In the 1920s, people on both the eastern and the western side of the game reserve were at the forefront of the witchcraft-cleansing movements that then swept the region.[49] The most famous Ngindo witchcraft cleanser, though, practiced at the end of the colonial period: Nguvumali became the subject of both Swahili praise poetry and an ethnographic study.[50] Further south in Lindi region, too, a Ngindo witchcraft cleanser accompanied the transition to Independence. People with Ngindo background were again involved in a spate of witchcraft cleansings in recent years, both on the coast and in Makonde – and Mwera – speaking areas.

It was in connection with these recent events that it was explained to me that Ngindo people made good witchcraft cleansers because the spirits found in Liwale (and whom the cleansers were assumed to communicate with) had a strong aversion against witchcraft.[51] It is likely, though requiring further investigation, that this view of Liwale's spirits is related also to the cult of a particular set of spirits, known as *mgende,* which at present is one of very few human activities inside the Selous Game Reserve and on its borders. The most accessible sites of this cult are reached from Liwale town, and attract visitors from as far away as the capital.[52] The *mgende* spirits are held to be very powerful if propitiated

48 Interview with Hamisi Mfaume Nyomole, Liwale 12 October 2000; conversations in and on way to Liwale.

49 Larson, Lorne E., 'Witchcraft eradication sequences among the people of the Mahenge (Ulanga) district, Tanzania' (seminar paper, University of Dar es Salaam, 1973).

50 Ismail, Hassan bin, *Swifa ya Nguvumali. The medicine man,* edited by Peter Lienhardt (Oxford: Clarendon Press, 1968).

51 I was told so in the Machenza household in Lindi, June 2004. The best-known example of a Ngindo witchcraft cleanser, and the best-known of all witchcraft cleansers in Southeast Tanzania is Nguvumali: see Ismail, *Swifa.*

52 I witnessed a party setting out to a *mgende* shrine in Liwale in August 2004. The men went in suits and carrying briefcases, rather as if visiting their bank manager. Conversations in the Litopite and Tengeneza households in Liwale, August 2004, provided further information on *mgende.*

appropriately, and highly vindictive if slighted. The experts working at the cult sites tend to be from Liwale region, again displaying the reputation of its inhabitants as indigenous, and associated with the esoteric knowledge of the wilderness. A succession of changing historical circumstances, then, has fed into the construction of Ngindo people as experts in witchcraft.

That new stereotypes may also arise fairly swiftly from an encounter of established ideas and changing context is made clear by recent assertions among Mwera villagers and coastal people about the Makonde people, inhabitants of the eponymous plateau. This region stands out in several regards. Firstly, it has throughout the last 100 years consistently been the most densely populated part of the region. Although water is very scarce on the plateau, its cassava-friendly soils and relatively reliable rains offer an unusual degree of food security, and during the pre and early colonial wars the escarpment served as additional security against invaders.[53] More recently, yet another agricultural feature of the plateau has become important: the altitude especially of its western reaches creates favourable conditions for the cultivation of cashew trees, the main cash crop of the region in the last fifty years.

Cashew production and marketing have revived over the last two decades, with new cultivation methods, intermittently stronger prices and the recovery of the infrastructure for distribution.[54] In consequence, Makonde traders have used cashew revenue to set themselves up in locations well beyond the plateau. In coastal towns and predominantly Mwera-speaking villages, these traders would be accused of sharp practice – to many peoples' mind the most persuasive explanation of their relative success. The accusation of shrewdness and dishonesty, moreover, extended to Makonde who were not professional traders.

In the early 2000s, after a particularly brutal cycle of boom and bust in the cashew trade that had enriched many producers in 2000, only to leave them in debt in 2001, another story was also making the rounds to

53 Tanzania National Archive, Newala District Books, vol. 1., H. Gillmann, 'Makonde bush fallowing'; Schmid, *Fruehzeit;* Nigmann, Ernst, *Geschichte der Kaiserlichen Schutztruppe fuer Deutsch-Ostafrika* (Berlin: Mittler, 1911).

54 Seppaelae, Pekka, 'The recovery of cashew production in Southern Tanzania', in Seppaelae and Koda (eds.), *Making,* pp. 118–138.

explain how some people, and especially Makonde, had survived the episode better than others.[55] It claimed that those who were prospering owed their good fortune to the local version of the zombie, the *ndondocha.* This notion is in itself not new: missionaries have described the belief in *ndondocha* from the 1930s onwards.[56] The basics of the notion appear constant. *Ndondocha* are people who were poisoned in such a way as to make them appear dead. Somehow, their future owner contrives to remove them from the shroud before burial and henceforth keeps them hidden at home, deprived of speech and independent will. No longer fully human, they are nevertheless precious manpower. The secrecy of zombie-keeping was expressed in the veiled accusation that someone 'had an extra room in his house', that is, one in which to keep the *ndondocha.*

Not only Makonde were rumoured to harbour *ndondocha*: a less specific mistrust against the wealthy could lead to the same accusation. In 2003, local Muslim radicals and administration officials, most of them from beyond the region, combined in the predominantly Mwera country town of Rwangwa to oppose the activities of a witchcraft cleanser who promised to rid the town of all forms of witchcraft, including *ndondocha.* In response, other townspeople concluded that both administrators and the sponsor of the Muslim radicals, a Mwera trader, were keepers of *ndondocha* who opposed witchcraft cleansing in order to keep their secret workers. According to some, *ndondocha* provided the explanation why the Mwera trader in question had been successful *without* being Makonde – which in turn implies that commercial success, probably by crooked means, was somehow natural for Makonde.

This recent example shows how an ethnic stereotype can arise fairly quickly from a changing economic context, condensing structural factors into personal characteristics. At the same time, the rise of these stereotypes of Makonde around their role in the regional cashew and retail trade could be said to form part of a time-honoured discourse. It is once

55 Chachage, Seithy L., and Joyce Nyoni, *Economic restructuring and the cashewnut industry in Tanzania: a research report* (Dar es Salaam: Tanzania Agriculture Situation Analysis, 2001).

56 Ndanda mission library, Joachim Amman, 'Sitten und Gebraeuche bei den Wamwera', undated typoscript (1930s).

again concerned with access to the lines of trans-regional exchange, as with the long-distance trade of a century ago.

Meanwhile, Tingatinga's depiction of the people of the south also represents one of the most fundamental, and arguably least political, elements of ethnic identity: livelihood, and in particular food. It was again on a bus journey that a young trader – most likely Makonde – exclaimed, on seeing me, that 'the world was coming to an end'. The reason? I had been eating *ming'oko,* a wild root that grows plentifully on the Makonde plateau, and is collected and traded widely between the plateau and the lowlands nearby. *Mzungu anakula ming'oko* – a white person is eating Ming'oko: this fact represented a degree of disorder to the young trader's mind that he, not entirely seriously, characterized as apocalyptic. One of his colleagues, though, promptly found a way to normalize my eating *ming'oko,* by analogy. White people, he pointed out, were known to be fond of eating carrot, so why shouldn't they also appreciate *ming'oko,* another root?

These references to livelihood indicate an understanding of ethnicity that is more fundamental and more organic than the official version of ethnicity as a matter of diverse cultural expression, of song, dance and oral tradition. At the same time, the trader's readiness to accept the eating of *ming'oko* as a parallel to the eating of carrot reminds us of the malleable nature of ethnic distinctions in the minds of Tanzanian observers, and the fact that they can be laid out to include and find connections as well as to assert difference.

Conclusion

The handful of cases outlined above is only part of the many ways ethnicity is talked about in present-day Tanzania. I have not dealt with narrations of origin and migration, which arguably are the mainstay of ethno-historical discourse.[57] Moreover, I have only touched on situations where interlocutors elaborate their own ethnicity, in claims starting, for instance, *sisi Wangindo,* 'we, the Wangindo'. Yet even the information given above may help appreciate that ethnic names can serve as starting points for accounts of one's self and network, help structure narratives of where one and one's neighbours came to be who and where they are.

Assertions of the kind that I have here dubbed stereotypes serve to explain historical outcomes – such as Chagga pre-eminence in government and the economy – or personal behaviour, as when a Mwera customer complains of a trader's sharp practice, dubbing him 'that Makonde'. But they are not treated as predictors of a person's behaviour, except to ostracize in an ongoing personal conflict. They are in many ways like a kind of oral knowledge that exists among a younger generation of Europeans who have spent time abroad: anecdotes swapped among Germans about the poor quality of British building work; anecdotes swapped among British people about the curt manners of German waiters and shop assistants, and so on. Yet while European travelers would often be wary of condensing such experiences into generalized claims, my Tanzanian interlocutors never expressed misgivings about the epistemic status of such observations, or about the ethics of making them. Nevertheless, they used them with great circumspecttion, often mitigated by a sense of humour.

Given that notions such as that of the forest-dwelling, medicine-wielding Ngindo resonate with so many layers of regional history, I do not find it plausible that they should be mere projections of the present into the past. Their significance and implications evidently change continuously, and it is likely that the 'cultural officers' of the present time encourage certain types of stereotypes and discourage others. But while the current meanings of ethnicity are continuously invented and embroidered, the

57 Maddox, *History,* chapter 4 and *passim.*

validity of ethnic distinctions is treated as given, as appears to have been the case already a hundred years ago. The fundamental mistake of colonial ethnographers was to treat the information they obtained on ethnic groups as the equivalent of a legal constitution, rather than as a snapshot of an on-going process of assertion and ascription.

It is striking, though, that at the level at which I have been examining ethnicity, the contours of the early colonial and the post-colonial period are easier to make out than those of the heyday of Indirect Rule, more commonly considered the crucial phase for the making of contemporary ethnic identities in Africa. In fact, I have skirted the issue that most bedevils the attempt to understand the role of ethnicity under colonialism: how it functioned as a lever of power. I have not discussed in what ways, if any, authority structures within clans, lineages and families may have been underpinned by ethnicity, and in what ways such structures may have changed in the process. Further questions could be asked, not only regarding the colonial period. My information is scant as to how stereotypes are reflected in action, rather than expressed in speech. Moreover, the state-sponsored notion of ethnicity as a cultural phenomenon is likely to have ramifications, to invite invention and maybe manipulation within state institutions, that would bear further investigation.

On the other hand, the perspective adopted here enables us to see a continuity in the history of ethnicity in this region that spans the pre- and post-colonial periods. Throughout, ethnic groups remained interspersed and the significance of ethnic terms highly malleable, while the set of ethnic names used was fairly stable. At the same time, the importance as well as difficulty of staying connected to the wider world was, in different ways, equally reflected in the stereotypes of the early twenty-first century, as in those of a century ago. While social relations within the region are less manifestly predatory now than they were then, considerable bitterness underlies assertions such as the attribution of economic success to zombie use. Tanzanians readily praise their government for having avoided ethnic confrontations, but it should be remembered that it was the exigencies of colonial rule that first led to the demilitarization of social relations in this area, and that the openness of ethnic categories for new significances also allows for the development of divisive ascriptions.

Bibliography

Adams, Alfons, 'Vom Nyassa-See nach Upogoro und Donde', *Mitteilungen aus den Deutschen Schutzgebieten* 11, 1898, pp. 251–254.

Adams, Alfons, *Im Dienste des Kreuzes* (Augsburg: Commissionsverlag Michael Seitz, 1899).

Alpers, Edward A., *Ivory and slaves in East Central Africa. Changing patterns of trade to the later nineteenth century* (London: Heinemann, 1975).

Becker, Felicitas, 'Traders, 'big men' and prophets: political continuity and crisis in the Maji Maji rebellion, 1905–07', *Journal of African History* 45(1), 2004, pp. 1–22.

Becker, Felicitas, *Becoming Muslim in Mainland Tanzania, 1890–2000* (Oxford and London: Oxford University Press for the British Academy, 2008).

Bennett, Norman Robert, *Mirambo of Tanzania, ca. 1840–1894* (New York: Oxford University Press, 1971).

Berman, Bruce, and John Lonsdale, *Unhappy valley: conflict in Kenya and Africa* (Oxford: James Currey, 1992).

Bravman, Bill, *Making ethnic ways: communities and their transformations in Taita, Kenya, 1800–1950* (Oxford: James Currey, 1998).

Busse, Walter, 'Forschungsreisen durch den südlichen Teil von Deutsch-Ostafrika', *Beihefte zum Tropenpflanzer* 3, 1902, pp. 93–119.

Chachage, Seithy L., and Joyce Nyoni, *Economic restructuring and the cashewnut industry in Tanzania: a research report* (Dar es Salaam: Tanzania Agriculture Situation Analysis, 2001).

Fields, Karen E., *Revival and rebellion in colonial Central Africa* (Princeton: Princeton University Press, 1985).

Giblin, James, *The politics of environmental control in northeastern Tanzania, 1840–1940* (Philadelphia: University of Pennsylvania Press, 1992).

Glassman, Jonathon, *Feasts and riot: revelry, rebellion, and popular consciousness on the Swahili coast, 1856–1888* (Oxford: James Currey, 1995).

Gwassa, Gilbert, 'African Methods of Warfare in the Maji Maji rising', in Bethwell A. Ogot (ed.), *War and Society in Africa* (London and Nairobi: Heinemann, 1972), pp. 123–149.

Gwassa, Gilbert, *The outbreak and development of the Maji maji war, 1905–07* (PhD thesis, University of Dar es Salaam, 1973).

Iliffe, John, *A modern history of Tanganyika* (Cambridge: Cambridge University Press, 1979).

Ismail, Hassan bin, *Swifa ya Nguvumali. The medicine man,* edited by Peter Lienhardt (Oxford: Clarendon Press, 1968).

King, Noel Q.; Klaus Fiedler, and Gavin White (eds.), *Robin Lamburn – from a missionary's notebook: the Yao of Tunduru and other essays* (Fort Lauderdale: Verlag Breitenbach, 1991).

Krumm, Bernhard, 'Grundriss einer Grammatik des Kimatumbi', *Mitteilungen des Seminars fuer Orientalische Sprachen* 15(3), 1912, pp. 1–63.

Larson, Lorne E., 'Witchcraft eradication sequences among the people of the Mahenge (Ulanga) district, Tanzania' (seminar paper, University of Dar es Salaam, 1973).

Larson, Lorne E., *A history of the Mahenge (Ulanga) district, ca. 1860–1957*, PhD thesis (University of Dar es Salaam, 1976).

Liebenow, J. Gus, *Colonial rule and political development in Tanzania: the case of the Makonde* (Nairobi: Heinemann, 1971).

Lumley, Edward K., *Forgotten mandate. A British district officer in Tanganyika* (London: Hurst, 1976).

Maddox, Gregory, with E.M. Kongola, *Practicing history in Central Tanzania* (Oxford: James Currey, 2006).

Mamdani, Mahmood, *Citizen and subject. Contemporary Africa and the legacy of late colonialism* (Princeton: Princeton University Press, 1996).

Maples, Chauncy, 'Masasi and the Rovuma District in East Africa', *Proceedings of the Royal Geographic Society* 2, 1880, pp. 338–353.

Maples, Chauncy, 'Results of the exploration of the country lying between Lake Nyasa and the Indian Ocean, 1880–88', *Journal of the Manchester Geographic Society* 1, 1885, pp. 69–85.

Mayer, Pater Ambrosius, 'Aus den Matumbibergen', *Missionsblaetter von St Ottilien* 14, 1910, pp. 115–118.

McGowan, Patrick J., and Patrick Bolland, *The political and social elite of Tanzania: an analysis of social background facts* (Syracuse University: Program of Eastern African Studies, Maxwell School of Citizenship and Public Affairs, 1971).

Nigmann, Ernst, *Geschichte der Kaiserlichen Schutztruppe fuer Deutsch-Ostafrika* (Berlin: Mittler, 1911).

Nurse, Derek, "Historical' classification of the Bantu languages', in John Sutton (ed.), *The growth of farming communities in Africa from the equator southwards* (Nairobi: BIEA, 1996), pp. 65–81.

Page, Melvin, 'The Manyema hordes of Tippu Tip', *International Journal of African Historical Studies* 7(1), 1974, pp. 69–84.

Prunier, Gérard, *The Rwanda crisis: history of a genocide* (New York: Columbia University Press, 1995).

Ranger, Terence O., 'European attitudes and African realities: the rise and fall of the Matola chiefs of South-East Tanzania', *Journal of African History* 20(1), 1979, pp. 63–82.

Redmond, Patrick, *The politics of power in Songea Ngoni society 1860–1962* (Chicago: Adams, 1985).

Rockel, Stephen, *Carriers of culture: labor on the road in nineteenth-century East Africa* (Portsmouth/NH: Heinemann, 2006).

Rodgers, W.A., 'Past Ngindo Settlement in the Selous Game Reserve', *Tanzania Notes and Records* 77, 1976, pp. 21–26.

Schmid, Rochus, *Aus kolonialer Fruehzeit* (Berlin: Safari Verlag, 1922).

Seppaelae, Pekka, 'The recovery of cashew production in Southern Tanzania', in Pekka Seppaelae and Berta Koda (eds.), *The making of a periphery* (Dar es Salaam: Mkuki na Nyota, 1998), pp. 118–138.

Sheriff, Abdul, *Slaves, Spices and Ivory in Zanzibar. The Integration of an East African commercial empire into the world economy, 1770–1873* (Oxford: James Currey, 1987).

Spear, Thomas, 'Neo-Traditionalism and the Limits of Invention in British Colonial Africa', *Journal of African History* 44(1), 2003, pp. 3–27.

Vail, Leroy (ed.), *The creation of tribalism in Southern Africa* (London: James Currey, 1989).

Weule, Karl, *Native life in East Africa,* translated by Alice Werner (London: Sir Isaac Pitman & Sons, 1909).

PART 2:

Coastal West Africa

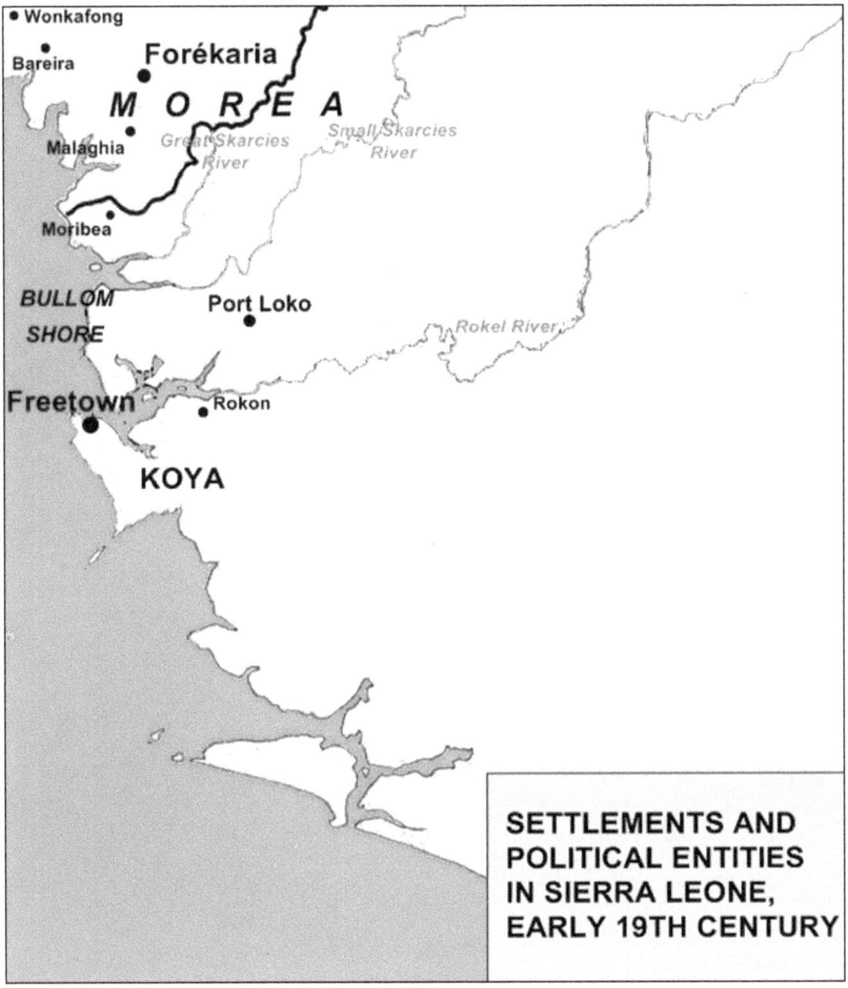

Settlements and Political Entities in Sierra Leone, early 19th century

Settlements and Group Labels in the Gold Coast (Ghana) – Togo Border Region, from 1800

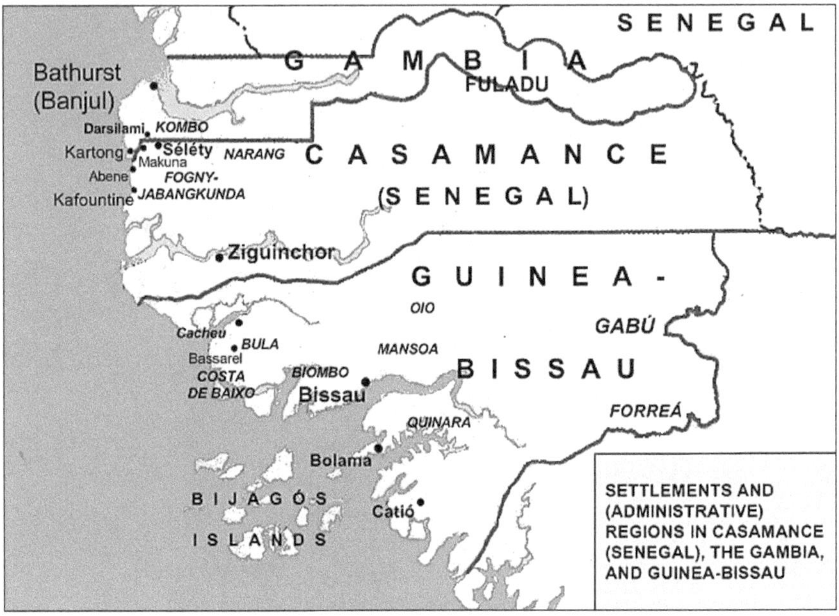

Settlements and (Administrative) Regions in Casamance (Senegal), the Gambia, and Guinea-Bissau

PAUL NUGENT*

The Historicity of Ethnicity: Mandinka/Jola and Ewe/Agotime Identities in the Nineteenth and Twentieth Centuries[1]

Introduction

The great debate about the roots of ethnicity in Africa has arguably reached the point of diminishing returns. This should not be construed as a negative outcome. On the contrary, the debate has greatly furthered our understanding of the dynamics associated with identity formation, and if the yields are now more meagre than before it is only because something like a broad consensus has emerged.[2] There are few Africanists today who would accept any straightforward notion that 'tribes' are rooted in a stable pre-colonial past, but equally the contention that they are colonial 'inventions' seems to obscure the historical sinews that hold many contemporary ethnicities together. In this respect, it is surely no accident that the case-studies that tended to dominate the early stages of

* Centre of African Studies, University of Edinburgh.

1 Research for different aspects of this article has been funded by the Nuffield Foundation (SGS/00910/G), the British Academy (SG-38667), the Carnegie Trust for the Universities of Scotland and both the Development Trust Research Fund and the Hayter Travel Fund of the University of Edinburgh.

2 For an analysis of the state of the field, see Spear, Thomas, 'Neo-Traditionalism and the Limits of Invention in British Colonial Africa', *Journal of African History* 44(1), 2003, pp. 3–27. Also, compare the earlier and later formulations by Terence Ranger in Ranger, Terence, 'The invention of tradition in colonial Africa', in Eric Hobsbawm and Terence Ranger (eds.), *The Invention of Tradition* (Cambridge: Cambridge University Press, 1983), pp. 211–262; and Ranger, Terence, 'The invention of tradition revisited: the case of colonial Africa', in Terence Ranger and Olufemi Vaughan (eds.) *Legitimacy and the State in Twentieth-Century Africa* (London: Macmillan, 1993), pp. 62–111.

the debate were drawn largely from Eastern and Southern Africa, and related to specific examples where a colonial Big Bang was plausible.[3] The West African literature tended to lag behind and to receive less attention.[4] However, it is clear that ethnicities have very deep roots across much of West Africa. This would be true of the Hausa and the Fulbe, but also of many other groups.

In a recent article which is a companion to the present piece, I have tried to demonstrate that in the case of two sets of paired identities – Mandinka/Jola in the Senegambia and Ewe/Agotime in the trans-Volta – it would be wrong to credit the colonial period, and far less colonial ad-

3 An early marker was laid down by Iliffe, John, *A Modern History of Tanganyika* (Cambridge: Cambridge University Press, 1979), p. 318. Some of the most important earlier case-studies are Ranger, Terence, 'Missionaries, migrants and the Manyika: the invention of ethnicity in Zimbabwe', in Leroy Vail (ed.), *The Creation of Tribalism in Southern Africa* (London: James Currey, 1989), pp. 118–150; Chimhundu, Herbert, 'Early missionaries and the ethnolinguistic factor during the 'invention of tribalism' in Zimbabwe', *Journal of African History* 33(1), 1992, pp. 86–109; Lonsdale, John, 'The moral economy of Mau Mau: the problem', in Bruce Berman and John Lonsdale, *Unhappy Valley: Conflict in Kenya and Africa* (London: James Currey, 1992), pp. 265–314; and *idem*, 'The moral economy of Mau Mau: wealth, poverty and civic virtue in Kikuyu political thought', in *ibid*, pp. 315–504; and Willis, Justin, 'The making of a tribe: Bondei identities and history', *Journal of African History* 33(2), 1992, pp. 191–208. It is worth pointing out that an even earlier literature on Swahili origins and identities, which pre-dated the ethnicity debate, can be revisited in a way that is compatible with the argument being made here.

4 The exception was the work of John Peel. See, for example, Peel, J.D.Y., 'The cultural work of Yoruba ethnogenesis', in Elizabeth Tonkin, Maryon Macdonald and Malcolm Chapman (eds.), *History and Ethnicity* (London: Routledge, 1989), pp. 198–215. Later studies, with more of a West African focus, are Killingray, David, 'Imagined martial communities: recruiting for the military and the police in colonial Ghana, 1860–1960', in Carola Lentz and Paul Nugent (eds.) *Ethnicity in Ghana: The Limits of Invention* (Basingstoke: Macmillan – New York: St. Martin's, 2000), pp. 119–136; Nugent, Paul, *Smugglers, Secessionists & Loyal Citizens on the Ghana-Togo Frontier: The Lie of the Borderlands Since 1914* (Athens/OH: Ohio University Press – Oxford: James Currey, 2002); Van den Bersselaar, Dmitri, 'Imagining home: migration and the Igbo village in colonial Nigeria', *Journal of African History* 40(1), 2005, pp. 51–73; Harneit-Sievers, Axel, *Constructions of Belonging: Igbo Communities and the Nigerian State in the Twentieth Century* (Rochester: University of Rochester Press, 2006); and Lentz, Carola, *Ethnicity and the Making of History in Northern Ghana* (Edinburgh: Edinburgh University Press/IAI, 2006).

ministrators, with the creation of these identities.[5] I argue that early European travellers borrowed ethnonyms that Africans used for each other, along with the stereotypes that went with them, and that these have enjoyed remarkable longevity. To take but one example, the colonial stereotype of the Mandinka as averse to physical labour and adept at sharp commercial practices, is one that can be found in the earliest European accounts at a time when the latter were heavily reliant on their African informants. Ironically, when colonial officials thought that they were identifying essential 'tribal' traits, and referred back to those earlier accounts for support, what they failed to appreciate was that these sources actually had an African provenance.

In this article, I will not repeat the first half of my argument about the much deeper roots of African ethnicities, but will concentrate on the second half in which the contention is that twentieth-century manifestations of ethnicity are best regarded as mutations from previous forms rather than as 'inventions' or ahistorical 'imaginings'. Using the same pairing of case-studies, I will concentrate on the period from the mid-nineteenth century onwards.

Ethnic Boundaries and Political Structures: Agotime and Ewe

In both of the case-study areas, the latter half of the nineteenth century was characterized by serious upheavals that had the effect of hardening some inter-group boundaries and softening others. These conflicts had some of their origins in the shifting contours of the economy of en-

5 A part of Paul Nugent's contribution has drawn upon material from within Nugent, Paul, 'Putting the History Back into Ethnicity: Enslavement Religion and Cultural Brokerage in the Construction of Mandinka/Jola and Ewe/Agotime Identities in West Africa c. 1650–1930', *Comparative Studies in Society and History* 50(4), 2008, pp. 920–948, © Society for the Comparative Study of Society and History, and published by Cambridge University Press. This part is reproduced with permission by the holders of the copyright.

slavement, although attempts to forge new political structures were arguably just as important. I will begin this account with a closer examination of the Agotime/Ewe case, before turning to Senegambia.

In the early nineteenth century, the assemblage of peoples we now call 'the Ewe' were divided into well over a hundred autonomous chiefdoms (*duko* sing., *dukowo* pl.). Many consisted of no more than a handful of villages. The *dukowo* that were the most substantial were those that successfully incorporated an Akan-style chieftaincy and related military forms. Asante may have provided the model, but closer to home it was the riverain state of Akwamu that was more important. Peki, which became the most powerful of the northern *dukowo*, was a close ally of Akwamu before leading a revolt against the latter in 1833–34. Anlo, which was the dominant Ewe polity at the coast, was closely involved at various times with Asante, Akwamu, Akyem and the Ga polities and inevitably borrowed much from its neighbours. There was a rough north-south divide, which was in part linguistic, and it could fairly be said that there was not a strong sense of being Ewe per se, given the absence of a context that might have made any such identity meaningful.

The Agotime, on the other hand, represent one fragment of a greater Adangbe diaspora that is scattered across the trans-Volta in what is now southeastern Ghana and southern Togo. The original Adangbe refugees left their homeland in the vicinity of Accra in the later seventeenth and reached their present homeland in the early eighteenth century. From the 1740s, they turn up fairly regularly in Danish documents as the suppliers of slaves to the coastal forts. By this point, they had already acquired their present name. Oral traditions are hotly disputed, but most agree that a group of Adangbes settled on land that was characterized by a profusion of fan-palms (which are still readily visible to this day) and made it their permanent home. The word Agotime (*Ago-ti-me*) is a compound that simply means '[the people] living amongst the fan-palms' and, in that sense, is a reference to a location rather than to a bloodline. From their first settlement at Afegame (literally 'in the big house/compound'), they fanned out to form a number of new settlements. The traditions of the neighbouring Adaklu-Ewe insist that the Adangbes requested land from them, and were allocated an area to the east.[6] The Adaklu claim is to have given a name to the refugees who would otherwise have had no identity. Adaklu sources are quick to point out that *Agotime* is an Ewe and not an Adangbe term, thereby underlining the unequal power relationship between them. By contrast, Agotime traditions are somewhat contradictory. In a long-running land dispute with Adaklu, some Agotime witnesses have asserted that their ancestors were the firstcomers, a claim that is distinctly implausible and is disputed by all their Ewe-speaking neighbours.[7] At other times, Agotime spokesmen have admitted that they arrived later, but have gone on to claim that they seized the land by force of arms, and thus were never placed in the position of supplicant. This might seem a mere point of detail, but it matters a great deal because Agotime claims to being a distinct 'people' hinge on their status as strangers or as conquerors.

In all likelihood, the first Adangbe settlers probably did request land from the Adaklu, but were quickly able to assert their autonomy. The Agotime key to future success lay in active participation in the slave trade, combined with the adoption of a client status to Akwamu. As with Peki, the Akwamu seemingly relied on the Agotime to exact tribute from the northern Ewe, and to retain their dominant position east of the Volta – and, by extension, that of Asante. The Agotime sold many slaves in return for guns, which gave them an advantage over their Ewe-speaking neighbours. The traditions of particular families and settlements make it clear that the Agotime incorporated many Ewe slaves into their own ranks. Even the most preliminary questioning throws up allusions to the forced marriage of defeated enemies and to entire quarters having descended from war captives. Indeed herein lies the basis for an Agotime identity: whereas the Adaklu and other Ewe sub-groups prided themselves on their prowess as farmers, the Agotime professed to be engaged purely in the pursuit of warfare and trade. Although chiefs now exist, there is general agreement that they are a recent creation. In the past, it is said, there were only warlords (*avafiawo* in Ewe) whose

6 Evidence led in 'Geze Anku and seven others vs Togbe Mahumansro and nine others in Ho District Native Court A at Ho', 1958 (copy in my possession).

7 For example, evidence of Nene Agbovi IV, before District Magistrate J.K. Ampiah, in the Adaklu-Agotime land case, sitting at Ho 6 November 1974 (copy in my possession).

leadership rested on success on the battlefield. Afegame claims to have provided a chief since the earliest times; however, in all likelihood this 'chief' was a priest. Indeed there appears to have been both a male and a female priest, each of whom was the custodian of a gendered 'fetish', now conveniently referred to as 'stools' in the Akan (and Ewe) fashion.

What one has to imagine is a small group of Adangbe settlers who rapidly augmented their numbers by incorporating Ewe captives. This strategy meant that over time the Adangbe element became smaller, which may have contributed to the expansion of the Ewe language in the towns that were most heavily involved in trade. The success of Kpetoe in incorporating captives, and thereby expanding its numbers, brought about a difference of opinion with Afegame whose leaders insisted on maintaining their exclusivity. Quite when the schism occurred is difficult to say, but it seems to date from at least the mid-nineteenth century, and remains deeply ingrained to this day when the people of Afegame are proud to assert that there are no non-Adangbes living in their midst. In the other towns, Ewes became Agotime through a process of absorption into kin groups, or spatially through the formation of separate wards. For the people of Kpetoe, this was a matter of pride rather than of shame because it brought demographic dividends, which gradually facilitated the geographical expansion of the polity. Whereas so much ethnic discourse today rests on the notion of distinct bloodlines, this was almost certainly alien to Agotime ways of thinking. However, considerable importance was attached to kinship – and not because slaves were anti-kin, but rather because it provided a set of rules for the incorporation of captives.[8]

The related pursuits of militarism and trade served the Agotime well until the last decades of the nineteenth century. The first turning point came in the 1830s. It began with the Ewe *duko* of Nyive requesting Agotime military assistance against Atikpui. This culminated in a dispute between Nyive and Agotime when the former failed to honour its side

8 Here, my interpretation comes closer to that of Miers and Kopytoff than Meillassoux. See Kopytoff, Igor, and Suzanne Miers, 'African slavery as an institution of marginality', in Suzanne Miers and Igor Kopytoff (eds.), *Slavery in Africa: Historical and Anthropological Perspectives* (Madison – London: University of Wisconsin Press, 1977), pp. 3–81; and Meillassoux, Claude, *The Anthropology of Slavery: The Womb of Iron and Gold* (London: Athlone Press, 1991).

of the bargain.[9] As the dispute escalated, many of Agotime's neighbours sided with Nyive, presumably in an attempt to end Agotime military dominance. On the other side, the Agotime received support from a Ga contingent, as well as from Peki and Akwamu. However, the line of fracture shifted when Peki fell out with Akwamu, apparently over the disposal of war captives, precipitating a wider revolt by the Ewe *dukowo* against Akwamu overlordship. On this occasion, the Agotime joined sides with Peki, and the grand alliance prevailed over an Akwamu-Anlo coalition. The Agotime were no doubt happy to have thrown off their allegiance to Akwamu, but now found themselves in a relatively weaker position. The fact that the external slave trade at the coast had ended did not help, although some slaves would have continued to pass through the ports along the Slave Coast. Peki attempted to capitalize on its leadership of the coalition, but was unable to secure the enduring loyalty of the other *dukowo*, which reverted to an autonomous existence. However, this successful co-operation of the northern Ewe – or Krepi – helped forge the germ of the idea about the benefits of unity.

The second turning point came with the Asante invasion of the trans-Volta in 1869.[10] The occupation, which lasted for some three years, was notionally about the restoration of Asante hegemony, but to all intents and purposes it was an exercise in pillage and slave raiding. Many Ewe *dukowo* capitulated in the hope of being spared, but this did not prevent their enslavement in large numbers. Others fled eastwards and into the Togoland hills where they endured great privation. The resistance to Asante was initially led by Kwadzo De IV of Peki and Dompre, a warlord from Akyem Kotoku, but after they were killed the mantle passed to the Ewe *duko* of Ho and to Agotime, who joined forces and fought a protracted guerrilla campaign. This was consistent with the

9 The fullest account of these events remains that of Reverend Carl Reindorf, even if it was published half a century later. Reindorf, Carl, *The History of the Gold Coast and Asante, Based on Traditions and Historical Facts Comprising a Period of More than Three Centuries From About 1500 to 1860* (Accra: Ghana Universities Press, 1966 [orig. 1889]).

10 The war aims of the Asante are discussed in Maier, D.J.E., 'Military acquisition of slaves in Asante', in David Henige and T.C. McCaskie (eds.), *West African Economic and Social History: Studies in Memory of Marion Johnson* (Madison: Wisconsin University African Studies Program, 1990), pp. 119–132.

Agotime image of itself as a polity forged in combat, and it reinforced a tendency to validate the pursuit of militarism as an end in itself. This was reflected in the emergence of a new war-chief who co-ordinated much of the fighting. There is some disagreement as to precisely what happened. One side maintains that the existing war-chief, Akoto Sah I – who had distinguished himself in previous campaigns against Agu – acknowledged the contribution of a young warrior Agbovi (a *nom de guerre*) and embraced him as a war-chief in his own right, but without relinquishing overall command. The other side avers that Agbovi I became the substantive leader of the Agotime in succession to Akoto Sah.[11] Whatever the truth of the matter, Agbovi I certainly rose to a position of leadership at a time of crisis. Although the Ho-Agotime coalition could not expect to defeat the Asante, they certainly wore them down, and Asante general Adu Bofo was eventually forced to retire to Kumasi without having prevailed. With the passage of time, this has been elevated to the status of military victory.

The withdrawal of the Asante and their Anlo allies led to a period of further turmoil. Those who had borne the brunt of the occupation visited retribution on the *dukowo* that had collaborated with the invaders. Heading the list was Taviefe, but it included Adaklu which had reputedly led the Asante armies straight to Kpetoe.[12] During this period, it seems likely that significant numbers of people were taken as slaves. We know, for example, that the village of Batome was founded by Agbovi I as a hamlet where he settled his personal slaves. There was also a measure of continuity in the manner in which Agotime absorbed other outsiders into its ranks. After the British defeat of Asante of 1874, the lines of north-south trade shifted to the land routes east of the Volta, placing Agotime in a strategic position. Shortly thereafter, Anlo traders became regular visitors and, after some time, requested permission to settle. This is perhaps surprising, given that the Anlo forces had fought alongside

11 Interviews with Nene Akoto Sah VII, Kpetoe, 5 September 2007; and Nene Todje-Agbo IV, Kpetoe, 7 September 2007.

12 See the short overview of the separate divisional histories by Captain R.S. Rattray from 1915 in Public Records and Administration Department, Ho, Ghana (PRAAD (Ho)), RAO 273, 'Togoland: A History of the Tribal Divisions of the District of Misahuhe and of the Sub-Districts of Ho and Kpandu'. See also the entries in PRAAD (Accra), ADM 39/4/4, 'District Record Book (Ho)'.

Asante, but one explanation may be that not all Anlo settlements were implicated in the war.[13] The Anlo were granted a portion of land just behind what is now the Kpetoe police station. Later, they were allowed to appoint their own chief, known as the *Anlofia* (or chief of the Anlos), who became a part of community decision-making. Over time, the Anlo became fully integrated, one index of which is that they ceased to send their bodies home for burial. Hence, the boundaries of inclusion still remained permeable at this point. Trade had always been highly esteemed by the Agotimes, and absorbing the Anlo helped the Agotime to perpetuate the strategy of demographic expansion, but also solidified certain links with towns at the coast.

Although militarism and trade, the twin bases of Agotime society, appeared to achieve a new lease of life, the emergence of European imperialism cut the ground from beneath the community. After the withdrawal of the Danes in 1850, the British had nominally acquired 'interests' in the trans-Volta. The British government was extremely reluctant to make territorial claims, but there was a desire to bring an end to warfare and to remove the internal barriers to trade.[14] The mixture of persuasion and pressure had some mileage for as long as the British were the only external actor, but the sudden intrusion of the Germans in 1884 presented a problem. The British hoped to capitalize on an incipient sense of Krepi solidarity under the leadership of Peki. The intention was to unite all the chiefs behind a collective agreement to accept British protection. The Germans lost no time in chalking up individual treaties in an attempt to stake claims of their own. At the centre of the rivalry between those two powers was Agotime. The British believed that they already had a binding agreement with Agotime, whereas the Germans managed to extract their own treaty from Agbovi I in 1886. In 1888, Agbovi and Akoto Sah 'signed' a declaration to the effect that they did not consider themselves beholden to Germany, while the British government seemed willing to argue a case based on the contention

13 Interview with Nene Dapaah VI, Kpetoe, 7 September 2007.

14 Johnson, Marion, 'Ashanti east of the Volta', *Transactions of the Historical Society of Ghana* 8, 1965, pp. 33–59, 56. For a detailed analysis, see Bryars, William Hudson, *The Evolution of British Imperial Policy on the Volta, 1857–1897: From Informal Opportunism to Formal Occupation* (unpublished PhD thesis, University of Birmingham, 1994).

that Agotime had previously accepted the leadership of the Peki 'king'. This was significant because in 1887 the British and German governments had entered into an agreement that determined 'to leave within the British Protectorate the countries of Aquamoo and Crepee (Peki)'. At the end of the day, greater geopolitical interests prevailed, and under the Heligoland Treaty of July 1890 Germany received most of its demands. While Peki proper passed to the Gold Coast, most of Krepi – including Agotime – was transferred to Germany. This outcome had serious implications for Agotime. Like the British, the Germans wanted to prevent a proliferation of firearms, to end the endemic conflict and to control the terms of regional trade. The last of these threatened to complicate British-German relations, given that both wished to tap the north-south trade routes, but they had an interest in working together on the other two items.

Like the British, the Germans were forced to work largely with the grain of African societies. But in placing the weight in one place rather than another, they tended to confer benefits on some groups rather than others, and hence reconfigured social relations in important ways. There is already a good literature on ways in which colonial rule made it easier for the Ewe peoples to think of themselves as sharing a common identity.[15] The Bremen Mission on the two sides of the border is credited with the creation of a standardized written version of Ewe, based on the Anlo dialect, which was propagated through church and school. Birgit Meyer has argued that championing a purified form of the Ewe language represented part of an attempt to reverse the division of mankind that had supposedly been brought about after the fall of the Tower of Babel.[16] By making the language a fitting receptacle for the Word of God, and by transcending the dialectical differences through a standardized written form, the missionaries hoped to reunify the Ewe and bring them back to their Creator. According to Sandra Greene, those missionaries

15 See especially, Welch, Claude, *Dream of Unity: Pan-Africanism and Political Unification in West Africa* (Ithaca: Cornell University Press, 1966), chapters 2–3; and Amenumey, D.E.K., *The Ewe Unification Movement: A Political History* (Accra: Ghana Universities Press, 1989). Also Nugent, *Smugglers*, chapters 4–5.

16 Meyer, Birgit, *Translating the Devil: Religion and Modernity Among the Ewe in Ghana* (Edinburgh – London: Edinburgh University Press for International Africa Institute, 1999), pp. 57–60.

also played an important role in codifying the Ewe cosmological system, raising *Mawu* to the status of a high God, and disseminating the legend of the flight from Notsie. The latter could be used to posit a unity of the Ewe that had once supposedly existed.[17] The warfare of the nineteenth century could be read as evidence for divisions that were perpetuated by heathen practices, but for Ewe converts the moments of co-operation at times of external oppression (in the 1830s and the 1870s) were equally striking. These events could also be given a Biblical slant, thereby making the reunification of the Ewe almost a divine enterprise. Although the Ewe case can be interpreted within an 'invention of tradition' paradigm, the danger lies in divorcing twentieth-century discourses from their earlier contexts. Many of those who became the converts would have been born in the midst of the turmoil of the 1870s, when questions about how the *dukowo* related to one another were very much to the fore. The efforts of early cultural nationalists therefore consisted of trying to bend older forms of self-identification to fit the colonial context.

The interventions of the German administration ran somewhat counter to that of the missionaries. Although the Bremen and Catholic missions had administrative structures of their own, which inevitably fed into local politics, their interest lay in building wider networks of co-believers. The political administration, on the other hand, tended to operate in ways that added greater weight to identities centered on the *dukowo*. Dr. Gruner, who presided over the Misahöhe district between 1890 and 1912,[18] spent a great deal of time fixing the land boundaries between *dukowo* on the basis of historical claims. This went together with a policy of recognizing 'superior' and village chiefs for all the *dukowo*. Hence, the Ewe were treated as belonging to their primary units, which was where the centre of administrative gravity subsequently lay. Although infrastructural developments in German Togo brought Ewe communities closer together, this did not over-ride the administrative tendency towards 'structured fragmentation'.

17 Greene, Sandra, *Sacred Sites and the Colonial Encounter: A History of Meaning and Memory in Ghana* (Bloomington – Indianapolis: Indiana University Press, 2002), chapter 1.

18 Knoll, Arthur J., *Togo Under Imperial Germany, 1884–1914* (Stanford: Hoover Institution Press, 1978), p. 44.

The Agotime were affected by German colonialism in ways that still retain a significant legacy. Neither the Bremen nor Catholic missions considered Agotime as a possible centre of operations.[19] Ho enjoyed an importance for the Bremen mission that pre-dated the Asante war, while Agu became a leading centre from 1901. Adaklu-Waya was downgraded to a sub-station, but retained some importance.[20] The Catholics initially focused on Hohoe, Kpalimé and Kpandu, but in 1908 they diverted some of their attention to Ho and Assahun, followed by Agu-Tomegbe two years later.[21] These all bordered onto the Agotime and, with the exception of Ho, had hitherto been considered as either rivals or 'vassals'. The net effect was that the Agotime fell behind in conversion to Christianity and in access to schooling. Moreover, neither of the missions regarded Adangbe as a language worthy of support, with the result that those who did attend school were forced to operate through the medium of Ewe. To all intents and purposes, the missionaries behaved as if the Agotime *were* Ewe.

Much the same could be said of the political administration. Whereas Kpandu and Ho were considered as important towns, Kpetoe was treated as a peripheral outpost. When J.T. Furley conducted interviews with all the chiefs in the region in 1918, only the chief of Atikpui indicated that he fell under Agotime division, whereas others, which would once have been tributary, had been hived off or constituted separate divisions in their own right. The German administration had also reconfigured power relations within Agotime. Rather than recognizing Agbovi or Akoto Sah, they opted instead to install one Keteku as the superior chief. Today, some people say that the latter was the guardian of the male fetish that had been taken from Afegame, whereas others claim that the Germans simply selected the person who arranged their

19 It is surely significant that Debrunner's very thorough history of the church makes very few references to Agotime. Debrunner, Hans, *A Church Between Colonial Powers: A Study of the Church in Togo* (London: Lutterworth Press, 1965). In fact, there are only three references for the post-1874 period. There appear to be none at all in Ustorf, Werner, *Bremen Missionaries in Togo and Ghana: 1847–1900* (Legon: Legon Theological Studies – Asempa, 2002).

20 Debrunner, *Church*, p. 109.

21 *ibid.*, p. 110.

lodgings.[22] What is generally agreed is that there had never been a paramount chief in Agotime up until this point.

Finally, Agotime made a difficult transition to colonial economic realities. In some respects, the Agotime were well-served by German investments in infrastructure. Kpetoe was located on the road that ran from Ho to the capital of Lomé. Moreover, the Lomé-Kpalimé railway line ran along the eastern edge of Agotime, with a station being opened at Amoussoukope. However, colonial commerce was dominated by European trading companies, or by Hausa traders who had travelled south. Having lost their niche in trade, and having been forced to give up the pursuit of militarism, the Agotime struggled to find an alternative vocation. The railhead at Amoussoukope provided a market for maize, and the authorities actively promoted cotton production in areas which they considered well-suited to the crop. But an Agotime aversion to farming remained deeply ingrained. The response of Agotime males was to turn to weaving as an occupation considered worthy of esteem. Many Agotime men migrated to the Eastern Province of the Gold Coast, where they combined work on cocoa farms with the skilled work of *kente* weaving.

After the First World War, the partition of Togoland was negotiated so as to bring the railways under French ownership.[23] This meant that a new border would need to be driven through the Ewe-speaking peoples, with the smaller section being transferred to British control. Although Eweland was divided, almost none of the individual *dukowo* were. By contrast, Agotime was cut into two unequal parts, with Kpetoe, Afegame and two smaller villages passing to Britain, and the rest of Agotime (13 villages) being allocated to France. The border became somewhat hard because of the opposition of the administering powers to the maintenance of any bonds of allegiance. The French insisted that the headchief in Kpetoe no longer had any call on their Agotime who were slotted into a different hierarchy. The British professed to be in the business of redressing excessive fragmentation by amalgamating chieftaincies, and because the Agotime headchief had so few subjects in

22 Interview with Nene Akoto Sah VII, Kpetoe, 5 September 2007.

23 'Memorandum on Togoland' (Confidential Print No 1065 (West Africa)), p. 9, enclosed in PRAAD (Accra), ADM 11/1620, 'Togoland Secret and Confidential Papers' (1918–1924).

British Togoland, he was required to come beneath the Ho paramountcy and was expected to forget about his kinsmen across the border.

In the years immediately after the Second World War, the Ewe unification movement endeavoured to mobilize Ewes in the Gold Coast, British and French Togoland to lobby for being placed beneath a single administration. The Agotime case was assumed to nest within the campaign of the Ewe people as a whole. In the years just before Ghanaian independence, it was apparent that strongly-held *duko* identities, and a residual hostility to Anlo, made the Ewe nationalist project unworkable. After the 1956 referendum on Togoland reunification, agitation for the unity of the Ewe people subsided remarkably quickly, which meant that the border was entrenched as a political reality. Interestingly, although the Agotime were directly affected by the border, most of those in British Togoland chose to vote for integration with the Gold Coast despite the fact that this would guarantee continued separation from their brethren in Togo. This is explicable if one recognizes that many 'British' Agotime had spent time as migrants in the Gold Coast and identified with it. It was also an exercise in distancing themselves from the northern Ewe leadership of the Togoland Congress who had presumed to speak on their behalf. In 1955, chiefs from the Anyigbe Local Council (including Agotime) claimed that they were unrelated to the northern Ewes of Ho District, but shared links with the coastal Anlo[24] – thus placing a construction on history that was vaguely plausible. In the referendum of 1956, the vote in Anyigbe was two to one in favour of integration. Bizarrely, therefore, an assertion of Agotime identity in the Gold Coast/British Togoland context involved a negation of a common Agotime identity straddling the border. Or, to put the matter differently, the border had been internalized so that 'being Agotime' now had a territorial frame of reference.

After independence, acrimonious relations between Ghana and Togo made it very difficult for local actors to raise matters relating to the border. In 1978, at a point when relations had momentarily thawed,

24 PRAAD (Ho), RAO/C749 ('Future of Togoland Under British Trusteeship'), 'Petition by the Natural Rulers of the Anyigbe Local Council Area praying for exemption from the forthcoming plebiscite and for the direct integration with the Gold Coast', 8 November 1955. The plebiscite itself is fully covered in Welch, *Dream*.

Agotime leaders decided to explore the possibility of restoring relations between their divided community. The decision was taken to initiate a cultural festival in which all Agotimes could participate. It was called *Avakeza* or roughly 'the festival to celebrate the ending of war'. According to one informant, this was a reworking of the pre-colonial principle that there needed to be a ritual cleansing following a period of conflict.[25] The first festival was held in Zukpe and the second, in 1981, in Amoussoukope, both of which are in Togo.[26] The third event was scheduled for Kpetoe, but chieftaincy disputes rendered this impossible. The closure of the border for much of the 1980s subsequently meant that the festival needed to be put on ice. It was only in 1995 that Nene Nuer Keteku III reactivated the idea of a festival through which all the Agotimes could take pride in their culture. But this initiative immediately raised questions about what it was being celebrated. The case against a revival of *Avakeza* was that it dredged up aspects of a controversial past. To focus on the military exploits of the Agotimes tapped memories of heroism – especially relating to the Asante wars – but it also raised what was now a problematic fact, namely that many Agotimes were descended from captives.

Nene Keteku considered it preferable to substitute a different kind of festival, called *Agbamevoza* (or the 'kente weaving festival'), to celebrate what made the Agotimes both special and different from their neighbours. The small problem was that weaving was associated with the towns on the Ghana side of the border, which was (in turn) related to the history of migration to the cocoa belt. The chiefs on the Togo side of the border observed that the wearing of *kente* was a Ghanaian fixation, and did not speak to their identity.[27] To compound matters, the centre-piece of any such event was a grand durbar in which the chiefs would sit 'in state'. But this raised acute difficulties because Nene Keteku was not a paramount chief in the Ghanaian context, whereas the Zukpe and Amossoukope chiefs had been elevated to *chefs de canton* in Togo.

25 Interview with Emmanuel Tetteh Kpeglo, Agotime-Akpokope (Ghana), 2 September 2003.

26 Interview with Togbe Apaloo, Agotime-Batome (Togo), 15 August 2002.

27 Interview with Togbe Apaloo, Agotime-Batome (Togo), 15 August 2002. See also the interview with Emmanuel Tetteh Kpeglo, Agotime-Akpokope (Ghana), 2 September 2003.

The fact that the festival was always held in Kpetoe was another consideration that impeded its acceptance in Togo. Furthermore, the *avafiawo* had not relinquished their claims to being the real community leaders. Although the grand durbar was presided over by Nene Keteku, the 'firing of musketry' on the previous day was a celebration of military feats in which Nene Akoto Sah and Nene Agbovi shared the limelight. They rode in their palanquins, something which Nene Keteku himself was not entitled to do. When Nene Keteku allowed the newly appointed chief of Akpokope to ride in a palanquin, he brought a storm upon his head. The *avafiawo* and other chiefs protested and there was talk of destooling him, before the matter was finally resolved. Getting the protocol right, therefore, was an almost impossible exercise, and ultimately it was the *avafiawo* in Kpetoe who were mollified and the Togolese chiefs who were made to feel less important. Hence they failed to attend most of the festivals – with the exception of the chief of Batome who had a special relationship with Kpetoe.

In the British period, identities became frozen in a way that was quite unlike the permeability of earlier times. But after 1920, British land and chieftaincy policies contributed to the emergence of a discourse of landlord and stranger which threatened to create perpetual hierarchies of insiders and outsiders. Land disputes became the issue on which disputes about belonging turned. Right across Ghana, festivals have become deeply embroiled in the politics of identity. In recent times, Nene Keteku, whose title is Konor of Agotime, has made a conscious effort to accentuate aspects of Agotime culture that are shared with other Adangbes. There has been an attempt, for example, to revive *dipo* rites for pubescent girls, which is popularly associated with the Krobos. Moreover, the Konor of Krobo has been an invited guest at *Agbamevoza*. At the same time, relations with Adaklu have sharply deteriorated. The land dispute that has been ongoing since the 1940s has now been further complicated by the creation of a new District for Adaklu, Agotime and Ziope. The Kufuor government had initially promised to site the capital at Adaklu-Waya, but changed its mind just before the 2004 elections. The choice of Kpetoe provoked a storm of protest in Adaklu where the point was forcefully made that because the Agotime were supposedly strangers, it would be perverse for the capital to be sited in Kpetoe. Given that the Parliamentary candidates for the two main parties were both Agotimes, the Adaklu put up an independent candidate who almost succeeded in taking a safe seat from the National Democratic Congress in 2004. In the midst of these tensions, there was speculation about open conflict. While the Adaklus boasted of their greater numbers, forgetting those in Togo, Agotime hardliners alluded to the military victories of old. Whether the Togolese Agotime would follow the war-chiefs in Kpetoe was a matter of debate. History had suddenly acquired a profound contemporary resonance. The tensions surrounding the issue of the District capital led to the suspension of *Agbamevoza* in 2006 for fear that it would be considered provocative. Although the two headchiefs did broker a compromise, which was followed by the Adaklu chief attending *Agbamevoza* as a special guest in 2007, communal tensions have only slightly subsided.[28]

Recent events underline that while there is a renewed effort to construct an Agotime identity – on different principles to those of the nineteenth century – it is not clear which elements ought to be considered paramount and whether it can be made to transcend the realities of the international boundary. The project is still very much work in progress, and whether it will succeed remains to be seen.

Ethnicity, Religion and Mobility: Mandinka and Jola

The second pairing is that of the Mandinka and the Jola located on the border between the Gambia and the Casamance region of Senegal. A pronounced sense of difference between the Mandinka and the so-called 'Floops' is attested to in an eighteenth-century account by Francis Moore.[29] In the era of the slave trade, the relationship was characterized by mutual avoidance at best and outright enmity at worst, with the Jola tending to be the victims of enslavement. By contrast, the turbulence of the mid-nineteenth century was not ethnic in nature. Within the

28 I was present at Agbamevoza in 2007 and many of the comments made here are based on informal discussions.

29 Moore, Francis, *Travels into the Inland Parts of Africa* (London: E. Cave, 1738), p. 36.

Mandinka kingdom of Kombo, a deep rift emerged between the old ruling lines, the 'Soninke', and Muslim converts led by the 'Marabouts'. The latter accused the former of engaging in practices that were incompatible with Islam, and eventually resolved to seize power. The military conflict was decided in favour of the Maraboutic cause in 1875, following which the winning side attempted to create a Muslim state. Under the leadership of Fodé Sylla, the new regime did not content itself with consolidating its position amongst the Mandinka, but proceeded to push southwards into the areas known as Narang and Fogny-Jabangkunda, where the population consisted largely of Jolas and remnants of the Bainunks, and eastwards into Fogny where the Jola predominated. Raiding of the Jola was justified in terms of a holy war conducted against pagans. Nevertheless, the forces of Sylla made rather tokenistic efforts to bring about conversion in the areas they conquered, although his supporters did point out that he built mosques and forbade the use of alcohol.[30] However his real interest lay in enslaving Jolas who could then be sold eastwards towards Fuladu in return for firearms and horses. The raids devastated the region and led to the flight of much of the population. The British and the French, who had agreed to a paper partition of the region in 1889, found the activities of Fodé Sylla increasingly problematic.[31] In 1894, the British finally decided to lance the boil by despatching an invasion force to Kombo. Fodé Sylla was captured by the French as he escaped across the border, and was sent into internal exile where he spent the rest of his life. This ended plans for the creation of a theocratic state and heralded the beginnings of colonial administration.

At the start of their tenure, the British and the French were aware of the mutual antagonism between Mandinka and Jola. In the minds of the Jola, it seems, there was a direct association between being

30 On Sylla, see Skinner, David, 'Islam in Kombo: the spirtual and militant jihad of Fode Ibrahim Ture', unpublished paper delivered at the African Studies Association conference, 1990, pp. 1–33. See also Nugent, Paul, 'Cyclical history in the Gambia/Casamance borderlands: refuge, settlement and Islam from 1880 to the present', *Journal of African History* 48(2), 2007, pp. 221–243.

31 National Records Service of the Gambia, Banjul (NRSTG), CSO, 1/120 ('Draft Despatches to Secretary of State'), R.B. Llewelyn, Administrator of the Gambia, to Marquess of Ripon, 18 December 1893.

Mandinka, practicing Islam and engaging in slave raiding. The first generation of administrators expressed sympathy for the Jola, as the putative victims, but quickly became exasperated by the refusal of the latter to embrace the civilizing mission – not least in the shape of taxation. The respective administrations were presented with a practical problem. Because the Jola did not have chiefs and the Europeans needed local intermediaries to collect taxes and enforce orders, they turned to Mandinka intermediaries to govern Jola populations. The appointed chiefs had little regard for the Jola placed beneath them, and not surprisingly the relationship was a highly abrasive one. In the early stages, there were many reports of Jola attacks on Mandinka itinerant traders, which the chiefs seemed powerless to stop. The annual report for 1901, for Fogni in the Gambia stated it thus:

> Crime in Fogni is excessive, the Jolahs they are continually committing murders & highway robberies. The hard part of a Commissioner's work in this District is his inability to make arrests, no Jolah will ever arrest another, & the Mandingos are afraid to; another point is that it is very hard indeed to get one Jolah to give evidence against another.[32]

At an early point, the British realized that it was better to find Jolas to serve not just as village chiefs (*alkalolu*), but also as superior chiefs (*seyfolu),* whereas the French persisted with the experiment of using Mandinkas until after the First World War.

The remarkable thing is that the mutual antagonism between Mandinka and Jola, which the Europeans regarded as destined to persist, dissipated in the first decades of colonial rule. Reform of chieftaincy structures undoubtedly helped by removing a point of friction, but even more important was the rapid conversion of the Jola to Islam. This took place in the context of a greatly enhanced level of mobility in the first decades of the twentieth century. Broadly speaking, three kinds of settlement emerged in the Gambia/Casamance borderlands. First of all, there were the historic Mandinka towns that retained their shape, but absorbed significant numbers of Jola and Karoninka migrants. Examples would be Kartong in the Gambia or Abéné in the Casamance. Secondly,

32 NRSTG, ARP 33/2, Report from the Travelling Commissioner, Sangster, 'Reports on Kombo, Foni and Kiang (1900–01 and 1906–07)', 26 September 1901.

there were older settlements that had been almost entirely taken over by immigrant populations. The best example is Makuda, whose original population fled at the end of the nineteenth century to escape the turmoil. Today, the village is made up almost entirely of Jolas, from different parts of the Casamance, and by Karoninkas. Another example would be Darsilami in the Gambia, where the largest segment of the population is Karoninka, but with significant numbers of Jolas, Manjaks, Balantas and Fulas adding to the mix. The final kind of settlement is the one that emerged *de novo*. The Narang forest became a particular focus for the Buluf-Jola who were entering a zone that had been de-populated and hence thought of themselves as pioneers. In each kind of settlement, the communities that took shape were extremely mixed – to an extent that any Ghanaian would find bewildering. There was general agreement that origins should matter less than one's contribution to the community. An attachment to Islam provided a powerful charter for the rights of the Jola immigrants. The net result was that a discourse of landlord and stranger was much more muted than in the Ghana/Togo example.

It is not possible to fully explore the reasons why the Jola converted so quickly, but much of the answer has to do with the missionary role played by Mauritanian marabouts like Cheikh Mahfoudz.[33] Their contribution was crucial because they helped to re-encode Islam as the religion of peace rather than of violence and enslavement. Jola converts who moved to Mandinka towns came to be accepted as co-religionists, while Mandinka marabouts began to win followers from amongst the ranks of the Jola. The relationship between ethnic and religious identities was a subtle one. Jola converts accepted Muslim modes of dress and address, but they retained their Jola names and, to that extent, did not relinquish their identities. At the same time, it was through the process of migration that the Jola became more fully conscious of an overarching identity, as opposed to more localized solidarities located on the village. In this, their experience was not unlike that of the Ewe, and the limitations of scaling up were equally apparent in the long-run. The boundary between Mandinka and Jola populations remained, as did many of the reciprocal stereotypes, but it mattered comparatively little as multi-ethnic communities proliferated across the southern Gambia and the Casamance.

33 Nugent, Paul, 'History', pp. 233–235.

The British and the French authorities were broadly in favour of this movement of population if it meant that the land was used more productively and greater revenues would flow into government coffers.[34]

In more recent times, the terrain has shifted in significant ways. In the Casamance, a heightened sense of Jola identity in the south and centre of the region had much to do with perceived neglect by Senegal's Socialist Party government since independence. In April 1990, separatist agitation entered a more militant phase when rebels of the Mouvement des Forces Démocratiques de la Casamance (MFDC) launched an armed assault on the Séléty border post. Although its leadership was predominantly Jola, the movement did claim to speak on behalf of Mandinkas as well, and could count some of the latter amongst its leadership.[35] The real focus of separatist hatred was the Wolof from northern Senegal who dominated the politics of the country and were thought to harbour imperialist intentions towards fertile land in the Casamance. The low-intensity conflict of subsequent years was immensely disruptive, and placed a considerable burden on Jola populations who were initially rather sympathetic to the MFDC.

This had some rather interesting consequences in Fogny-Jabangkunda and Narang. The Mandinka populations generally regarded the MFDC rebels as a scourge, and in the former case they formed a Fogny-Jabangkunda association whose objective was to rebuild links between old Mandinka towns, which had become attenuated since the nineteenth century, and to drive the MFDC from their midst. A residual sense of identification with the pre-colonial unit of Fogny-Jabangkunda was therefore used to promote a contemporary agenda. The second consequence was the surfacing of internal divisions within the Jola fold. Some Jola from Fogny proper and from Fogny-Jabangkunda accused the

34 This was reflected in the competition for migrants.

35 On the MFDC rebellion, see Marut, Jean-Claude, 'Le dessous des cartes casamançaises: une approche géopolitique du conflit casamançais', in François-George Barbier-Wiesser (ed.), *Comprendre la Casamance: chronique d'une intégration contrastée* (Paris: Karthala, 1994), pp. 193–211; and *ibid*, 'Le problème casamançais: est-il soluble dans l'état-nation?', in Momar-Coumba Diop (ed.) *Le Sénégal contemporain* (Paris: Karthala, 2002), pp. 425–458. Also Gasser, Geneviève, ''Manger ou s'en aller': que veulent les opposants armés casamançais?', in *ibid.*, pp. 459–498; and Evans, Martin, 'Senegal: Mouvement des Forces Démocratiques de la Casamance', Chatham House, Briefing Paper 04/02, November 2004.

Buluf-Jola migrants of having brought the rebels with them. However, the greatest backlash came from the Karoninka population. Their original homeland is located in the peninsula and islands south of Kafountine, but they have moved into the border zone in considerable numbers since the 1980s. Colonial ethnography defined the Karoninkas as a branch of the Jola, but this was now openly refuted by those who claimed to speak for them: Karoninka intellectuals insisted that they were quite distinct from the Jola and that they should be recognized as a distinct ethnic group, namely as the 'Kalorn'. Their self-professed spokesmen have been quick to assert that the Kalorn are not recent arrivals or strangers in the border region, but had been regular visitors to Kombo from time immemorial. I myself have been rapped over the knuckles for suggesting that the Bainunks were the 'autochthons' who were absorbed into the Mandinka and Jola populations from the seventeenth century. My critics have insisted that it was the Kalorn who were there first to settle and provided the place names, which mean nothing in Mandinka. Recapturing the 'true history' of the Kalorn is a project that receives a great deal of attention, but it is a history that tends to be inscribed in landscape rather than being captured in discrete events.

The Karoninka were late converts to Islam, and approached the experience from a rather different angle to the Jola. In the Mandinka towns of Kombo and Fogny-Jabangkunda they did not merely adopt the new religion, but typically switched their ethnic identity as well. That is, converts adopted Mandinka names, relocated their homes and cut themselves off from their 'pagan' kin back in Karone. Kayong Kalorn, the ethnic association that was founded in 1994, was somewhat hostile to the Jola, but its attitude towards the Mandinka was very different. It was quick to accept that the relationship between the two peoples had always been friendly, given that Mandinka landlords had often served as patrons to Kalorn/Karoninka seasonal migrants and to those who later became substantive settlers. But one point the association did insist upon was that the Kalorn could be both good Muslims and Kalorn, without the need to assume a Mandinka identity.[36]

36 Interviews with Paul Jarjue, Secretary of Kayong Kalorn, Banjul, 3 April 2004, and with Sonkal Jasseh, Abéné (Casamance), 14 February 2004.

This ethnic project is also very much work in progress. It has made considerable strides in the Gambia where the government has been very encouraging towards Karoninka immigration, as part of its attempt to re-jig the ethnic arithmetic of the country. The Gambian authorities have permitted the Kalorn/Karoninka to have their own radio programmes, which is valued for its importance in the promotion of the language amongst the younger generation that has been born in the Gambia. Kayong Kalorn also organizes its own annual festival which, like that of the Agotime, aims to highlight and promote elements of a common culture. While the association claims simply to be preserving what is already in existence, it is also engaged in a self-conscious attempt to filter out what is considered desirable from that which can be dispensed with. A great deal of emphasis is placed upon education, especially for girls.[37] Not surprisingly, there is an intensive debate about what it means to be Kalorn. The festival is always held in rotation between towns on the Gambian side of the border, whereas those who live in Senegal have largely been relegated to the role of observers. This is ironic, given that the Karoninkas are originally Senegalese, but the political climate in the Casamance may not be as conducive to this kind of activity. Moreover, Kayong Kalorn is eager to make the case that the Kalorn are really an indigenous people of the Gambia – whose presence there allegedly pre-dates that of the Mandinka and the Jola – and hence it is reluctant to muddy the waters by extending its operations into Senegal. Hence, as with the Agotime, the existence of the border has helped to shape the way in which ethnicity is articulated.

Conclusion

In the Ewe-Agotime case, it is evident that memories run very deep, but as the context has shifted, it has become a problem to press history into the service of the present because it is potentially divisive. The mechanisms that had once forged Agotime social structure rested on enslave-

37 *Kayong Kalorn Perspective* (undated pamphlet), p. 4.

ment, which is a subject that tends to be avoided today for fear of creating offence. The self-conscious search for new symbols of a common identity, after decades of having been treated as a kind of proxy Ewe, arises out of this underlying reality. Moreover, the international border has greatly complicated the search for a means of uniting the Agotime behind a common ethnic project, which relies to a large extent on the oxygen provided by the land dispute with Adaklu. In the Mandinka-Jola case, it is possible to demonstrate the existence of a clear distinction in the eighteenth century. This relationship became still more antagonistic in the nineteenth century in the context of slave raiding. But Jola migration and conversion to Islam in the early colonial period combined to produce a very different chemistry. Although the Jola were becoming more aware of what they had in common, they also invested in the identity associated with being a Muslim.

Like the Ewe, the Jola also retained a strong attachment to their places of origin, and these internal contradictions were never entirely resolved. Like the Ewe unification movement, the MFDC endeavoured to simultaneously mobilize its chosen ethnic constituency (the Jola) while allaying the fears of other groups who would be affected by a territorial reorganization (mainly the Mandinka). The failure of Ewe secessionism in the 1950s has been mirrored in more recent times by the emergence of multiple splits in the Casamance separatist movement. In some respects, lower-order identities have asserted themselves, and this is especially true of the Karoninka. The latter have to all intents and purposes ceased to be regarded as part of the greater Jola family. But Karoninka ethnic brokers, like their Agotime counterparts, have also had to face the problem of defining what it is that makes them a people apart. In a very similar fashion, the success in redefining identity has preceded at an uneven pace on the two sides of the border. Indeed, to a large extent, the international boundaries have acted as an effective barrier to the realization of the ethnic project, even when they have been extremely porous. While history often stubbornly refuses to be pressed into service, boundaries have created a bifurcated set of political imaginings.

Bibliography

Amenumey, D.E.K., *The Ewe Unification Movement: A Political History* (Accra: Ghana Universities Press, 1989).

Bryars, William Hudson, *The Evolution of British Imperial Policy on the Volta, 1857–1897: From Informal Opportunism to Formal Occupation* (unpublished PhD thesis, University of Birmingham, 1994).

Chimhundu, Herbert, 'Early missionaries and the ethnolinguistic factor during the 'invention of tribalism' in Zimbabwe', *Journal of African History* 33(1), 1992, pp. 87–109.

Debrunner, Hans, *A Church Between Colonial Powers: A Study of the Church in Togo* (London: Lutterworth Press, 1965).

Evans, Martin, 'Senegal: Mouvement des Forces Démocratiques de la Casamance', Chatham House, Briefing Paper 04/02, November 2004.

Gasser, Geneviève, "Manger ou s'en aller': que veulent les opposants armés casamançais?', in Momar-Coumba Diop (ed.) *Le Sénégal contemporain* (Paris: Karthala, 2002), pp. 459–498.

Greene, Sandra, *Sacred Sites and the Colonial Encounter: A History of Meaning and Memory in Ghana* (Bloomington – Indianapolis: Indiana University Press, 2002).

Harneit-Sievers, Axel, *Constructions of Belonging: Igbo Communities and the Nigerian State in the Twentieth Century* (Rochester: University of Rochester Press, 2006).

Iliffe, John, *A Modern History of Tanganyika* (Cambridge: Cambridge University Press, 1979).

Johnson, Marion, 'Ashanti east of the Volta', *Transactions of the Historical Society of Ghana* 8, 1965, pp. 33–59.

Killingray, David, 'Imagined martial communities: recruiting for the military and the police in colonial Ghana, 1860–1960', in Carola Lentz and Paul Nugent (eds.) *Ethnicity in Ghana: The Limits of Invention* (Basingstoke: Macmillan – New York: St. Martin's, 2000), pp. 119–136.

Knoll, Arthur J., *Togo Under Imperial Germany, 1884–1914* (Stanford: Hoover Institution Press, 1978).

Kopytoff, Igor, and Suzanne Miers, 'African slavery as an institution of marginality', in Suzanne Miers and Igor Kopytoff (eds.), *Slavery in Africa: Historical and Anthropological Perspectives* (Madison – London: Wisconsin University Press, 1977), pp. 3–81.

Lentz, Carola, *Ethnicity and the Making of History in Northern Ghana* (Edinburgh: Edinburgh University Press/IAI, 2006).

Lonsdale, John, 'The moral economy of Mau Mau: the problem', in Bruce Berman and John Lonsdale, *Unhappy Valley: Conflict in Kenya and Africa* (London: James Currey, 1992), pp. 265–314.

Lonsdale, John, 'The moral economy of Mau Mau: wealth, poverty and civic virtue in Kikuyu political thought', in Bruce Berman and John Lonsdale, *Unhappy Valley: Conflict in Kenya and Africa* (London: James Currey, 1992), pp. 315–504.

Maier, D.J.E., 'Military acquisition of slaves in Asante', in David Henige and T.C. McCaskie (eds.), *West African Economic and Social History: Studies in Memory of Marion Johnson* (Madison: Wisconsin University African Studies Program, 1990), pp. 119–132.

Marut, Jean-Claude, 'Le dessous des cartes casamançaises: une approche géopolitique du conflit casamançais', in François-George Barbier-Wiesser (ed.), *Comprendre la Casamance: chronique d'une intégration contrastée* (Paris: Karthala, 1994), pp. 193–211.

Marut, Jean-Claude, 'Le problème casamançais: est-il soluble dans l'état-nation?', in Momar-Coumba Diop (ed.), *Le Sénégal contemporain* (Paris: Karthala, 2002), pp. 425–458.

Meillassoux, Claude, *The Anthropology of Slavery: The Womb of Iron and Gold* (London: Athlone Press, 1991).

Meyer, Birgit, *Translating the Devil: Religion and Modernity Among the Ewe in Ghana* (Edinburgh – London: Edinburgh University Press for International Africa Institute, 1999).

Nugent, Paul, *Smugglers, Secessionists & Loyal Citizens on the Ghana-Togo Frontier: The Lie of the Borderlands Since 1914* (Athens/OH: Ohio University Press – Oxford: James Currey, 2002).

Nugent, Paul, 'Cyclical history in the Gambia/Casamance borderlands: refuge, settlement and Islam from c.1880 to the present', *Journal of African History* 48(2), 2007, pp. 221–243.

Nugent, Paul, 'Putting the history back into ethnicity: enslavement, religion and cultural brokerage in the construction of the Mandinka/Jola and Ewe/Agotime identities in West Africa, c.1650–1930', *Comparative Studies in Society and History* 50(4), 2008, pp. 920–948.

Peel, J.D.Y., 'The cultural work of Yoruba ethnogenesis', in Elizabeth Tonkin, Maryon Macdonald, and Malcolm Chapman (eds.), *History and Ethnicity* (London: Routledge, 1989), pp. 198–215.

Ranger, Terence, 'The invention of tradition in colonial Africa', in Eric Hobsbawm and Terence Ranger (eds.), *The Invention of Tradition* (Cambridge: Cambridge University Press, 1983), pp. 211–262.

Ranger, Terence, 'Missionaries, migrants and the Manyika: the invention of ethnicity in Zimbabwe', in Leroy Vail (ed.), *The Creation of Tribalism in Southern Africa* (London: James Currey, 1989), pp. 118–150.

Ranger, Terence, 'The invention of tradition revisited: the case of colonial Africa', in Terence Ranger and Olufemi Vaughan (eds.) *Legitimacy and the State in Twentieth-Century Africa* (London: Macmillan, 1993), pp. 62–111.

Reindorf, Carl, *The History of the Gold Coast and Asante, Based on Traditions and Historical Facts Comprising a Period of More than Three Centuries From About 1500 to 1860* (Accra: Ghana Universities Press, 1966 [orig. 1889]).

Skinner, David, 'Islam in Kombo: the spirtual and militant jihad of Fode Ibrahim Ture', unpublished paper delivered at the African Studies Association conference, 1990, pp. 1–33.

Spear, Thomas, 'Neo-Traditionalism and the Limits of Invention in British Colonial Africa', *Journal of African History* 44(1), 2003, pp. 3–27.

Ustorf, Werner, *Bremen Missionaries in Togo and Ghana: 1847–1900* (Legon: Legon Theological Studies – Asempa, 2002).

Van den Bersselaar, Dmitri, 'Imagining home: migration and the Igbo village in colonial Nigeria', *Journal of African History* 40(1), 2005, pp. 51–73.

Welch, Claude, *Dream of Unity: Pan-Africanism and Political Unification in West Africa* (Ithaca: Cornell University Press, 1966).

Willis, Justin, 'The making of a tribe: Bondei identities and history', *Journal of African History* 33(2), 1992, pp. 191–208.

PHILIP J. HAVIK*[1]

Tchon i Renansa: Colonial Governance, Appointed Chiefs and Political change in 'Portuguese' Guinea

Introduction

Over the last decades, the literature on sub-Saharan Africa denotes a lively debate providing new perspectives on the complex question of ethnicity, which has been characterized as a veritable 'minefield'.[2] Invariably linked to race, nationalism and governance, as well as a variety of tropes regarding African societies, the topical nature of the notion of ethnicity has been highlighted as a result of political conflicts in Africa. The case of Rwanda/Burundi provoked many reactions, reinforcing the idea of 'myth making'[3], 'invented traditions'[4] and 'politicised identities'.[5] Some suggested the existence of astute '*ethnic entrepreneurs*' who

* IICT, Lisbon.

1 Instituto de Investigação Científica Tropical (IICT), Lisbon, Portugal with the support of the Fundação para a Ciência e Tecnologia (FCT).

2 Green, Elliot D., 'What is an Ethnic Group? Political Economy, constructivism and the common language approach to ethnicity', Working Paper (London: London School of Economics, 2005).

3 Lemarchand, René, 'Ethnicity as a Myth: a view from Central Africa', occasional paper (Copenhagen, CAS, 1999).

4 Ranger, Terence, 'The invention of tradition in colonial Africa', in Eric Hobsbawm and Terence Ranger (eds.), *The Invention of Tradition* (Cambridge: Cambridge University Press, 1983), pp. 212–262; Ranger, Terence, 'The Invention of Tradition revisited: the case of colonial Africa', in Preben Kaarsholen and Jan Holten (eds.) *Inventions and Boundaries: Historical and Anthropological Approaches to the Study of Ethnicity and Nationalism* (Roskilde: University of Roskilde, 1994), pp. 5–50.

5 Mamdani, Mahmoud, *Citizen and Subject: contemporary Africa and the legacy of late colonialism* (Princeton: Princeton University Press, 1996).

manipulated ethnicity playing upon its 'demonic and seductive traits'[6], whilst others reflecting upon the growth of nationalism concluded that we were dealing with the search for historical legitimacy by means of '*imagined communities*'.[7] The twin concepts of '*moral ethnicity*' and '*political tribalism*' as introduced by John Lonsdale, which have gained broad acceptance among africanists, and the question of 'invented chieftaincy' during colonial times, highlight the contested space between politics and identities that has come to dominate much of the debate on the (fragility of the) African state.[8] These approaches have not only touched upon ethnical tropes and their evolution, but also linked 'ethnicities' to the competition between indigenous groups and communities for resources.

In a recent contribution to the discussion, Bruce Berman employed these concepts to underpin his analysis of the 'resurgence of the politics of identity and ethnicity' in the era of multiparty elections. He and his co-authors argue that 'ethnicities are constructed from diverse indigenous and foreign cultural materials' and are 'continually redefined and recreated' at a local level.[9] Colonial bureaucracies have been credited with an important role in the shaping of 'ethnicities', not only in terms of representations but also by means of 'native' policies. The genealogy of the crisis of the African state has over the last decade been traced to the colonial enterprise which turned custom and thereby porous 'tribal' identities into rigid legal categories.[10] One of the issues at the forefront of an analysis of colonial governance is the role of the appointed 'ethnic' chiefs which formed the basis for different forms of 'indirect rule' in British, French and Portuguese colonies.[11] This brings us to the principal

6 Lemarchand, 'Ethnicity'.

7 Anderson, Benedict, *Imagined Communities: reflections on the origin and spread of nationalism* (New York: Verso, 1991).

8 Lonsdale, John, 'Moral Ethnicity and Political Tribalism', in Preben Kaarsholen and Jan Holten (eds.) *Inventions and Boundaries: Historical and Anthropological Approaches to the Study of Ethnicity and Nationalism* (Roskilde: University of Roskilde, 1994), pp. 131–150.

9 Berman, Bruce; Dickson Eyoh, and Will Kymlicka, 'Introduction: Ethnicity & the Politics of Democratic Nation-Building in Africa', in Bruce Berman, Dickson Eyoh, and Will Kymlicka (eds.), *Ethnicity and Democracy in Africa* (Oxford: James Currey – Athens/OH: Ohio University Press, 2004), pp. 1–21, 4.

10 Mamdani, *Citizen*.

11 This issue gave rise to an intensive debate amongst anthropologists. 'Indirect rule'

question that Mamdani dealt with in his 'Citizen and Subject', namely the reliance on 'native auxiliaries', and in particular on '*decentralised despots*' and the anti-bodies they unleashed amongst their respective constituencies.[12] Some scholars have contested the idea of an almost unbridled capacity of the colonial powers to reinvent and manipulate chieftaincy in order to achieve domination over African societies.[13] The tensions between officials' attempts to instrumentalize tradition for political ends and chiefs' local legitimacy based upon their ability to act as providers and patrons, actually conditioned and limited the colonial state's options. These limitations are also highlighted by Terence Ranger and Bruce Berman who argue that the small stratum of administrators 'desperately needed local allies' and entered into 'patron–client relationships' or 'patriarchal alliances' with chiefs, transforming them from patrons into clients.[14] As we will demonstrate below, 'the relation of unstable and contradictory mutual dependence' to which it gave rise ultimately depended upon the ability of administrators to manipulate local political actors, and of incumbent and aspiring chiefs to 'deliver' while taking advantage of the formers' patronage.[15] Case studies have focused on the ambivalent position of 'administrative chiefs', their legitimacy and capacity for intervention, popular support and resistance, as well as the relation between ethnographic knowledge and colonial governance.[16]

---

made British colonies an obvious target; see for example Max Gluckman's pioneering essay, Gluckman, Max, 'The Village Headman in British Central Africa', *Africa* 19(2), 1949, pp. 89–106, and the Manchester School's (contested) notion of the 'dual spheres'.

12 Mamdani, *Citizen.*

13 Spear, Thomas, 'Neo-Traditionalism and the Limits of Invention in British Colonial Africa', *Journal of African History* 44(1), 2003, pp. 3–27.

14 Ranger, 'Invention revisited'; Berman, Bruce J., 'Ethnicity, Patronage and the African State: the politics of uncivil nationalism', *African Affairs* 97(388), 1998, pp. 305–341.

15 Berman, 'Ethnicity', p. 317.

16 Newbury, Catherine, 'Colonialism, Ethnicity and Rural Political Protest: Rwanda and Zanzibar in Comparative Perspective', *Comparative Politics* 15(3), 1983, pp. 253–280; Geschiere, Peter L., 'Chiefs and Colonial Rule in Cameroon: inventing chieftaincy, French and British style', *Africa* 63(2), 1993, pp. 151–175; Van Nieuwaal, A.B. van Rouveroy, 'Chieftaincy in Africa: three facets of a hybrid role', in A.B. van Rouveroy van Nieuwaal and R. van Dijk (eds.), *Rethinking Chieftaincy in Africa: African chieftaincy in a new socio-political landscape* (Münster: LIT, 1999), pp. 21–

The case of Portuguese Guinea has been the subject of numerous attempts to define the core essence of resistance to colonialism, owing to the successful struggle waged by a nationalist movement which resulted in independence in 1974.[17] Forced labour, taxes and the chieftainship system were key issues not only in Guinea but also in Angola and Mozambique, and were subsequently transformed into political causes by resistance movements from the 1950s. The appointment of chiefs ('*régulos*' in Guinea and Mozambique, *sobas* in Angola) became a cornerstone of colonial rule in all of Portugal's continental African territories in the early twentieth century. Its implementation occurred just as Portugal was seeking to dominate African societies by military means. As a result, those dignitaries who allied themselves with colonial interests were rewarded with chieftainships, thus in effect becoming 'agents of pacification'. The creation of an intermediate, auxiliary layer between 'citizens and subjects' at once allowed regimes to claim customary authenticity, as well as giving them a regional political base. At the same time, these chieftainships formed an integral part of the broader notion of 'native' policy or '*política indígena*': the introduction of this 'modern' concept of governance entailed the juxtaposition of administrative dichotomies such as 'citizen' (*civilizado,* civilized person) and 'subject' (*indígena*, native).

Rather than 'tribal' these chieftainships were essentially 'territorial' obeying to an administrative, geo-political rationale, in which a number of chieftaincies (*regulados*) and communities were integrated and subsumed into administrative districts. However, in this respect, administrators pursued largely personalized and improvised arrangements instead of consistent policies or strategies. The rapid turnover of officials, arbitrary appointments of chiefs and their intervention in quarrels over succession tended to absorb much of their time and efforts, leading them to make and break chiefly aspirations to act as local leaders. The example of Portuguese Guinea shows that tax collection was one of the principal vectors of a paradigm shift that occurred in a colonial context

---

47; Ginio, Ruth, 'French Colonial Reading of Ethnographic Research: the case of the 'desertion' of the Abron King and its aftermath', *Cahiers d'Etudes Africaines* 42(166), 2002, pp. 337–357.

17 For an insightful analysis of the colonial regime and the evolution of its relations with civil (rural) society, see Forrest, Joshua B., *Lineages of State Fragility: rural civil society in Guinea Bissau* (Athens/OH: Ohio University Press, 2003).

from 'ethnic' to 'domestic' spaces, thereby decisively contributing to a fragmentation of political authority, both in an 'ethnic' and an administrative sense. By taking stratified societies as a 'model' for government and by obliging their dignitaries to guarantee the extraction of (tax) revenue and the recruitment of labour, the need for understanding regional and local power structures was generally sacrificed for reasons of political expediency. The fact that the population inhabiting districts and *regulados* was often heterogeneous, further contributed to the dilution and fragmentation of 'identities', while inter and intra-community conflicts often remained undetected, or even purposefully hidden by local actors, until they spun out of control. Although reports produced recommendations and successive administrations and officials debated the issue, a consensus proved hard to come to given the perceived lack of alternatives. Eventually, administrative knowledge and control was weakened by its own extractive practices which resulted in solutions by default, leaving many a chiefly post vacant or in the hands of caretakers. While the anti-colonial war would eventually confront the colonial and metropolitan administration with the consequences of their negligence, post-independence politics were to demonstrate the ineptitude of the new leaders to solve the imbroglio of local governance.[18]

18 On the question of the *regulados* after independence, the Manjaco region has been best studied; see Crowley, Eve L., *Contacts with the Spirits: religion, asylum and ethnic identity in the Cacheu region of Guinea Bissau* (unpublished PhD thesis, Yale University, 1990); Gable, Eric, *Modern Manjaco: the ethos of power in West African society* (unpublished PhD dissertation, University of Virginia, 1990), and *idem*, 'Manjaco Rulers after a Revolution', *Africa* 72(1), 2003, pp. 88–112; and also Carvalho, Clara, *Ritos de Poder e Recriação da Tradição: os régulos manjaco da Guiné Bissau* (unpublished PhD dissertation, ISCTE Lisbon, 1999).

New Borders and Changing Identities: War and Migration

The military campaigns which began in the 1890s and resulted in the conquest of continental Portuguese Guinea in 1915 within the borders drawn by the Berlin Conference (1884–85) and the Franco-Portuguese treaty (1886) decisively altered the situation on the ground. Although this strategy for domination – just like the resistance against it – was apparently oriented by 'ethnic' vectors by dealing separately with every group, it ended up by demonstrating the importance of the territorial organization of African societies.[19] Colonial governance was confronted with the fact that Guinea was inhabited by fifteen different 'ethnic' groups – or 'races' as the authorities would have it – which diverged considerably in terms of language, customs and traditions. Early fifteenth and sixteenth-century travelers' accounts had defined the principal '*nações*' or 'nations' of the '*gentio*' or 'heathen' as they were then known. The early definition of these tropes and their continuity up to the present would then contradict the idea that these labels were only recently 'invented'.[20] Originally, eight groups were classified, i.e. the Felupe/Jola, the Balanta, the Bañun, the Biafada, the Pepel, the Bijagó, the Soninke/Mandinka, and the Fula. While the first two long remained wary of direct contact and trade, the other groups acted as suppliers or intermediaries of the

19 For an analysis of the 'ethnic' and inter-'ethnic' formations and concomitant representations from first contact to the first decade of the twentieth century, see Havik, Philip J., *Silences and Soundbytes: the gendered dynamics of trade and brokerage in the pre-colonial Guinea Bissau region* (Münster: LIT – New Brunswick: Transaction Publ., 2004), pp. 86–147. The emergence of a Creole language with an Afro-Portuguese lexical base, i.e. Kriol, which became the *lingua franca* in coastal regions from the sixteenth century, reflects the self-definition of communities by their ancestral territory, i.e. '*tchon*' (derived from Portuguese *chão* or land) and those in authority as the '*dunus di tchon*' or lords of the land (derived from Portuguese *dono* or owner).

20 Many of the terms used were based upon existing ethnonyms employed by communities in region. See Almeida, António de, *Das Etnonimias da Guiné Portuguesa, do Arquipélago de Cabo Verde e das Ilhas de São Tomé e Príncipe* (Lisbon: ISCSPU, 1965/66).

Atlantic slave and goods trade.[21] The introduction of export crops (above all peanuts) from the 1830s would provoke large scale out-migration in Senegambia, leading to increasing cross-cultural ties between different groups and areas. The aptitude and productivity of the indigenous population with regard to the cultivation of certain crops begins to be discussed, contributing to a redefinition of 'ethnic' attributes as they had grown out of early contact and were consolidated by the slave trade. However, by the late nineteenth century when the scramble was on, many Portuguese authors still quoted from these travelers' accounts when describing the region's populations.

Military campaigns were further complicated by the terrain, which ranged from coastal mangrove floodplains where rice was cultivated, to savannah plateaus in the interior better suited to cereals such as millet and sorghum; marshes and densely forested areas provided populations with natural defenses. These circumstances illustrated the need for studying the region's topography, and the political and social organization of communities that still had to be 'conquered'.[22] As one governor succinctly put it: '(…) nominally Guinea pertains to the Portuguese Crown, but in reality the Mandinkas, Soninkés, Balantas, Pepel etc. exercise sovereignty over it'.[23] Local communities and lineage clusters joined in order to counter offensives which attempted to penetrate their respective ancestral territory or *tchon,* villages or *tabankas* and compounds or *moransas*.[24] In fact, some scholars concluded that the conflict did forge inter-'ethnic' alliances[25], while the involvement of Christianised communities such as the Kriston in the fighting alongside 'animist' groups such as the Pepel reinforced multi-

21 Although the coastal populations of the Guinea-Bissau region migrated over a period of five centuries, the ancestral roots of these communities are still located in the areas originally indicated in travelers' accounts.

22 Arquivo Histórico Ultramarino, Lisbon (AHU), Direcção Geral do Ultramar (DGU), Repartição Militar, Cx. 6. João Augusto Muzanty, Bolama, to Overseas Ministry, Lisbon, 28 Aug. 1908.

23 AHU, DGU, Guiné, 1ª Repartição, Cx. 8, Alfredo Cardoso de Soveral Martins, Governor of Portuguese Guinea, Bolama, *Relatório do governador*, 12 Oct. 1903.

24 Forrest, *Lineages*, pp. 105–123.

25 *ibid.*, pp. 85–104.

cultural aspects of co-operation.[26] The creation of new collective labels showed that territorial criteria on some occasions overrode 'ethnic' identification. By resisting Portuguese domination, the inhabitants of the Oio province which had once formed part of the Soninke-ruled Kaabú federation, gained the reputation of fearsome, 'invincible' fighters, symbolized by the 'ethno-regional' epithet *Oincas*.[27] The close co-operation between different resident communities, i.e. Soninke, Mandinka and Balanta, led colonial forces who largely ignored local cultures, to adopt the term which was thereafter reproduced in publications alongside other 'ethnic' groups.[28]

The fact that the 'pacification' of littoral 'animist' communities was achieved mainly with the aid of a large number of African mercenaries and auxiliaries from stratified, Islamised groups, such as the Fula and Mandinka, would also hold significant implications for inter-community relations. The influx of members of such stratified, Islamised communities into the *tchon* of largely segmentary 'animist' groups, not only as *djila* (Dyula) or itinerant traders and *murus* or *marabouts,* but also as soldiers, *cipaios* (guards), and ultimately as appointed chiefs or *régulos* as a reward for their loyalty would give rise to tensions and quarrels. Policies pursued by the French administration in neighbouring French West Africa (AOF) and in particular among the Jola in the Casamance region which had a common border with Portuguese Guinea would lead to similar results.[29] Whereas the policy of appointing non-ethnic chiefs was discontinued in the aforementioned region in Senegal, it remained in place in Guinea throughout the colonial period. Besides the Balanta, similar policies were pursued in relations to the Mandinka on whom Fula chiefs were imposed. Relations between these stranger chiefs and their non-'ethnic' subjects were complex and above all localized, rather than being

26 Pélissier, René, *La Naissance de la Guiné: Portugais et Africains en Sénégambie (1841–1936)* (Orgeval: Pélissier, 1989).

27 Forrest, *Lineages*, p. 88.

28 See for example, Pereira, Carlos, *La Guinée Portugaise (subsides pour son étude)* (Lisbon: A Editora Lda, 1914), p. 29. The author, a former governor, defined the Oincas as an 'ethnic group'.

29 See for the appointment of Islamised *Wolof* chiefs, former soldiers, among the Jola in the Casamance region from the 1880s, Roche, Christian, *Histoire de la Casamance: conquête et résistance: 1850–1920* (Paris: Karthala, 1985), pp. 268–274.

based upon 'ethnic' animosities. Essentially, they were seen as officials, as agents and extensions of the colonial administration, and not as 'non-ethnic' peers.

The appointment of chiefs was essentially based on their perceived loyalty to the colonial cause or personal ties with district administrators, rather than their ethnic affiliation or traditional claim to the chieftaincy. The warning given by a governor during the campaigns in the early 1900s to the effect that the 'territory was divided up between twelve different races, [so that] only a carefully pondered native policy could maintain the province in a state of equilibrium (...)' was meant exclusively for metropolitan ears.[30] The fact that chiefs received a significant percentage of the hut tax – introduced in 1903 – they collected in the area under their control, indicated to what extent power was shared in this transitional phase.[31] As the protracted military conflict drew to a close, divide-and-rule tactics were abundantly used by European officers and African auxiliaries, who took an ever-greater share of taxes and tribute. By associating chieftainships with geo-political and above all fiscal interests, the loyalty shown by natives as auxiliaries in Portuguese-led military or tax campaigns – and not their customary title to the chieftaincy – had become the norm for confirming their nomination. In some strategic areas this 'policy' consisted of the appointment of non-ethnic 'foreigners' to the posts or the invention of *regulados* were none existed before, in order to guarantee a measure of political control and of tax revenue.

The case of the mercenary Abdul Injai and his appointment as *régulo* of the Oio region is symptomatic in this respect. The region in question was inhabited by an amalgam of different 'ethnic' groups, including Balanta and Soninke, who had long defied colonial occupation. Once occupying the post of *regedor* or *régulo* in the Oio region as a reward

30 AHU, Guiné, Repartição Militar, Cx. 6, João Augusto de Muzanty to Ministério da Marinha e do Ultramar, Bolama, 18 July 1907.

31 As the advance of military incursions into the interior proceeded but overall territorial control was still beyond reach, the share of tax receipts accruing to chiefs varied between thirty-five and forty percent of the total; see AHU, Fundo Viegas, Processo 8, *Arrolamento, cobrança e recenseamento da população indígena de 1902 a 1911*, Note: The dossier in question contains several documents from the said period, and the references are taken from different ones.

for his active support in conquering it, Injai was to pose a serious problem for the colonial authorities. After establishing his own fiefdom in the area based upon wide-scale intimidation and arbitrary tribute, authorities branded him a troublemaker and regarded him as a threat to Portuguese authority. Accused of jeopardising the '*política indigena*' or native affairs policy and calling the prestige of the colonial authorities in question, he was subsequently deposed and banned into exile in 1919.[32] Such objections indicated that in a colonial perspective he had exploited his position of a mere administrative auxiliary to attain the status of an African ruler or warlord. His power, which was based upon military strength, relied upon troops that were a multi-cultural amalgam of personnel with widely differing origins, including Wolof, Fula, Mandinka, Tukolor, Sarakole and Susu. Interestingly, officials failed to agree on Injai's own 'ethnic' origins, which ranged from Fulbe and Wolof to Sereer. He was described by the vociferous local opposition as the 'ferocious enemy of all the races in Guinea', suggesting a broad consensus against the stranger-invader.[33] The Portuguese governor concluded that rather than selecting *régulos* from the beaten tribes, those pertaining to the victorious groups were being appointed instead. The latter solely lived from the booty they pillaged, such as Abdul Injai. As a result, the governor argued, such 'French chiefs' were sending for their countryfolk, who were populating the region in question and committing atrocities against its 'native inhabitants'.[34]

In the meantime, the war had also engendered the emergence of a political conscience among urban social strata, with many political deportees among them, which resulted in a proto-nativist movement. The first formal proponents of a 'Guinean' identity were the self-styled

32 Bowman, Joye L., *Ominous Transition: commerce and colonial expansion in the Senegambia and Guinea, 1857–1919* (Aldershot: Avebury, 1997), pp. 141–163.

33 The administration regularly played upon these antagonistic sentiments by threatening to send the mercenary leader over to 'take their cattle and their women'. For an account by the 'Guinean' opposition, see Loff de Vasconcellos, Luís, *Contestação dos Presos Políticos Implicados na Suposta Rebelião de Bissau* (Bolama: Imprensa Nacional, 1916), p. 3. After his forced departure, Mandinkas attempted to regain their former hegemony over the Fula in the Oio region.

34 AHU, Fundo do Governo da Guiné (FGG), L. 177, Francelino Pimentel, Governor of Portuguese Guinea, to Ministério da Marinha e do Ultramar, 6 Oct. 1909.

'natives of Guinea' who established the *Liga Guineense* (Guinean League) in 1911.[35] In the course of the war, the expression '*Guinés*' was also used as a pejorative term for urbanised strata with political aspirations, and who opposed the colonial regime.[36] The mainstay of the association were the Kriston who had long acted as go-betweens in the riverine relay trade and formed trade lineages in coastal towns such as Bissau, Cacheu, Geba and Bolama.[37] Acting as intermediaries, the Kriston fostered alliances between pro-nativist urban strata and lineage chiefs in the interior against Abdul Injai, 'the Senegalese', who was portrayed as a foreign bandit and bloodthirsty terrorist.[38] Pamphlets vehemently attacked authorities for allying themselves with him, sounding a proto-nationalist note, much influenced by the turmoil in the metropole following the fall of the monarchy in 1910. These events showed that such alliances were not only regrouping urban strata but for the first time also extended beyond them into rural areas, thus blurring spatial and social boundaries while heightening the perception of immediate threat on the part of military and administrative authorities. Subsequent colonial policies based upon the legal distinction between *civilizados* ('civilized persons' with Portuguese nationality) and *indígenas* (natives) were clearly meant to avoid a repetition of such a situation. Therefore, the political and economic changes that took place as a result of armed conflict and the establishment of an administration caused new tropes to emerge, which did not necessarily follow well-trodden 'ethnic' patterns dating back to first contact in the fifteenth century. Rather, they shifted attention to

35 See *Estatutos da Liga Guineense* (Lisbon: Typ. da Parceria António Maria Pereira, 1911). The League was eventually outlawed in 1915 for having allegedly conspired against the authorities and for having incited chiefs to rebel against the administration. Also see Mendy, Peter Karibe, *Colonialismo Português em África: a tradição de resistência na Guiné Bissau (1879–1959)* (Bissau: Instituto Nacional de Estudos e Pesquisa (INEP), 1994), pp. 328–343; and Havik, Philip J., 'Mundasson i Kambansa: espaço social e movimentos politicos na Guiné Bissau', *Revista Internacional de Estudos Africanos* 18–22, 1995–1999, pp. 115–167, 120–123.

36 Loff de Vasconcellos, Luís, *A Defeza das Victimas da Guerra de Bissau: o extermínio da Guiné* (Lisbon: Imprensa Libânio da Silva, 1916), p. 86.

37 See Pélissier, *Naissance*, pp. 295–300; Mendy, *Colonialismo*, pp. 329–335; Havik, 'Mundasson', pp. 120–125; Havik, *Silences*, pp. 340–343.

38 See for example, Loff de Vasconcellos, *Defeza*, and *idem*, *Presos*.

'modern' categories which were directly associated with the imposition of colonial rule.

Modernizing Governance: From 'Ethnic' to 'Administrative' Paradigms

The modern use of 'ethnic' terminology, for example in population censuses and ethnographic surveys from the early twentieth century, shows to what extent it permeated the colonial science and its 'external' definition of social identities.[39] While the first demographic and tax censuses in the 1920s employed the 'ethnic' classifications mentioned above, they became increasingly detailed as a result of ethnographic surveys which 'discovered' ever more subdivisions and smaller entities. Whereas in the mid-1800s the number of groups mentioned for 'Portuguese Guinea' was about twelve, by 1915 there were twenty and by the 1950s the 'official' count was thirty-two. As the process of classification was transformed into a statistical exercise, anthropometric and demographic measurements came to be standardized so that categories multiplied.

In the case of the Guinea-Bissau region it can be argued that 'ethnic' paradigms are the result of an ongoing interaction between 'internally' and 'externally' generated tropes. Although they were and still are subject to redefinition, their longevity, grounded in pre-colonial ethnogenesis, is surprising. Not only colonial authorities but also nationalist movements abundantly used 'ethnic' identities to classify populations and further certain political ends, thus demonstrating the existence of an apparent consensus on the matter. However, these tropes were not the only way in which African societies were categorized, given that the colonial period would introduce certain modern paradigms that were to shift the emphasis to eminently geo-political concerns. The military and administrative occupation of African soil produced a plethora of data

39 See Carreira, António, 'Organização Social e Económica dos Povos da Guiné Portuguesa', *Boletim Cultural da Guiné Portuguesa* (BOGP) 16(64), 1961, pp. 641–735, for a comprehensive overview of 'ethnic' classifications and groups.

whose extraction and processing followed an administrative logic which in turn bred a new terminology regarding 'native' societies, discarding 'tribalist' identities. But at the same time, it fragmented the information collected by superimposing administrative borders upon existing territorial divisions, which had evolved over the centuries by mutual accord between the founding lineages of communities. The introduction of the '*residências*', i.e. administrative districts, in 1908 led local populations to protest against them for wanting to pertain to the same administrative divisions, which in their eyes failed to respect the 'ethnic character of the peoples in question'.[40] Responses to questionnaires on these districts and their inhabitants also included interesting information on traditional chiefs, the rules of succession, their power and authority, the existence of any local opposition, and their relations with administrative officials.[41] In some areas, they noted that 'natives were becoming increasingly convinced that the *régulos* only want(ed) to extort them', which led inhabitants to seek the mediation of administrators.[42]

The reforms of Guinea's administration of 1912, created seven districts many of which were initially named after the majority resident 'ethnic' group, the names gradually being replaced by the district capitals.[43] Until 1918 when the administration was formally handed over to civil authorities, military posts in the interior also carried 'ethnic' labels. The primary responsibility of conducting 'native policy' and the 'pacification' in the area under their jurisdiction pertained to district administrators. In order to do so, they were instructed to acquaint themselves with the relations between the different *régulos* and village chiefs, and frequently travel and reconnoitre their district. Indigenous authorities were to act as the mediators of administrative orders, liaising with

40 AHU, FGG, 177, Francelino Pimentel, Bolama, to Ministro da Marinha e do Ultramar, 29 Nov. 1909.

41 See 'Relatórios das Residências', *Boletim Oficial da Guiné Portuguesa* (BOGP), Supplement, 30 Sep. 1911.

42 See José António de Castro Fernandes, *Relatório da Residência de Buba*, Buba, 31 May 1911, BOGP, 30 Sep. 1911.

43 For example the 'Brame region' or the 'Balanta region', which were eventually dropped in the 1920s; in other cases, districts were named after existing chieftaincies, i.e. the 'Oio region'.

the population by means of local elders or *grandes*.[44] The law stipulated that the *régulos* were regarded as indigenous authorities, being subordinate to the district administrators, while the village heads were the delegates of their chiefs; succession was regulated in accordance with local custom.[45] Given that the *régulo* responded directly to the administrator, in effect the *regulados* were subsumed into the colonial administration, thus representing its lowest tier.[46] They were expected to assist district and local authorities in the recruitment of labour for public works and the collection of taxes, which were listed as their prime responsibilities, closely watched by the former. The administrators' brief was broad and extensive, to the extent that in the absence of regular supervision and inspection, they had a considerable margin with regard to the application of 'indigenous policy'. Those administrators who remained in place for a number of years, were able to build patron–client relations which relied upon the malleability of *régulos*. In some cases these relations became prebendial, which could include the support for certain candidates in return for favours as well as the sharing of the proceeds of illegal transactions. In other instances, traditional lineage chiefs would co-operate with the authorities as a trade-off for retaining their power and prestige in areas that were inaccessible to the latter.[47]

The implementation of appointed chieftainships was to have a profound impact upon relations between African societies and colonial authorities, as well as between the communities themselves. In one particular case the appointment of a mercenary to the position of (non-ethnic) chief in an area regarded as rebellious, would be the source of frequent conflict with local communities and pose innumerous problems for a weak ad-

44 Pereira, *Guinée*, p. 36.

45 *Regulamento das Circunscrições Civis*, 1912, art. 45, 46 & 47; in Pereira, *Guinée*, pp. 33–83.

46 Schoenmakers, Hans, 'Old Men and New State Structures in Guinea Bissau', *Journal of Legal Pluralism* 25/26, 1987, pp. 99–138, 109–110.

47 See the case of Queen Pampa of Orango (an island in the Bijagó archipelago) who levied taxes, built roads and produced palm kernels, without any direct intervention of the authorities; see Centre des Archives d'Outre-Mer (CAOM), FM 1AffPol/1291, Gustave de Coutouly, French vice-consul in Bissau, Portuguese Guinea, to French Foreign Ministry, 6 Oct. 1917.

ministration.[48] During the war, certain lineage chiefs were executed as in the case of Pepel *djagras* who had combated against colonial and auxiliary forces, ending their autonomy and replacing them by more pliant dignitaries.[49] In some cases, existing paramount chiefs were dethroned and 'kingdoms' dismembered, such as in the case of the Manjaks of the *Costa de Baixo* and their capital Bassarel, leaving a large number of fragmented *regulados* without a central leadership.[50] In the case of the Mancanhe *regulados* of Bula and Có, the settlement of Balanta farmers seeking new paddy rice-fields provoked 'ethnic' animosities which still linger to the present day. The armed conflict between Mancanhe and Pepel on the island of Bissau actually led to a redrawing of administrative frontiers and the de-annexation of the Pepel *chão* or territory of Biombo from the Cacheu district. The creation of *regulados* in segmentary societies such as the Balanta and the appointment of non-'ethnic' strangers to these posts, also caused considerable unrest and tense relations. In other cases, existing former 'kingdoms' such as Fuladú were broken up into smaller, easily controllable units, and dissected by new administrative borders whereby they fell under different district administrators.

Military incursions and the extension of colonial rule to the interior also 'opened up' certain *tchon*, thereby allowing neighbouring communities to penetrate areas previously inaccessible to outsiders. The forays of the Manjaks into Felupe/Jola territories in order to collect rubber, provoked quarrels with the local population on account of the perceived threat to the latter's control over natural resources and sites of ancestral worship. Seasonal migration of the Pepel from the island of Bissau to the Bijagós Islands to harvest palm kernels, also caused tensions between them and the islanders who complained to the administration. The penetration by the Mancanhe into the neighbouring Pepel *tchon* of the island of Bissau, where they cultivated plots and successfully marketed crops, would eventually erupt into violent clashes in the 1930s.

48 See Bowman, Joye L., 'Abdul Injai: ally and enemy of the Portuguese', *Journal of African History*, 27(3), 1986, pp. 463–479.

49 See Loff de Vasconcellos, *Defeza*, p. 36.

50 Carreira, 'Organização', pp. 49–50; Crowley, *Contacts*; Crowley, Eve L., 'Chefes de Posto and Chefes de Terra: the dynamics of domination and self-determination in the Cacheu region, Guinea Bissau' (Conference paper, Bissau, September 1991); Forrest, *Lineages*, pp. 148–156.

Those clashes have been characterized as a 'tribal' or inter-'ethnic' war ending in a 'massacre'.[51] Official reports emphasise that the 'numerous Mancanhe natives were victims only for pertaining to a tribe which for some time had been quarreling with the Pepel tribe'. However, the same reports indicate that the multi-'ethnic' Kriston, described as 'assimilated natives', played a prominent role in the outburst of violence, for having instigated the Pepel to take up arms. The fact that the accusations focused on the 'acts of treason' committed by the Kriston rather than the Pepel, and that the former received harsher sentences, confirmed this angle which evoked strong parallels with the events that had occurred between 1913 and 1915.[52] By condemning and deporting Pepel chiefs, elders and village heads while invoking the exclusive responsibility of the Department of Native Affairs for the resolution of conflicts, the administration clearly took a dim view of appointed chiefs and, by implication, of its own *política indígena* or native policy.[53]

The tradition among certain male Balanta age sets to steal cattle gave rise to numerous problems throughout the colonial period, not only affecting inter-'ethnic' relations but also within the communities themselves. Whereas they were initially thought to live 'in complete anarchy', only recognizing the authority of the 'head of family' and choosing their village heads from amongst the 'most valiant or most famous thief of their tribe'[54], the existence of 'ethnic' institutions in their midst

51 See João José Soares Zilhão, Bôr, 20 Oct. 1931, *BOGP* 39, 1931; and also Pélissier, Guiné, pp. 374–376. According to estimates, hundreds of Mancanhe resident on the island of Bissau died as a result of Pepel *razzias*. The state of siege was declared on 30 September 1931 and a military command post was set up in one of the Pepel *regulados* (Bor) of the island, but only three days after the fighting started; see João José Soares Zilhão, Bissau, 30 Sept. 1931, *BOGP* 36, 1931.

52 *ibid*: Zilhão, 30 Sept. 1931.

53 According to French sources, dissatisfaction among the Mancanhe population was widespread, on account of the lack of protection offered by colonial authorities during the three days of the uprising; see Archives du Ministère des Affaires Etrangères, Paris (MAE), KAfr, PP6, Hostains, French Consul in Bissau, to French Foreign Ministry, Paris, 15 Nov. 1931.

54 Cesar Ludgero Barbosa, *Relatório da Residência de Cacheu*, Cacheu, 11 Jan. 1911; *BOGP*, 30 Sep. 1911.

came to be recognized in ethnographic surveys in the 1920s.[55] The emergence during the wars of pacification of the native figure of the *sargento* (or sergeant) who aided the village heads and acted as liaison with colonial authorities points to shifts in patterns of mediation. Reports also indicated the existence of quarrels between rival factions in Balanta villages which in some cases boasted two heads.[56] Given that appointed stranger chiefs in these areas proved incapable of settling these disputes, traditional and administrative authorities were frequently called upon to intervene, often bypassing and marginalizing the former.

The gradual acculturation of Balanta farmers as a result of Mandinka influence (hence *mandinguisation*) had already resulted in the emergence of the Balanta-Mané (also called Balanta-Batcha) as a separate identity. Similar processes took place with regard to the Biafada of Quínara who after being exposed for centuries to Mandinka influence were gradually but superficially Islamised by the invading Fula from the late nineteenth century. The migration of Mancanhe and Manjaks into the region as a result of groundnut cultivation in the mid-1800s also resulted in their peaceful settlement along the banks of the Rio Grande inlet. The settlement of Balanta rice farmers in the Nalú *tchon* in the Catió area in the South during the 1920s was actually negotiated with the latter at village level, given the complementary nature of agricultural practice. The imposition of new borders, both inter-colonial (with the AOF) and administrative (within Portuguese Guinea), also challenged 'ethnic' solidarities. As ancestral territories were divided by political frontiers demarcated by a joint Franco-Portuguese mission, villages came to be separated from each other and integrated into different administrative systems and traditions, creating regional disparities. Given the imprecision of borders, disputes about their course as well as regarding land titles between divided communities were not uncommon.[57]

55 For example, the role of Balanta authorities in the settlement of disputes over rice fields, the kidnapping of women and the theft of cattle was recorded in an ethnographic survey in the 1920s; see Alberto Gomes Pimentel, *Resposta ao Questionário de Inquérito sobre as Raças da Guiné e seus caracteres étnicos*, BOGP 50, 10 Dec. 1927, pp. 14–15.

56 See Pimentel, *Resposta*, BOGP 50, 10 Dec. 1927, p. 15.

57 The first Franco-Portuguese convention which regulated the legality of these titles and the transit of harvests was only signed in 1931; see Archives Nationales Sénégalaises (ANS) 21G 36, *Convention [du 22 Déc. 1931, entre Mr. Chesse Henri, Chef*

The crossing of these frontiers which were largely unguarded gave rise to border incidents, some of which led police and the armed forces to intervene, sometimes producing fatal casualties. Besides seasonal migration, these demographic fluxes were also a function of actions undertaken by the administration on both sides: taxes, military recruitment drives, and forced labour.[58] The settlement of migrant farmers from neighbouring French Guinea in the East of the territory provoked infighting between rival lineages straddling the border, thereby necessitating the active involvement of 'traditional' authorities. The frequent kidnapping of women not only caused regular consultation between Portuguese and French authorities, but also created great animosities between co-'ethnic' communities. The intense cross-border smuggling often prompted authorities on both sides to intervene, but the forging of cross-cultural bonds regularly enabled traders and migrants to escape or remain undetected.

The question here is to what extent colonial intervention in African societies affected pre-existing 'ethnic' affinities and tropes that had been nurtured and reproduced for almost five centuries. The complex pattern of migration and cross-cultural relations that resulted from export crop cultivation, the Scramble for Africa and the imposition of colonial rule were to affect these notions. 'Ethnic' tropes also adapted to the new conjuncture as a result of the intense migratory fluxes and the growing interaction between the different communities which took place, becoming diluted as a result of trade, co-settlement and intermarriage. Population censuses and taxation also redefined 'external' notions of Africans, creating a parallel set of social parameters that challenged the 'ethnic' paradigm. In this respect, the question of chieftainships and their incorporation into the colonial hierarchy was a barometer for the way in which 'ethnic', territorial, administrative and personal criteria contributed to the progressive fragmentation of 'ethnic' concepts.

Administratif des Colonies et de la Casamance, et José Peixoto Ponces de Carvalho, Director of Serviços de Negócios Indígenas], 22 Dec. 1931.

58 Havik, Philip J., 'Estradas sem Fim: O Trabalho Forçado e a Política Indígena na Guiné, 1915–1945', in Centro de Estudos Africanos da Universidade do Porto (ed.), *Trabalho Forçado Africano: experiências coloniais comparadas* (Porto: Campo das Letras, 2006), pp. 229–247.

Chopping and Changing: 'Native' policy and Appointed chiefs

The *Reforma Administrativa Ultramarina* (1933) or *RAU* for short, by means of which the *Estado Novo* (1926–1974) reorganised colonial administration, included the codification of the appointment of native chiefs throughout the Portuguese 'empire'.[59] Its timing was metropolitan and formed part of a change of policy towards centralization and corporatist rule from the late 1920s, but in the Guinean case it came at a time when the administration was still recovering from a coup by dissenting republicans and from domestic, inter-ethnic troubles.[60] District administrators retained their wide-ranging powers, being responsible for the application of 'native policy' in all its regional aspects. They determined the territorial limits of the *regedorias* or *regulados,* which should fall within district borders, and appointed (or deposed) *régulos*. A novel distinction was made between *regedores indígenas,* i.e. regional chiefs, and *chefes de povoação* or village heads, both appointed by the district administrator upon proposals submitted by local dignitaries in accordance with local custom. Whilst it was strictly forbidden for the former to levy taxes, this task now expressly pertained to the village heads with regard to the area within their jurisdiction.[61] These changes effectively created a second stratum of appointed chiefs, dependent upon and remunerated by the administration whilst owing formal allegiance to the *régulos.*

District administrators were now viewed as 'men of action' rather than bureaucrats (*RAU*, art. 406), whose decisions in terms of the *política indígena* were subject to superior consent. Local officials were held to consult 'native authorities' and elders who proposed a representative

59 Lisbon, Ministério das Colónias, *Reforma Administrativa Ultramarina (RAU)*, Decreto Lei 23.229, 15 Nov. 1933 (Lisbon: Imprensa Nacional, 1934).

60 A short-lived coup by dissenting republicans, mostly from the military ranks, in 1931 shook the otherwise tranquil political scene, following the revolutionary events in the Azores and Madeira; see 'Ao Povo da Guiné', Junta Governativa, BOGP, 10, 17 April 1931, The violent outbursts between Pepel and Mancanhe groups on the island of Bissau in 1933 and the belated intervention by the authorities, also sent shockwaves through the colony and its administration.

61 *Reforma Administrativa Ultramarina (RAU)*, art. 108 (1), and art. 116.

member from their midst. Although administrators were subject to superior scrutiny when appointing *régulos*, in the case of village heads, however, their appointment was the exclusive responsibility of the European official. Whereas appointed chiefs and heads could be exempted from the payment of taxes and administrators were entitled to reward them monetarily for services rendered, the law was rather vague leaving it in effect to the official's discretion.

In 'Portuguese' Guinea, the question of the *regulados* illustrated the curious and ambivalent mixture of 'ethnic' and territorial divisions, sometimes revealing conflicting notions of *ius soli* and *ius sanguinis*. The example of the Gabú district in the East of the colony was often quoted as an example of how not to proceed. By instituting a system whereby appointments were based upon racial-ethnic instead of territorial criteria, the district became 'ungovernable'. The number of pretenders who invoked 'royal privileges' multiplied while intrigue and tensions mounted, 'contrary to indigenous interests and undermining native traditions which should be respected'.[62] The never-ending quarrels over succession in the district led the then-governor to order an enquiry in the mid-1930s which resulted in the formal designation of territories with fixed boundaries within which customary succession was to be maintained. The question was seen as crucial given the importance of the Gabú region as a source of export crops (groundnuts) and as an area with a well developed commercial infrastructure that linked up with neighbouring AOF territories. In other areas chiefs were deposed, leaving only village heads as legitimate native representatives, i.e. at the micro-level.[63]

The case of Balanta territories to which Fula or Mandinka, i.e. non-'ethnic' *régulos* were appointed, demonstrated the inconsistencies of the 'system'. Besides the fact that the (s)election of chiefs did not correspond to territorial authority or to 'ethnic' identities, it also ran counter to acephalous traditions in segmentary societies. Therefore, their appointment was treated as a purely administrative affair. Most of the

62 AHU, Inspecção Superior da Administração Ultramarina (ISAU), 1667, Luiz António Carvalho Viegas, Bolama, *Relatório da Colónia da Guiné*, 28 June 1937.

63 *Portaria* 45, 1936; in Viegas, Luíz António de Carvalho, *Guiné Portuguesa*, vol. II (Lisbon, Typ. Severas, Freitas, Mega & Companhia, 1939), pp. 149–150. The main 'ethnic' groups in the district in question were designated as 'Fula Forro', 'Fula Preto', and 'Mandinga'.

thirteen *regulados* of the Mansoa district, the Balanta's core *tchon*, were occupied by strangers who had been invested since pacification. As a result the Balanta would first encounter 'a native from Fula or Mandinga origin who did not speak their language and imitated the ways of the European, then a *chefe de posto* (usually a Capeverdean) and further up an administrator (generally a Portuguese)'. Thus the appointment of non-ethnic chiefs (Fula, Mandinga or Biafada) in Balanta-dominated areas came to be increasingly frowned upon, on account of the unrest it caused, and by fomenting cross-border (e)migration.[64] But attempts to appoint Balanta *régulos* also failed, because their own people did not obey them; so that some *régulos* were not replaced, leaving authority in the hands of village chiefs.[65] As a result, administrative authorities were obliged to effectively acknowledge customary indigenous authorities and deal directly with them.

An inspection report concluded that in Guinea the institution of appointed chiefs left much to be desired, and sometimes appeared not to exist at all.[66] In most cases they were 'badly dressed natives without any prestige whatsoever, insulted and slandered by the same administrative authorities that appointed them'; in fact, it was not unusual for the latter to be whipped in front of their own people.[67] Their monetary reward (which was only half of what policemen or guards earned) for having to extract taxes from their subjects was pitiful. Administrative authorities generally detested these 'servants of colonisation', did not educate or

64 AHU, ISAU, 64, Sacramento Monteiro, Administrator of Mansoa, to Central Department of Civil Administration Services (*Repartição Central dos Serviços de Administração Civil*), Bissau, 4 April 1942, in Nunes de Oliveira, *Relatório da Inspecção Geral aos Serviços Centrais da Colónia da Guiné,* 1st August 1942. The administrator questioned the policy of appointing *régulos* of Fula, Mandinga or Biafada extraction to areas inhabited by Balanta and proposed that the Balantas community itself elect its chief.

65 AHU, ISAU, 1725, A.F. Borja Santos, Bissau, *Relatório do Curador Geral, 1942*, 20 Oct. 1943.

66 AHU, ISAU, 1669, Henrique Jones de Silveira, *Relatório de Inspecção Administrativa, 1940*, 20 May 1941, p. 13.

67 For example, reports mention the case of one administrator who had the most influential of all Manjaco *régulos*, Joaquim Batican Ferreira, of the Costa de Baixo, beaten by a guard in front of all his own subjects; see AHU, ISAU, 2245, Mário Costa, *Relatório da Inspecção Administrativa, 1944–5*, without date.

support them, and even attempted to undermine their authority. Above all this was true for many *chefes de posto,* because in some cases chiefs were uncomfortable witnesses of malpractice. Chiefs with a 'good' reputation were those who were able to rapidly deliver greater tax returns, thereby ingratiating themselves with officials but not with their people. In fact, chiefs themselves were collecting taxes, which although manifestly illegal, was common in certain areas.[68] Those who in the eyes of administrators did not produce the expected tax revenue were treated roughly or deposed. But the opposite would also occur, i.e. that administrators would depose a *régulo* who complied with instructions and replace him by an intriguing rival.[69]

Then again, the case of Fula chiefs in the Forreá region in the south of Guinea showed how the 'ominous' policies conducted by certain administrators who persecuted natives and imprisoned chiefs had provoked a population exodus, significantly reduced tax income and completely discredited local dignitaries who proved unable to reverse the situation.[70] Often administrators, who had the exclusive power to appoint them, created new chieftainships, thereby multiplying their number; the tensions that ensued would then lead the governor to force chiefs to resign and replace them, largely without detailed knowledge of the actual situation. Rather than applying 'ethnic' criteria to the *regulados,* arbitrary intervention often failed to respect lineal succession, i.e. in the male line in Islamised communities (such as the Fula and Mandinka) and matrilineal amongst stratified, littoral groups (such as the Manjaks, Mancanhe, Pepel and Biafada). This in turn created considerable confusion and raised suspicions of the administration's motives on the part of the local population, which advocated the maintenance of their own institutions and the hereditary nature of succession, i.e. the transfer of the *reinansa* or governance. Some

68 AHU, ISAU, 1731, Vaz Monteiro, Bissau, *Guiné: processo referente à Conferência dos Adminstradores, 1944*, 2 Jan. 1945. The then-governor of the colony stated that *régulos* received a standard *abono de gratificação* for their services based upon the number of *palhotas* or huts under their jurisdiction, while questioning the method of counting these huts. The latter was based upon the fiscal census carried out annually by the tax clerks under the auspices of the *chefes de posto.*

69 AHU, ISAU, 64, Nunes de Oliveira, Lisbon, General Inspector, to Central Services of the Colony of Guinea-Bissau, 1st August 1942.

70 AHU, DGAPC, 997, Calvet de Magalhães, *Ponte de Corubal,* February 1927.

régulos even proposed to appoint their successor by means of a will, in order to ensure the peaceful transition to a person of their choice beyond the strict circle of siblings or collateral kin.[71] In some instances, however, deposed chiefs continued to be regarded as the legitimate heirs to the position, despite having incurred the anger of officials or of their peers for any irregular practices committed.[72]

Apart from chiefs who had collaborated with military pacification campaigns, and those who succeeded their relatives, others owed their appointment to having been the administrators' chauffeurs, guards or cooks. According to metropolitan inspectors, that was not the most appropriate way in which to approach the establishment of an (indigenous) aristocracy, which was supposed to act as intermediary between the 'tribes' and the authorities, and 'as a guide, model or leader of the indigenous masses'[73]. Some distinguished between the majority of 'tribes' that wished to keep *régulos* and a minority including the Felupe and Balanta that emphatically rejected them. At the same time, the authority of appointed chiefs was to be based upon local customs and traditions and not to be charged with administrative tasks or with the policing of their subjects.[74] Despite the fact that complaints were often well-founded and justified, authorities generally ignored them, thus creating serious impediments for effective and sustained 'indirect rule'. But at the same time, many *régulos* who were appointed often acted in an arbitrary and repressive fashion which caused the population to seek refuge elsewhere. Such cases led prestigious academics – who taught at the colonial school in the metropole – to conclude that in their opinion '*régulos*' did not produce any benefits for the administration'.[75] Even those who were in favour of maintaining the *régulo* system agreed that

71 See Government of the Colony of Portuguese Guinea, *Colónia da Guiné: Conferência dos Administradores 1941* (Bolama: Imprensa Nacional, 1942), pp. 64–65.

72 See the case of the Fula chief Monjur Embaló, who despite having been deposed a number of times by the colonial authorities would, according to locals, always be the greatest '*grande*' of the Gabú region; Caroço, Jorge Vellez, *Monjur: o Gabú e a sua História* (Bissau: Centro de Estudos da Guiné Portuguesa, 1948), pp. 267–268.

73 AHU, ISAU, 2245, Mário Costa to Minister of Colonies in Lisbon, 15 March 1945.

74 *ibid.*

75 AHU, ISAU, 1697, António de Almeida to Minister of Colonies, Lisbon, *Parecer*, 17 Dec. 1946.

Guinea's rural inhabitants – except the Balanta and Felupe –, while understanding the need for *traditional* chiefs, had difficulties to accept administrative appointments.[76] Nevertheless, inspectors disapproved of the common practice of appointing caretakers whose nomination was not subsequently confirmed.[77]

District administrators appeared to be divided on the question of the *regulados* and the utility of their office. Opinions ranged from those who defended the right of succession as established by traditional custom (which varied from region to region) and those who favoured their abolition. The former argued for a selection process based upon recommendations made by the local community, while arguing for imposing limits upon the margin for manoeuvre of *chefes de posto* in order to counter the appointment of the wrong candidates by inexperienced officials.[78] The latter preferred to abolish the *regulados* altogether given that there was no valid reason to maintain them in most of the administrative districts.[79] According to the latter current of thought, the evidence was overwhelming: all political agitation had ended in the areas where the chieftaincy system had been abolished. 'As soon as the *régulos* disappear, all politicking would be over.' Some complained that '*régulos* only contributed, by means of plunder and exactions, to worsen the lot of the natives, who were already suffering from other (unnamed) abuses'[80]; they also sought to bolster their personal prestige by any means at their disposal, in ways reminiscent of Mamdani's 'decentralized despots'.[81] In the case of areas where *régulos* were imposed, as in districts (such as Mansoa) with a Balanta majority, administrators failed to understand the reasons for such a policy. Given that the chiefs were not co-ethnic, the population distrusted them profoundly and treated them as officials;

76 AHU, ISAU, 2245, Mário Costa, *Relatório de Inspecção Admininistrativa*, 1944–45, Lisbon, 1945.

77 AHU, ISAU, 2245, Mário Costa, *Circunscrição de Farim*, in *Relatório de Inspecção Administrativa*, 1944–45.

78 Government of the Colony of Portuguese Guinea, *Conferência (1941)*, pp. 130–131, 184–186. Some administrators stated unequivocally that the 'intervention of whites and civilizados' had provoked 'political agitation', *ibid.*, p. 130.

79 *ibid.*, p. 362.

80 *ibid.*

81 *ibid.*, p. 301.

thus, in effect, there were no go-betweens to mediate quarrels.[82] As a result, the officials compared appointed chiefs to 'miniature *chefes de posto*' who ostensibly enjoyed the *régulo*'s privileges while being largely ignored by the local inhabitants.[83] Most administrators defended some form of phasing out the chiefs, for example by not replacing them once the incumbent died.[84] They were also particularly concerned about the formation of parties or factions that pledged their support to alternative candidates, inventing 'imaginary titles' in the process and once appointed being subjected to 'maquiavellian intrigue' by their rivals. Their principal motive was material gain (and personal vanity – i.e. *ronko*) and had little or nothing to do with traditional rights.[85] The maintenance of (appointed) village heads as exclusive intermediaries was considered to be the most viable option.

A report by an experienced district administrator shed some new light on a subject which in his opinion had been seriously neglected by his predecessors. By listing the various consecutive alterations of district borders, which were not based upon any intimate knowledge of the region, his account shows just how the instability of administrative divisions negatively impacted upon their development.[86] Despite the fact that the district encompassed the territories of five different 'ethnic' groups, reliable census data or ethnographic studies were still unavailable. Local conflicts over the *reinansas* and chiefly succession had actually spread during the last decades, 'infecting' neighbouring areas, also as a result of administrative incompetence. It had all started in the largest and richest of all *reinansas*, the so-called Costa de Baixo, where the election of a chief along customary lines had antagonized part of the population.

82 Government of the Colony of Portuguese Guinea, *Conferência (1941)*, p. 249. Administrators in Felupe areas commented that those proposed by villagers always lacked prestige and wealth, 'because according to the natives as they did not produce or own anything, they had nothing to lose'. *Ibid.*, p. 65.

83 *ibid.*

84 See for example, *ibid.*, pp. 300–301.

85 The question of dress was important, and depending on the specific *regulado* and the personal preferences of the administrator, uniforms were supplied to incumbents, who thereby acquired a military status.

86 AHU, António Carreira, *Relatório da Circunscrição Civil de Cacheu de 1945*, 23 March 1946.

The subsequent confirmation of this appointment by the colonial authorities, ignoring local tradition with regard to succession and the transmission of the *bens de reinança*, caused such a stir among the region's inhabitants that the chief in question was deposed (only to be reinstated six months later). The district had been in turmoil ever since, as native dignitaries and colonial officials instigated campaigns in favour of certain parties involved. The notable demographic exodus to neighbouring regions including the AOF was in the opinion of the official in charge, directly related to the flaring up of these quarrels. Upon these conflicts, the long-standing socio-economic inequalities characteristic of Manjak society, and chiefly privileges with regard to the usufruct of land and labour, had a strong bearing. The intervention of district officials in these disputes had drawn them and the administration as a whole into the maelstrom becoming targets of invective and convenient scapegoats, constantly harassed by intriguing *agents provocateurs*.[87] By actively conditioning the choice of village heads whose investiture amounted to a 'sale of jobs' to the highest bidder, promoted by paramount chiefs who rented plots to them, the administration had become a player in highly complex ethnic politics. The fact that the administration could not dispense with chiefs, given that it would not be accepted by the population, while being unable to redistribute the plots pertaining to the *reinansas,* meant that the assets of office had to be taken into account when selecting its titleholders.

The governor appointed immediately after World War II, who was later to become Minister of Colonies in the 1950s, was the first to publicly defend the abolition of the *regulado* system.[88] He proposed direct intervention in the question of chiefly appointments, succession and inheritances in order to gradually remove powers from indigenous authorities, recommending the progresssive dwindling away of *régulos*: 'the fewer chiefs, the weaker they were, the better'. He added significantly

87 The same administrator also listed a number of professional agitators, some of whom had been actively destabilizing the region since the end of the pacification campaigns. Some of them had been tried and deported, sometimes more than once, to other Portuguese colonies following incidents and disruptive action, while others were banned from holding office and forced to resettle.

88 Sarmento Rodrigues, M.M. *No Governo da Guiné: discursos e afirmações* (Lisbon: Agência Geral das Colónias, 1949), p. 116.

that 'for some reason they wanted to impose them on the Balanta who never had chiefs, which was going backwards, and without any justification'. Indeed, official reports demonstrate that by the 1950s most *regulados* had no effective occupants and only caretakers. And many posts were left vacant, sometimes for decades, so that relations with colonial authorities were essentially maintained through *chefes de povoação* or village chiefs. But highly critical reports on the (lack or inconsistency of) 'native' policies, showed that there was no consensus on the issue, be it in the metropole or in the colonies. Some officials proposed that the titles to *reinansas* should be thoroughly researched in case of quarrels over succession, in order to select chiefs and determine the legitimacy of their claims. Others preferred to simply ignore them. Although the ethnographic survey carried out in 1946 did produce a comprehensive body of knowledge on 'ethnic' traditions, which would be published, it was to have little practical impact.[89] In fact, it was rarely used to good effect by officials who far from being knowledgeable 'men of action' spent most of their time on deskwork rather than in the field. Thus, authorities maintained an ambivalent attitude: whilst continuing to employ 'ethnic' classifications and at least formally subscribe to the *régulo* system, in practice they preferred to bypass regional and 'ethnic' politics by relying upon intermediaries at micro, village, and compound level. As a result, far from redesigning outdated and ineffective policies, the regime abandoned the notion of a coherent 'native policy' built round 'ethnic' paramount chiefs, leaving local and district administrators to deal with situations on an ad-hoc basis.

Conclusion

The problems associated with the creation of chieftaincies or *regulados,* which were by no means unique to Guinea or Portuguese colonies in general, show that these entities never actually became institutions, and remained, to a great extent, foreign bodies in the local landscape. The idea of

89 Teixeira da Mota, A., *Inquérito Etnográfico* (Bissau: Governo da Colónia da Guiné, 1947).

incorporating *régulos*, *paramount chiefs*, *chefs supérieurs* or *Häuptlinge* into the colonial administration was common to most colonial dominions, induced by the need to reinforce their authority over rural African populations.[90] At the same time efforts were made to 'traditionalize' these chieftaincies, both by colonial and by indigenous authorities, keen to bolster their position. In some cases officials wrote what seemed like oral histories or even novels about prestigious chiefs, describing their military feats and political prowess whilst praising the services rendered to colonial overlords during military operations.[91] Their authors did not hesitate however to counter-balance this 'positive' image with information concerning less attractive aspects of their careers, including slave raids, extortion and arbitrary justice, thus delineating the limits of 'invention'.

After a period of redrawing boundaries and appointing chiefs for the loyalty shown during the wars of 'pacification', official reports began to gain a critical tone when discussing the issue from the 1930s. By highlighting the tendency of pretenders to state exaggerated claims invoking imaginary rights while fomenting intrigue, which in turn led to social unrest and economic disruption, those reports would indicate growing misgivings on the part of colonial decision makers. The latter increasingly recognized the shortcomings of policies that had eliminated paramount chiefs, thereby exposing the weaknesses of an intermediate stratum – village clusters or *grupos de povoações* – to which customary succession did not apply. The recognition that 'in many areas *régulos* were merely decorative figures who enjoy the prestige that we wish to give them and which they lack in a personal or traditional sense'[92] actually implied a change in attitude towards native issues. This shift was justified on the grounds that colonial in(ter)vention had considerably weakened the 'traditionalism' of chiefly functions, which was now generally applauded, for having reduced or eliminated powers that conflicted with colonial sovereignty.[93] Exceptions were only made when political authority was indissolubly linked to religious prestige whereupon the

90 Geschiere, 'Chiefs', p. 153.

91 Duarte, Fausto, *A Revolta!* (Porto: Livraria Latina Editora, 1942); Caroço, *Monjur*.

92 Duarte, *Revolta!*.

93 Viegas, Luíz António de Carvalho, *Guiné Portuguesa*, vol. III (Lisbon: Typ. Severas, Freitas, Mega & Companhia, 1940), p. 38.

performance of certain key ceremonial acts depended, for example in connection with the seasonal cycle.

Thus the vacant 'thrones', the appointment of caretakers and the incorporation of existing chiefs as wage earners, against which local dignitaries protested in the 1940s and 1950s, signified a sea-change in 'indigenous politics'. Having grown weary of the complexities associated with the latter, authorities resorted to direct rule by default, relying on the basic, community level. Although this tendency was most marked in the case of segmentary societies, the fragmentation of customary authority in some areas inhabited by stratified groups had also favoured political atomization. Eventually, by dealing with the heads of villages or directly with heads of residential compounds, which was regarded as a salutary development benefiting the local population[94], the administration by implication recognized the failure of attempts to invent or impose traditions by assuming the role of chief-makers and instituting warrant chiefs. If – as was officially stated – native policy essentially hinged upon the prestige attributed to chiefs and their transformation into 'Portuguese authorities', colonial history clearly demonstrated its failure. By making chiefs' permanence in office dependent upon their pursuance of 'national' interests, metropolitan policy-makers adhered to the rationale that it was easier to co-opt and convert a few chiefs to the cause than the population at large.[95] By the 1940s colonial governors had come to the conclusion that while the *regulado* system should continue for the time being in order to guarantee the implementation of administrative policies, it was in the long run only feasible in 'tribes' where similar positions had already existed, i.e. in centralized and stratified communities.[96]

The Guinean case shows that taxation played an important – but so far underestimated – role in the process of the weakening of chiefly authority as well as in the gradual shift in emphasis from 'ethnic' to village and compound-oriented concepts in a colonial context. Metropolitan considerations were not shared by district administrators and *chefes de*

94 Viegas, *Guiné*, vol. 2, p. 152.

95 Monteiro, Armindo, *As Grandes Directrizes da Governação Ultramarina no Período que Decorreu entre as Duas Guerras Mundiais* (Lisbon: Bertrand, 1942), p. 63.

96 Vaz Monteiro, 9 Dec. 1941, in Government of the Colony of Portuguese Guinea, *Conferência (1941)*, p. 65.

posto whose immediate concern was to control or eliminate cumbersome go-betweens. At the same time, reports also show that there was a latent – and sometimes open – rivalry between administrators and 'their' *chefes de posto*, whose competence to implement native affairs was called into question by the former. The erosion of the authority and functions of the *chefes de posto*, which resulted from the introduction of administrative reforms in the 1930s, was indeed the subject of complaints by students of the *Escola Superior Colonial*, where future colonial officials received their training.[97] The two most contentious issues in this respect were taxation and the *política indígena* or 'native affairs', and most notably relations with warrant chiefs. That these questions turned out to be potentially divisive in various ways was by no means surprising, given that administrative intervention was geared primarily to tax collection and labour recruitment to the exclusion of almost all other issues. This tendency had even been reinforced by the budgetary priorities of the corporatist *Estado Novo* regime from the 1930s. Officials found that they could augment income and labour inputs by a two-pronged approach, i.e. simply bypassing or eliminating cumbersome intermediaries on the one hand, and getting chiefs to act on the basis of 'direct persuasion or intimidation' on the other hand.[98] While increasing administrative malpractice and the incidence of disciplinary measures against officials, these policies also reinforced the tendency of communities to 'negotiate governance' with local officials, on an *ad-hoc* basis. However, the passive and active resistance of African communities accelerated the weakening of chiefly rule and the progressive fragmentation of political superstructures. In a move to capitalize on existing discontent, the leader of the nationalist opposition denounced 'destruction of African political life' and the use of chiefs as 'puppets', for example in cases of non coethnic appointees.[99] Most of the arbitrary divisions introduced during and after military occupation would in fact not stand the test of time and

97 Letter, Associação Académica da Escola Superior Colonial to Minister of Colonies, Lisbon , 27 Nov. 1944.

98 The minister of colonies in the 1930s favoured this approach; see Monteiro, *Directrizes*, p. 64.

99 Cabral, Amílcar, 'The Facts about Portugal's African Colonies (1960)', in Amílcar Cabral, *Unity and Struggle: speeches and writings* (London: Heinemann, 1980), pp. 17–27, 26.

proved to be invented or artificial *regulados*[100], despite belated efforts to 'reinvent' co-ethnic chieftaincies in the final stages of the colonial war.[101] Among the few exceptions were some Islamised chiefs whose reputation was founded upon religious rather than ethnic identity, and non-Islamised headmen whose authority was essentially anchored in socio-economic privileges pertaining to ruling lineages.

One of the key factors that triggered and deepened this trend towards community and 'ethnic' fragmentation was precisely the emphasis upon – or obsession with – tax collection and the mobilization of labour in Portugal's African colonies. This shift largely dictated the gradual abandonment of early colonial strategies based upon the instrumentalization of warrant chiefs, the *regedores*, *régulos* or *sobas*. However, the trend towards the replacement of the hut by the head tax in most colonies by the 1930s, whether Portuguese, French or British, was not followed in the Guinean case until the 1950s. By then many *regulados* had become practically inoperative or were simply bypassed and had lost their former 'intermediary' roles. Extracting local revenue directly ensured that villages, i.e. village heads, and compounds (heads of 'family' or 'household') constituted the main targets of intervention, to the detriment of 'ethnic' communities 'invented' by a colonial 'bureaucratic culture'. Besides a few notable exceptions, most of the chiefs that remained were regarded as mere ceremonial figures dressed in uniforms, ridiculed and cajoled by officials.[102]. The fact that after World War II official reports began to stress that appointed chiefs should receive 'their' percentage of the hut tax, rather than being treated as officials with a fixed wage, with a residence built and paid by the government'[103], underlines this paradigm shift from native chief to administrative clerk. Despite demands for just compensation, many local chiefs failed to receive any share of the tax

100 Dias, José Manuel de Braga, *Mudança Sócio-Cultural na Guiné Portuguesa (contribuição para o seu estudo)* (unpublished PhD dissertation, Lisbon, ISCSPU, Universidade Técnica de Lisboa, 1974), pp. 67–103.

101 Belchior, Manuel, *Os Congressos do Povo da Guiné: um novo caminho?* (Lisbon: Arcádia, 1973).

102 See Caroço, *Monjur*, p. 172, commented that 'chiefs were replaced with the same ease as one changes one's shirt'.

103 AHU, ISAU, Henrique Jones da Silveira, *Relatório da Inspecção Administrativa, 1950–51* (without number), 30 June 1951.

revenue at all when the total amount collected did not attain the minimum sum stipulated for the region in question. What reports failed to mention was that the problems surrounding chieftainships and succession were directly related to the fact that the material benefits accruing from colonial taxation had actually become part of the *bens de reinansa* in stratified societies, i.e. especially those characterized by patrilineal succession. Like the right to organize work parties, these prerogatives constituted – and were viewed by the incumbents – as an extension of existing customary privileges and therefore additional income, also for non co-ethnic chiefs. Other communities without chiefly traditions or where the (colonial) office never took root, generally remained hostile to such modernities.

At first glance the allocation of 'perks of office' gave the administration an additional 'prebendial' leverage with regard to appointments and remuneration.[104] However, widespread ignorance of traditions and kinship relations as it was typical among colonial officials, and the complexities of 'indigenous politics', seriously undermined the intended impact of those patron–client relationships, by fomenting dissension and conflict. Although for the first time providing ample data on African societies and their traditions, the ethnographic surveys carried out immediately after World War II – by the administrators themselves – had little impact upon administrative policies and practice.[105] The latter were thus far from 'ethnically' or 'tribally' oriented as some scholars have suggested, and varied considerably, even within a small colony like Portuguese Guinea. The widespread resistance of African societies to compliance with the payment of a 'tribute of submission' in the form of tax or labour, which generally gave rise to out-migration or straightforward emigration, only accelerated the process of the chiefs' loss of prestige and authority. However, it also weakened colonial authorities' capacity to control the native population. The high turnover of officials, and the increasing difficulty in filling vacancies at *chefe de posto* level, meant that from the 1950s onwards many posts remained unoccupied or temporar-

104 Berman, 'Ethnicity', p. 316.

105 See for example Talal Asad's claim that 'The role of anthropologists in maintaining structures of imperial domination has (...) usually been trivial', Asad, Talal, 'Afterword', in George W. Stocking, *Colonial Situations: essays in the contextualization of ethnographic knowledge* (Madison: University of Wisconsin Press, 1991), pp. 314–324, 315.

ily filled by 'apprentices', just like in the case of village chiefs and *régulos*. Despite signs that power relations in Africa were shifting, and that cross-border and urban migration was affecting social stratification and internal stability of the small enclave of 'Portuguese' Guinea, political reforms failed to materialize. Metropolitan policy-makers preferred to focus upon the 'jewels of empire', i.e. Angola and Mozambique. By the 1950s this process of political erosion had advanced to such an extent in Guinea that nationalist movements encountered a fertile ground for their campaigns and succeeded in rekindling alliances between rural and urban strata that the colonial regime had suppressed in the past, but this time failed to counter.

Bibliography

Almeida, António de, *Das Etnonimias da Guiné Portuguesa, do Arquipélago de Cabo Verde e das Ilhas de São Tomé e Príncipe* (Lisbon: ISCSPU, 1965/66).

Anderson, Benedict, *Imagined Communities: reflections on the origin and spread of nationalism* (New York: Verso, 1991).

Asad, Talal, 'Afterword', in George W. Stocking, *Colonial Situations: essays in the contextualization of ethnographic knowledge* (Madison: University of Wisconsin Press, 1991), pp. 314–324.

Belchior, Manuel, *Os Congressos do Povo da Guiné: um novo caminho?* (Lisbon: Arcádia, 1973).

Berman, Bruce, 'Ethnicity, Patronage and the African State: the politics of uncivil nationalism', *African Affairs* 97(388), 1998, pp. 305–341.

Bowman, Joye L., 'Abdul Injai: ally and enemy of the Portuguese', *Journal of African History,* 27(3), 1986, pp. 463–479.

Bowman, Joye L., *Ominous Transition: commerce and colonial expansion in the Senegambia and Guinea, 1857–1919* (Aldershot: Avebury, 1997).

Berman, Bruce; Dickson Eyoh, and Will Kymlicka, 'Introduction: Ethnicity & the Politics of Democratic Nation-Building in Africa', in Bruce Berman, Dickson Eyoh, and Will Kymlicka (eds.), *Ethnicity and Democracy in Africa* (Oxford: James Currey – Athens/OH: Ohio University Press, 2004), pp. 1–21.

Cabral, Amílcar, 'The Facts about Portugal's African Colonies (1960)', in Amílcar Cabral, *Unity and Struggle: speeches and writings* (London; Heinemann, 1980), pp. 17–27.

Carreira, António, 'Organização Social e Económica dos Povos da Guiné Portuguesa', *Boletim Cultural da Guiné Portuguesa* (BOGP) 16(64), 1961, pp. 641–735.

Carvalho, Clara, *Ritos de Poder e Recriação da Tradição: os régulos manjaco da Guiné Bissau* (unpublished PhD dissertation, ISCTE Lisbon, 1999).

Caroço, Jorge Vellez, *Monjur: o Gabú e a sua História* (Bissau: Centro de Estudos da Guiné Portuguesa, 1948).

Crowley, Eve L., *Contacts with the Spirits: religion, asylum and ethnic identity in the Cacheu region of Guinea Bissau* (unpublished PhD thesis, Yale University, 1990).

Crowley, Eve L., 'Chefes de Posto and Chefes de Terra: the dynamics of domination and self-determination in the Cacheu region, Guinea Bissau' (Conference paper, Bissau, September 1991).

Dias, José Manuel de Braga, *Mudança Sócio-Cultural na Guiné Portuguesa (contribuição para o seu estudo)* (unpublished PhD dissertation, Lisbon, ISCSPU, Universidade Técnica de Lisboa, 1974), pp. 67–103.

Duarte, Fausto, *A Revolta!* (Porto: Livraria Latina Editora, 1942).

Forrest, Joshua B., *Lineages of State Fragility: rural civil society in Guinea Bissau* (Athens/OH: Ohio University Press, 2003).

Gable, Eric, *Modern Manjaco: the ethos of power in West African society* (unpublished PhD dissertation, University of Virginia, 1990).

Gable, Eric, 'Manjaco Rulers after a Revolution', *Africa* 72(1), 2003, pp. 88–112.

Geschiere, Peter L., 'Chiefs and Colonial Rule in Cameroon: inventing chieftaincy, French and British style', *Africa* 63(2), 1993, pp. 151–175.

Ginio, Ruth, 'French Colonial Reading of Ethnographic Research: the case of the 'desertion' of the Abron King and its aftermath', *Cahiers d'Etudes Africaines* 42(166), 2002, pp. 337–357.

Gluckman, Max, 'The Village Headman in British Central Africa', *Africa* 19(2), 1949, pp. 89–106.

Government of the Colony of Portuguese Guinea, *Colónia da Guiné: Conferência dos Administradores 1941* (Bolama: Imprensa Nacional, 1942).

Green, Elliot D., 'What is an Ethnic Group? Political Economy, constructivism and the common language approach to ethnicity', Working Paper (London: London School of Economics, 2005).

Havik, Philip J., 'Mundasson i Kambansa: espaço social e movimentos políticos na Guiné Bissau', *Revista Internacional de Estudos Africanos* 18–22, 1995–1999, pp. 115–167.

Havik, Philip J., *Silences and Soundbytes: the gendered dynamics of trade and brokerage in the pre-colonial Guinea Bissau region* (Münster: LIT – New Brunswick: Transaction Publ., 2004).

Havik, Philip J., 'Estradas sem Fim: O Trabalho Forçado e a Política Indígena na Guiné, 1915–1945', in Centro de Estudos Africanos da Universidade do Porto (ed.), *Trabalho Forçado Africano: experiências coloniais comparadas* (Porto: Campo das Letras, 2006), pp. 229–247.

Lemarchand, René, 'Ethnicity as a Myth: a view from Central Africa', occasional paper (Copenhagen, CAS, 1999).

Loff de Vasconcellos, Luís, *A Defeza das Vitimas da Guerra de Bissau: o extermínio da Guiné* (Lisbon: Imprensa Libânio da Silva, 1916).

Loff de Vasconcellos, Luís, *Contestação dos Presos Políticos Implicados na Suposta Rebelião de Bissau* (Bolama: Imprensa Nacional, 1916).

Lonsdale, John, 'Moral Ethnicity and Political Tribalism', in Preben Kaarsholen and Jan Holten (eds.) *Inventions and Boundaries: Historical and Anthropological Approaches to the Study of Ethnicity and Nationalism* (Roskilde: University of Roskilde, 1994), pp. 131–150.

Mamdani, Mahmoud, *Citizen and Subject: contemporary Africa and the legacy of late colonialism* (Princeton: Princeton University Press, 1996).

Mendy, Peter Karibe, *Colonialismo Português em África: a tradição de resistência na Guiné Bissau (1879–1959)* (Bissau: Instituto Nacional de Estudos e Pesquisa (INEP), 1994).

Monteiro, Armindo, *As Grandes Directrizes da Governação Ultramarina no Período que Decorreu entre as Duas Guerras Mundiais* (Lisbon: Bertrand, 1942).

Newbury, Catherine, 'Colonialism, Ethnicity and Rural Political Protest: Rwanda and Zanzibar in Comparative Perspective', *Comparative Politics* 15(3), 1983, pp. 253–280.

Pélissier, René, *La Naissance de la Guiné: Portugais et Africains en Sénégambie (1841–1936)* (Orgeval: Pélissier, 1989).

Pereira, Carlos, *La Guinée Portugaise (subsides pour son étude)* (Lisbon: A Editora Lda, 1914).

Ranger, Terence, 'The invention of tradition in colonial Africa', in Eric Hobsbawm and Terence Ranger (eds.), *The Invention of Tradition* (Cambridge: Cambridge University Press, 1983), p. 211–262.

Ranger, Terence, 'The Invention of Tradition revisited: the case of colonial Africa', in Preben Kaarsholen and Jan Holten (eds.), *Inventions and Boundaries: Historical and Anthropological Approaches to the Study of Ethnicity and Nationalism* (Roskilde: University of Roskilde, 1994), pp. 5–50.

Roche, Christian, *Histoire de la Casamance: conquête et résistance: 1850–1920* (Paris: Karthala, 1985).

Sarmento Rodrigues, M.M. *No Governo da Guiné: discursos e afirmações* (Lisbon: Agência Geral das Colónias, 1949).

Schoenmakers, Hans, 'Old Men and New State Structures in Guinea Bissau', *Journal of Legal Pluralism* 25/26, 1987, pp. 99–138.

Spear, Thomas, 'Neo-Traditionalism and the Limits of Invention in British Colonial Africa', *Journal of African History* 44(1), 2003, pp. 3–27.

Teixeira da Mota, A., *Inquêrito Etnográfico* (Bissau: Governo da Colónia da Guiné, 1947).

Van Nieuwaal, A.B. van Rouveroy, 'Chieftaincy in Africa: three facets of a hybrid role', in A.B. van Rouveroy van Nieuwaal and R. van Dijk (eds.), *Rethinking Chieftaincy in Africa: African chieftaincy in a new socio-political landscape* (Münster: LIT, 1999), pp. 21–47.

Viegas, Luiz António de Carvalho, *Guiné Portuguesa*, 3 vols. (Lisbon: Typ. Severas, Freitas, Mega & Companhia, 1936, 1939 & 1940).

ALEXANDER KEESE*[1]

Who's King Tom? Being a 'Temne', 'Mandinka' or 'Susu' between Identity, Solidarity and Ethnic Shifts in Early Nineteenth-Century Sierra Leone

Sierra Leone knew many struggles between local groups in the second half of the eighteenth century and in the first half of the nineteenth century. Besides the Gold Coast and Portuguese Angola, the Sierra Leonean coast probably is the place from where we have most detailed reports on battles between different local populations. This fact comes from the particular circumstances of European, that is, mainly, British presence on Sierra Leone's coast. Contrary to other European settlements that had had their origins in participation in the slave trade, the British colony of Freetown fulfilled a completely different purpose.[2] The city, future capital of Sierra Leone, was a symbol for the abolition of slavery to come, for the liberation of the once enslaved peoples, and for their settlement on a coast that seemed appropriate for them from a racial and early colonialist point of view. British commitment to stop the slave trade drew the European administration of the colony into the complex wars and conflicts of local communities in the 'interior',

* CEAUP, University of Porto.

1 The author is grateful for generous funding of his project by the Holcim Foundation, Holderbank, Switzerland.

2 On the typical limited interest of European merchant-administrators in regional politics, and their concentration on the slave trade, as expressed in European sources from West Africa, see Strickrodt, Silke, 'A Neglected Source for the History of Little Popo: The Thomas Miles Papers ca. 1789–1796', *History in Africa* 28, 2001, pp. 293–330; and Lovejoy, Paul E. and David Richardson, '"This Horrid Hole": Royal Authority, Commerce and Credit at Bonny, 1690–1840', *Journal of African History* 45(3), 2004, pp. 363–392.

because the administrators wished to establish their presence and to convince local rulers to abstain from the 'wicked traffic'.

The British military commanders and governors particularly believed they faced the Temne (called 'Timmaneys' by British officials) as a group enemy. Most of the neighbours of the settlement of Freetown on the Sierra Leone Peninsula were Temne-speakers, and the British side had to engage in violent operations to protect the second settler colony from destruction, after a first project for a colony had indeed gone up in flames when attacked by the troops of a local Temne-speaking chief. Apart from that diplomatic and military activity, the British government of Sierra Leone was also engaged in occasional negotiations with rulers of the region farther to the north, in the Skarcies and beyond, as those rulers were suspected of being major furnishers of slaves. The populations to be found there did not speak Temne, they employed other languages such as Mandinka, Susu, or Bullom, but they were used to having contact with the 'Timmaney kings' of the south.

In the long-term perspective from first British settlement to decolonisation in 1961 and into the post-colonial state, the constellation changed. Today, the Temne are undisputed as one of the two leading ethno-cultural groups in Sierra Leone, besides the Mende that live in the more southern and southeastern regions of the country. Before the Civil War of the late 1980s and 1990s, ethno-cultural identity was one of the principles by which to explain political solidarity and animosity. Scholars have demonstrated that the voting behaviour in the late colonial state and under post-colonial conditions depended strongly on ethno-cultural affiliation. However, we have to ask ourselves what 'being a Temne' or being one of the members of the other groups mentioned above would mean two hundred years earlier.

To understand aspects of group identity in context, it is useful to look particularly at the region between the Skarcies Rivers and the Kisi River, which lies in the border area between present-day Sierra Leone and Guinea-Conakry. Here we find one of the centres of political gravity in the region: the 'kingdom' or 'federation' of Morea, which was in 1800 in constant contact with both the Temne and the British administration of Freetown. Researchers assume that Morea was a conglomerate of small towns and trade posts, those being dominated by immigrant Dyula families (both as traders, mercenary leaders and Muslim scholars), as had happened elsewhere in the coastal regions of Western Africa.[3] However, the question of how the latter's activity fits into the pattern of local identities is not answered. We profit from excellent interpretations about those families' commitment to Islam and about their engagement in active proselytisation. Less convincingly, David Skinner and Bruce Mouser concluded that those local identities are blurred and that ethnicity is not a central factor for identity in the area.[4] Most historians nevertheless use ethnic labels in their descriptions and do not explain what they mean by the solidarities inside of such groups. They come somehow to the astonishing conclusion that the succession conflict for the 'kingship' of Morea in the early nineteenth century (which we will discuss below, because it is linked to the extradition of King Tom) was resolved according to a 'new spirit of Djula/Mande nationalism'.[5] It must be said that such a terminology is dubious; it is necessary to elaborate more accurately on those questions, not by omitting the role of Dyula traders as an identity group, but by regarding as well the solidarities within the population groups amongst which those traders lived. Naturally, as our sources are written by Europeans, historians attempting to use them for an understanding of processes of ethnic group formation in Sierra Leone and West Africa have to be extremely careful. Nevertheless, given a necessary amount of prudence, those documents are an extremely rich source, which sheds light on the question of whether ethnicity was already a valid concept in what is today northern Sierra Leone at the beginning of the nineteenth century.

3 Brooks, George E., *Eurafricans in Western Africa: Commerce, Social Status, Gender, and Religious Observance from the Sixteenth to the Eighteenth Century* (Athens: Ohio University Press – London: James Currey, 2003), pp. 37–49.

4 Skinner, David E., 'Mande Settlement and the Development of Islamic Institutions in Sierra Leone', *International Journal of African Historical Studies* 11(1), 1978, pp. 32–62, 55; Mouser, Bruce L., 'Rebellion, Marronage and Jihād: Strategies of Resistance to Slavery on the Sierra Leone Coast, c. 1783–1796', *Journal of African History* 48(1), 2007, pp. 27–44, 32–33.

5 Mouser, Bruce L., 'The 1805 Forékariah Conference: A Case of Political Intrigue, Economic Advantage, Network Building', *History in Africa* 25, 1998, pp. 219–262, 231.

The Setting: King Tom's Attacks on Freetown and the British Diplomatic Missions Towards Morea

Already for a decade, the black settlers of Freetown and the British governor of the colony had feared an attack by the indigenous groups neighbouring the settlement. On 18 November 1801, this attack finally happened. A large group of armed inhabitants of the area surrounding the colony attempted to overrun the city and the fort. Under the heavy musket fire of the attackers, the British side lost a considerable number of subjects and soldiers. Even Governor William Dawes was wounded in what the British would call a 'treacherous and unprovoked aggression'. However, the attackers failed in their attempt to take the fortress of Freetown. They suffered high losses; they subsequently halted the offensive and were unsuccessful with an attempt at siege. Profiting from reinforcements of armed settlers and from the arrival of a group of friendly Mandinka-speaking warriors led by a headman of Rokon and famous slave trader, Gumbo Smart (which was ironic enough, as the government of Sierra Leone regarded themselves the champions of the end of the slave trade in the region), the British troops finally drove the assailants away.[6]

British reports are now quite congruent in the interpretation of this 'treacherous attack'. They identified the local ruler of a region called Koya as the responsible person behind the attacks. Koya was a region and group of Temne-speaking and Loko-speaking villages that was directly adjacent to the Sierra Leone Peninsula, the settlement area of Freetown. The indigenous name or title of the ruler in question was probably Pa Kokelly, but he was called 'King Tom' by other indigenous leaders and by the British settlers and subjects. It seems that meanwhile he had himself adopted this name.[7]

6 The National Archives (TNA), Public Record Office, London (PRO), CO/270/8, *Sierra Leone House* (without number), 12 Feb. 1802, pp. 1–4.

7 Fyfe, Christopher, *A History of Sierra Leone* (London: Oxford University Press, 1962), p. 74.

For a long time, it had already become obvious that the problems with this unruly neighbour would end in violent dispute. In March 1800, King Tom had stopped labour migration from his territory to Freetown, and in spite of the many concessions the chief had obtained concerning rights on the tariffs in Saint George's Bay near the settlement, conceded by British Governor Thomas Ludlam, the tensions remained a permanent problem.[8] Senhor Domingo and Pa Dick, two chiefs of adjacent villages, both allied to King Tom, disputed the colony's proprietorship of various agricultural zones.[9] Also, King Tom and other local rulers were rather discontent with what they considered to be exaggerated prices for European merchandise available in Freetown. Lack of credits was another issue of conflict. The tensions got worse because some leading Black settlers from Freetown – former so-called *hundredors* of the colony – who had originally been important promoters of the settlement project, had left the colony altogether and found exile with King Tom.[10] This furthered hostilities. On 9 October 1801, after sunset, groups of armed indigenous warriors from King Tom's community had marched through Freetown to threaten the settlers.[11] Everyone involved in the politics of the area remembered that the late King Jimmy who had burned the first British model colony some years before, had gone away with that unpunished.[12]

But if King Tom had counted on British passivity, he would have erred. Sierra Leone was now more than just an idealistic settlement project supported by philanthropists among London's city gentlemen. The Sierra Leone Company, administering the city of Freetown, enjoyed the unconditional support of the British government, which transformed the

8 TNA, PRO, CO/270/5, Ludlam, British Acting Governor of Sierra Leone, *Council Notes* (without number), 8 March 1800.

9 TNA, PRO, CO/270/6, *Sierra Leone Council Notes*, 31 Jan. 1801, pp. 59–61.

10 TNA, PRO, CO/270/5, Wansey; Word; Haywood; Wilbee; Stober; Elliott, and White, representatives of Black settler community in Freetown, *The following list of Grievances were presented by the Hundredors & Tythingmen to the Governor & Council* (without number), 13 Feb. 1800.

11 TNA, PRO, CO/270/6, *Sierra Leone Council Notes*, 9 Oct. 1801.

12 Braidwood, Stephen J., *Black Poor and White Philanthropists* (Liverpool: Liverpool University Press, 1994), pp. 206–207; Fyfe, *History*, pp. 24–25.

possibility of military action into a real option.[13] Military support made it possible for the settlers to defend the town during the first half of 1802.[14]

The British commitment to the cause of the colony became clear when King Tom attempted to attack Freetown for a second time. He obviously had good hopes of being more successful than before, being supported this time by allied warriors from the Kisi River region north of the peninsula. Nevertheless, the second attack failed in complete disaster. The British troops were able to strike back harder and to undertake a pillaging campaign in the area of Koya, King Tom's country. Surprised by this sudden turn of the tide, King Tom obviously feared for his life. He left his community and fled with some supporters to the Kisi River region, where he was received by his ally Fatima Fodi in the city of Malaghia.[15]

From now on, British engagement in relation to the future of King Tom was strong, as the British were obsessed with completely neutralising this persistent enemy. The documentation of their efforts in this direction gives us some outstanding material from which we gain a clearer idea of the structures of local group organisation. The British efforts concern in particular the three missions of Reverend Bright and of Alexander Smith to the region of the Kisi River. Their detailed reports have already been partly utilised to analyse British early colonial policy in Sierra Leone, to describe local Islamisation and to understand trade dynasties and networks. This being said, they have never been analysed thoroughly and critically to gain information about processes of ethnogenesis and identity building.[16]

13 Braidwood, *Poor*, p. 249.

14 TNA, PRO, CO/270/8, Wilson, Carr, and Macmillan to Governor and Council of Sierra Leone (without number), 2 Jan. 1802, pp. 2–3.

15 Fyfe, *History*, p. 90.

16 Those appear in *ibid.*

The 'Temne' King Tom: Alliances, Diplomacy, and Adaptation of a Temne Ruler

Who was then King Tom, the persistent enemy of the British settlement project? Where did he seek his allies? Did ethno-cultural group identity play a role in finding alliances? The British observers of the political struggle after 1800 were consistent in their analysis of what they regarded as clear facts. According to those reports, their enemy was the 'king of the Timmaney nation', the highest-ranking authority of a homogenous realm, or pre-colonial state. The offensive action of armed warriors against the British settlement would thus have been due to the hostility of a homogeneous population group. Other 'nations', homogeneous 'tribes' as well, would have chosen the side of the British colony:

> This treacherous and unprovoked aggression is exclusively attributed to the Timmanys, and it appears to have strongly the indignation of many of the neighbouring African Chiefs, several of whom had repaired with a considerable number of Men to the assistance of the Settlement and had joined in the excursions which were undertaken against the enemy.[17]

The British administration of Sierra Leone retaliated exactly according to those stereotype categories. 'King Firama', which was the English variant of Bai Farimer, another 'Timmaney' ruler, would be subject to collective punishment. He was assaulted by British troops, his main settlement went up in flames, and the Governor in Freetown demanded a part of Bai Farimer's land as a compensation for the damage caused to the colony by 'his tribe'.[18]

At the same time, the British Governor Dawes prepared a diplomatic mission. This mission was sent out to approach the 'king' of the 'Mandingo nation', Setáfa Setantomani, in order to petition for the extradition of King Tom and of the rebellious settlers in his entourage. It was natural from the point of view of the British administrative officers,

17 TNA, PRO, CO/270/8, *Sierra Leone House* (without number), 12 Feb. 1802, p. 5.

18 TNA, PRO, CO/270/8, *Questions proposed by Commodore Hallowell, with the Governor & Councils answers* (without number), 12 Jan. 1803, pp. 20–21.

that the 'Mandingoes' as a group were, like the Temne, more or less homogenous. From the British point of view, this meant that one would deal with their 'king' to lay hands on the 'foreigners'.[19]

From our knowledge of how politics in Sierra Leone would develop in the nineteenth and, in particular, in the twentieth century, it might seem plausible at first glance that different ethnic groups were already the main political actors in the violent encounters during the first twenty years of the settlement on the Sierra Leone Peninsula. In a memorandum of the Freetown Aborigines Department from 1887, composed by Government Interpreter Thomas George Lawson and by his successor, James Christopher Parkes, both 'Creoles', the authors imagined the space of Sierra Leone as territories of different 'tribes'. On this imaginary map, the British located specific territories as the propriety of the 'Temne', the 'Mende', the 'Sherbro', the 'Bullom', the 'Susu', and, eventually, the 'Mandingoes'.[20]

Undoubtedly, ethnic arguments were to play a leading and even crucial role in Sierra Leonean politics of the twentieth century, from the moment when it came to the implementation of parliamentary structures in Sierra Leone. In late colonial and post-colonial Sierra Leone, tendencies to ethno-cultural homogeneity of political leadership circles would even sharpen.[21] Whole governments would be dominated by ethnic groups – this being the fact for the cabinets of Milton and Albert Margai, predominantly 'Mende', as well as the successor cabinet of Siaka Stevens, led by 'Temne'.[22] Ethnic confrontation would only be overshadowed by warlordism and civil war from the 1980s, and in this period of generalised disorder it would lose much of its importance as a binding principle.[23]

19 TNA, PRO, CO/270/8, Reverend J. Bright, *Journal of Mr. Bright's Expedition to the Mandingo Country performed in Septr and Octr 1802* (in the following as *Bright Journal*), pp. 33, 35.

20 TNA, PRO, CO/267/172, Madden, *Report of Commissioner of Inquiry on the Western Coast of Africa. Second Part. Sierra Leone* (without number), 31 July 1841, p. 7.

21 Harvey, M.E., 'Social Change and Ethnic Relocation in Developing Africa: The Sierra Leone Example', *Geografiska Annaler* 53B, 1971, pp. 94–106.

22 Kandeh, Jimmy D., 'Politicization of Ethnic Identities in Sierra Leone', *African Studies Review* 35(1), 1992, pp. 81–99.

23 See, on the group experiences in the period of the civil war, the analyses of Richards, Paul, *Fighting for the Rain Forest: War, Youth and Resources in Sierra Leone*

What do we encounter of similar logics in the early phase of British presence in Sierra Leone? Around 1800, it was of course already possible to distinguish Temne-speakers from groups using one of the Mande languages, such as the Susu or Mandinka. This is evident from both European reports and Temne oral tradition.[24] Nevertheless, we also have to take into consideration the existence of a number of 'inter-ethnic' marriages and of individuals of mixed descent, as Wylie pointed out for the first half of the nineteenth century.[25] Moreover, within several political units present in the region around 1800, we can observe that clans of different language were involved in joint political leadership. Thus, in the territory of Port-Loko, the Susu-speaking family of the Sanko ruled over Temne-speaking 'sub-chiefs'.[26] Finally, scholars working on pre-colonial Sierra Leone admit that the perpetual local wars took place inside one 'ethnic group' as well as between 'ethnic entities'.[27] This fact balances well the idea of conflict in Africa as a permanent conflict between 'tribes'. However, most scholars continue to focus on ethnic differentiation rather than on the flexibility of identities, and without looking at particular moments of mobilisation and at strategies of shifts of allegiance. Even when

(Oxford: International African Institute in association with James Currey – Portsmouth/NH: Heinemann, 1996); Hirsch, John L., *Sierra Leone: Diamonds and the Struggle for Democracy* (Boulder – London: Lynne Rienner, 2001); Kandeh, Jimmy D., 'In Search of Legitimacy: The 1996 Elections', in Ibrahim Abdullah (ed.), *Between Democracy and Terror: The Sierra Leone Civil War* (Dakar: CODESRIA, 2004), pp. 123–143; Keen, David, *Conflict and Collusion in Sierra Leone* (Oxford: James Currey, 2005).

24 Winterbottom, Thomas M., *An account of the native Africans in the neighbourhood of Sierra Leone to which is added an account of the present state of medicine among them* (London: 2nd edn Frank Cass, 1969 [1803]), pp. 10–11, 75–76; Laing, Alexander Gordon, *Travels in the Timannee, Kooranko, and Soolima Countries, in Western Africa* (London: John Murray, 1825), pp. 32, 36, 66.

25 Wylie, Kenneth C., 1977, *The Political Kingdoms of the Temne: Temne Government in Sierra Leone 1825–1910* (New York: Africana Publications), pp. 21–22.

26 Wylie, *Kingdoms*, pp. 38–39.

27 Abraham, Arthur, *An Introduction to the Pre-Colonial History of the Mende of Sierra Leone* (Lewiston – Queenston – Lampeter: Edwin Mellen Press, 2003), p. 51; Wylie, *Kingdoms*, p. 63.

they discuss existing cultural exchange between the groups involved, they treat them as clearly distinguishable ethno-cultural entities.[28]

If a political structure following the simple logic of ethnicity had existed in the region of the Kisi River, the task of the British envoys sent thereto to demand the extradition of King Tom would have been easier. But the reality was different. On 28 September 1802, the Reverend Bright, member of the governing council of Sierra Leone, started a journey to Forékaria, the main city of the 'country' of Morea. This urban centre (today in Guinea-Conakry) was then considered the heart of the 'Mandingo region' of the Upper Guinea Coast. Bright's idea was nothing less than meeting a 'King of the Mandingoes' who could, through his authority, force his subjects to give the 'foreigner' King Tom into the hands of the representative of the British crown.[29] At first attempt, this mission was more difficult to carry out than expected, because Setáfa Setantomani had died in the meantime. Nevertheless, Bright remained optimistic and confident that the election of a new king would soon bring a solution to this problem. Those hopes would rapidly be frustrated. The Almamy of Forékaria, Setan Sulimani, formally the 'governor' of the city on behalf of the vacant throne of Morea, claimed to be in support of Bright's mission and anxious to see a successor crowned in the shortest possible interval. The different headmen of the city seemed friendly to Bright's wishes. Yet nothing further happened.[30] The British diplomat initiated another public relations campaign in two urban centres of the region, Wonkafong and Bareira, to proceed with the extradition of King Tom. Again, the effort showed little success.

Instead of seeing the case resolved by the strong hand of an ethnic 'Mandingo' paramount chief, as Bright had hoped, the British envoy had to invest considerable sums of money to win over an intermediary for

28 Mouser, 'Conference', p. 232. Compare for assumptions about similar processes among the Mende in Sierra Leone, Abraham, 'Introduction', pp. 37–38. Odile Goerg, while pointing to the manipulation of ethnic association in Freetown, speaks of the 'classic' ethnic groups, see Goerg, Odile, 'Chefs de quartier et 'Tribal Headmen'. Deux visions des colonisés en ville', in Jean-Pierre Chrétien and Gérard Prunier (eds.), *Les ethnies ont une histoire* (Paris: 2nd edn Karthala, 2003), pp. 267–282.

29 TNA, PRO, CO/270/8, *Bright Journal*, p. 5.

30 *ibid.*, pp. 13, 37, 39–40.

his cause. This intermediary was 'Miss' Betsy Heard, a female Anglo-African merchant and town headwoman from Bareira.[31] She would bribe the headmen of Malaghia with part of the sums furnished by Bright. Thus, in December 1802 a subsequent British diplomatic mission under Alexander Smith finally took into custody the rebellious settlers from Freetown, Wansey and Carey.[32] Still the Malaghians continued to refuse to hand over King Tom. Some days later, Bright himself tried his luck again, this time directly in Malaghia. However, Fatima Fodi, the nephew of the deceased Setantomani, and the other headmen of the town responded that King Tom was 'a free man' and that they had no right whatsoever to hand him over to the British crown. Frustrated in his effort, Bright could do nothing more than return with empty hands.[33] In spring 1803, King Tom finally left Malaghia to join Mori Kanu, another local ruler at the coast. Mori Kanu resided on the so-called Bullom Shore and was extremely feared by the British officials in Freetown, because of his canoe fleet.[34] King Tom would remain in the territory of Mori Kanu until the latter ran into war problems in the subsequent years. In the end, in 1807, the chief of Koya would sign a peace treaty with the British administration of Freetown, which set a term to the long-lasting conflict and allowed King Tom to return from his exile.[35]

Who was King Tom in the eyes of his hosts? Speaking undoubtedly Temne with his direct subjects, he did not have any problems in communicating with the Mandinkas of Malaghia. The reports we have about the discussions of Smith and his interpreter Miss Heard, on one side, King Tom and his 'prime minister' Bana as a second, and the Mandinka headmen of Malaghia as a third party, show that there was plenty of common

31 TNA, PRO, CO/270/8, *Bright Journal*, pp. 44–46.

32 TNA, PRO, CO/270/8, Alexander Smith, *Journal of a Voyage from Sierra Leone to the River Kisi, Dec. – in the Schooner King Kanta of Sierra Leone by Mr. Alex.r Smith – pursuant to an order from Gov. Dawes* (in the following as *Smith Journal*) (without number), p. 4.

33 TNA, PRO, CO/270/8, *Sierra Leone Council Notes* (without number), 17 Dec. 1802, 3/193.

34 TNA, PRO, CO/879/25/332, Hay, Administrator-in-Chief of Sierra Leone, to Stanhope (n° 425), 6 Nov. 1886, p. 18.

35 Fyfe, *History*, p. 92.

ground in using Mandinka as a *lingua franca*.[36] In that context, towards the headmen of Malaghia, King Tom insisted that he was a former client of Setantomani, and, consequently, a vassal of Setantomani's sons after the death of the old ruler. Thus, Setantomani's sons would be obliged to defend him against the schemes of his enemies.[37]

In light of the discussions about the fate of King Tom, being held in Forékaria, Bareira, Wonkafong or Malaghia, the issue of a Temne identity of the refugee was not even mentioned. An ethno-cultural perspective did not play any role, and King Tom was not considered a stranger.[38] Religion also did not matter, although religious hostility would have been possible between the 'animist' King Tom and the family of Setan Sulimani, the ruler of Forékaria, who was a convert to Islam.[39] Religious strife and bloody wars out of religious motivation were not atypical for the Kisi River Region around 1800. The Jihad of a Mahdi in the 1780s that had cost several 'infidel' rulers their lives is a vivid example of the force religion could exert in the region of Upper Guinea, if this card was played by a charismatic leader.[40] However, such was not the case with King Tom. In spite of religious tensions, the latter was never characterised as a Pagan Temne.

'Mandingos', 'Susus', 'Bulloms', and the Flexibilities of Group Affiliation in the Kisi River Region

Who were the hosts of the refugee King Tom in terms of group affiliation?

Reverend Bright attempted to understand the complex diplomatic pattern in the region of Forékaria relating to group identity, but he

36 TNA, PRO, CO/270/8, *Smith Journal*, pp. 3–4.

37 TNA, PRO, CO/270/8, *Sierra Leone Council Notes* (without number), 8 Dec. 1802, 2/182.

38 TNA, PRO, CO/270/8, *Bright Journal*, pp. 5, 13, 16, 18, 24, 33–34, 59.

39 *ibid.*, p. 26.

40 Winterbottom, *Account*, pp. 246–250; TNA, PRO, CO/270/8, *Bright Journal*, p. 19.

quickly found his limits. He did not inquire into some questions that seemed to him too confusing. Such a problem was the question of which ethnic groups would be eligible for the throne of Morea – or what Bright saw as 'the Mandingo area' around Forékaria. To find a successor to Setáfa Setantomani, the headmen of the region were scheduled to participate in the election process.[41] Before Amara obtained the turban as a compromise candidate in 1805, the discussions were not conclusive, but they show the political reasoning of the headmen of the region.[42] Besides Setan Sulimani, many influential headmen of Morea also considered Finda Modu an option, being himself a headman and acting Almami of Wonkafong.[43] In this position, Finda Modu represented, at the same time, the 'capital of the Soosoo country'.[44] Considering that both population groups, Mandinkas and Susus, were speakers of a Mande language, it is extremely difficult to decide whether Finda Modu presented himself towards his local subjects as a 'Susu ruler' or as 'Mandinka'.[45] What is obvious is the fact that in diplomatic exchange with Forékaria and in the issue of Setáfa Setantomani's succession, he defined himself indeed as a Mandinka. He emphasised this aspect of his identity in his conversation with Reverend Bright:

> I had some private conversation today with Finda Moodoo in which he told me that king Tom would not be permitted to leave Malghia; and that we should soon hear some good news. We had nothing to fear from the Mandingoes. Speaking of the present state of the Country, he said, it could be settled only by himself and

41 TNA, PRO, CO/270/8, *Bright Journal*, p. 6.

42 TNA, PRO, CO/270/8, *Smith Journal*, pp. 10–11.

43 TNA, PRO, CO/270/8, *Bright Journal*, p. 23.

44 *ibid.*, pp. 65, 68.

45 Regarding the hypotheses around the immigration of 'Mandingos' and 'Susu' and the installation of individuals as successful 'strangers' among local 'landlords', see Mouser, Bruce L., 'Landlords-Strangers: A Process of Accommodation and Assimilation', *International Journal of African Historical Studies* 8(2), 1975, pp. 425–440, 427–428. On the complexities to distinguish 'Soosoo' and 'Mandingoes', see a the report from Church Missionary Society (CMS) missionary Hartwig, Church Missionary Society Archives, University Library of Birmingham (CMS) C A1/E1, 96b, Hartwig, *Answers to 21. Queries addressed to me by Gov.r Ludlam, with the approbation of Committee of Correspondence* (without number), 12 Jan. 1807, p. 11.

> three other persons. He meant to propose a headman for the country, who might afterwards, if he appeared to be capable and worthy, be elected king.[46]

Again, religious conflict complicated what could have been (but was not) an ethnic divide. Wonkafong was situated still, during the first decade of the nineteenth century, on the other side of the religious gulf. This particular constellation meant that Finda Modu as a candidate to the throne of Morea, a kingdom whose main centre lay in the now-Muslim community of Forékaria, would be the ruler of an 'animist' municipality. In the town of Wonkafong attempts at Islamic mission had still failed in the late eighteenth century. The Muslim scholars who had tried to get a foothold there were too strongly implicated in local slave trade to be fully accepted by the townsmen.[47] Religious strife explains as well why the Almami Inta Selli of Moribea, a city under the domination of Wonkafong but revolting against the rulers of the latter, found support in Setan Sulimani and the Mandinka headmen of Forékaria.[48] For the following war, this led to a constellation in which the troops of the Muslim Mandinka Almami of Forékaria were confronting the warriors of Finda Modu, who was Mandinka or Susu according to the situation, but who represented, as a Muslim, a non-Muslim community![49] Despite his leading role in the community, there were no traces of Islamisation in Wonkafong when the town was reached in May 1806 by a Church Missionary Society missionary who, despite all his shortcomings in describing accurately Susu societies, was very aware of a possible presence of Muslim scholars in the area.[50] The Susu of the area of Wonkafong, including their leader, promised shelter and support to the Christians.[51] Such an attitude was obviously not at all contradictory for a Dyula having become a landlord in a non-Muslim town.

46 TNA, PRO, CO/270/8, *Bright Journal*, p. 52.

47 *ibid.*, pp. 50–51.

48 The practice of employing war-chiefs independently of their ethnic affiliation makes the complex coalitions of the war between Wonkafong and Moribea less surprising, see Dorjahn, Vernon R., 'The Changing Political System of the Temne', *Africa (London)* 30(2), 1960, pp. 110–140, 121–122.

49 TNA, PRO, CO/270/8, *Bright Journal*, p. 41.

50 CMS C A1/E1 – 59, Hartwig to Pratt (without number), 10 May 1806, p. 1.

51 CMS C A1/E1 – 83b, Hartwig to Ludlam (without number), 13 May 1806.

However, on the side of the rebels from Moribea we also find Mori Kanu. He appears as a devout Muslim during his presence at palavers in Forékaria.[52] However, Mori Kanu counted otherwise as a Bullom leader and had thus to represent the coastal populations that were no friends of Islam at all. Ironically, as far as it concerns the shifting game around alliances, ethnic identity and religion, the Almamy Inta Selli broke his promise: after winning the war and securing the 'liberation' of the Moribeans' communitary from their tributary relation to Wonkafong, he suddenly changed his mind and refused a mass conversion of the locals to Islam.[53]

Mori Kanu, the chief who ruled the coast north of Freetown and who was feared by the British administrators, is another case of fluid ethnic identity. He had a force of Bullom warriors under his command and conversed using the language of this population group.[54] Various headmen of the Mandinkas assured Reverend Bright, during his first mission, that Mori Kanu exerted 'no influence over any people in the Mandingo Country'.[55] However, looking closer at the elements of the internal debates in Morea, it becomes obvious that such comments were formulated to satisfy the British conversation partners. The Bullom Chief certainly had a leading position in the quest for the nomination of a successor of the late Setáfa Setantomani. He was coming to Forékaria to participate in the election and the coronation, and he was expected to do so by the headmen of the whole region.[56] At the same time, Mori Kanu appears as a patron for the Temne-speakers of Koya and of the area adjacent to the Sierra Leone Peninsula. After King Tom had fled into the territory ruled by Mori Kanu in the beginning of 1803, the latter assembled for a conference 'King' Farimer, Pa London, Senhor Domingo, and 'other Timmaney Chiefs'.[57]

52 TNA, PRO, CO/270/8, *Smith Journal*, p. 30.

53 TNA, PRO, CO/270/8, *Bright Journal*, pp.42–43.

54 The Bullom were clearly defined, on linguistic terms, as a distinct group in the early nineteenth century, see on that Hair, P.E.H., 'Ethnolinguistic Continuity on the Guinea Coast', *Journal of African History* 8(2), 1967, pp. 247–268, 253–255.

55 TNA, PRO, CO/270/8, *Bright Journal*, p. 64.

56 *ibid.*, p. 53.

57 TNA, PRO CO/270/8, Dawes, Ludlam, and Bright, *Copy of a Letter from the Governor & Council of Sierra Leone to Commodore Hallowell* (without number), 12 June 1803, pp. 3–4.

We thus have a number of proofs that both ethnic and religious definitions were somewhat fluid in the region of present-day Sierra Leone. Even leading rulers, such as King Tom, Finda Modu or Mori Kanu utilised them in a flexible way, according to the situation they were facing. The threshold to change one's group identity in that way was obviously low. However, this does not mean that we do not find any conscience of the differences between local languages and cultural ties. Those could be formulated and used for processes of exclusion, in a circumscribed way, as the following examples will show.

When do 'Ethnic Groups' Clash in Pre-colonial West Africa? Two Examples

In spite of the principle of fluidity in group affiliation, processes of ongoing ethnic confrontation already existed in the pre-colonial period of Sierra Leone. However, they mostly appear under the shadow of massive military threats. This is in itself not surprising, as the wars between the rulers of the relatively small areas were frequently pursued until the complete destruction of one of the communities. The losing side had to face death or slavery.[58] These extremely dangerous situations made it necessary to use all means of mobilisation and morale boost. This again led sometimes to a stronger expression of an ethnic bond between the members of different communities, which was not imaginable under 'normal' circumstances.

Two examples from Wonkafong are to illustrate this context. In the 1780s, Morisalia, the ruler of Bareira, prepared a campaign against Wonkafong, after the inhabitants of the latter town had expelled the Muslim marabouts that were, theoretically, under Morisalia's protection. After Morisalia's troops had conquered and laid waste to Mungatta, a small town in the surroundings of Wonkapong, the conflict had changed, for the

58 TNA, PRO, CO/267/149, Campbell, Governor of Sierra Leone, to Glenelg, Secretary of State for War and the Colonies (without number), 19 May 1838, pp. 1–2.

inhabitants of Wonkafong, into an existential threat. Fearing the worst, they played the ethnic card to strengthen their fighting morale. They started to emphasise their Susu identity, in contrast to the alien invaders who were presented as the 'other', the 'Mandingos'. This strategy met with final success. The Mandinka from Bareira were defeated in several battles and finally stopped their campaign in the area.[59]

Other threats in the region were farther away in geographic terms, but they nevertheless led to a strategy of mobilisation with reference to ethnic distinctiveness. This concerned the Empire of Timbo in the Fuuta Jallon area, which the inhabitants of the Kisi River Region regarded as a constant danger.[60] Those worries did also concern the Mandinka of Forékaria, although the latter were occasionally allied with the Almami of Timbo to co-operate in military campaigns in order to convert the 'infidels' of their immediate neighbourhood.[61] However, the military power of the 'Fulas' was a consistent source of uneasiness. The rulers of the Kisi River Region were quite aware of the fact that Timbo had immense military means at its disposal that were not comparable to those of any of the other local potentates.[62] Unsurprisingly, the worries were greatest among the headmen of Wonkafong because of the religious divide. Several occasions show that the religious conflict with the Muslim empire of Timbo had already led the inhabitants of the city into protracted wars with the Almami. In the first decade of the nineteenth century, the community of Wonkafong feared nothing more than another, more persistent military campaign of 'the Fulas'.[63] Those fears erupted from time to time in the form of an emphasis on enmity that was formulated in ethnic terms. Bright could himself witness this sort of 'ethnic mobilisation' during his

59 TNA, PRO, CO/270/8, *Bright Journal*, pp. 23–24; Winterbottom, *Account*, pp. 154–155.

60 On the influence of the 'Fula force' on the reliability of the trade routes to the coast, see Mouser, Bruce L., 'Trade, Coasters, and Conflict in the Rio Pongo from 1790 to 1808', *Journal of African History* 14(3), 1973, p. 45–64, 57–58. Campaigns of troops from Timbo engaging to change trade conditions in their favour were frequent. Already in 1806, Fula troops were indeed present in the Rio Pongas, see CMS C A1/E1 – 39, Hartwig to Pratt (without number), 18 March 1806, p. 1.

61 TNA, PRO, CO/270/8, *Bright Journal*, p. 59.

62 *ibid.*, p. 27.

63 *ibid.*, p. 78.

mission, when Finda Modu invited him to see the performance of a *maray*, a specialised swordsman in the service of the headmen of Wonkafong:

> He [the maray] then made the feint of an attack, calling his followers to the spot with a growl and a bark, and parrying and thrusting with his sword. Observing a poor Foula among the numerous spectators, with threatening gestures he commanded him from the spot.[64]

Indeed, 'the Fulas' were regarded by the different rulers and inhabitants of Susu-speaking communities as a homogeneous group, and as a single danger. This is visible from the different versions we have about an abortive 'Fula invasion' in the territory of Kanosi.[65] Although the ruler of Timbo denied any involvement in the affair, the leaders of the different Susu-speaking villages eagerly prepared a vengeance attack that was directed collectively against 'the Fula'.[66]

These examples show that playing on ethnic difference *could* in fact be a feasible strategy for mobilisation. Consequently, political actors sometimes emphasised such differences to influence or motivate their followers. However, ethnic difference has to be seen as only one option in a pattern of various parallel modes of behaviour.

Conclusion

We thus find indeed in British documents *some* situations in which precolonial conflict in Sierra Leone and adjacent regions has a visible ethnic side. Clashes that were interpreted through ethno-cultural distinctiveness occurred particularly under circumstances of devastating war, in which leaders felt obviously motivated to call on ethnic, meaning linguistic and ethno-cultural solidarity. This technique could strengthen the internal

64 TNA, PRO, CO/270/8, *Bright Journal*, p. 57.

65 See CMS C A1/E3 – 23, Klein to Pratt (without number), 5 Nov. 1812, pp. 4–5; CMS C A1/E3 – 39, Renner to Pratt (without number), 24 Dec. 1812, pp. 1–4, 8, 12.

66 CMS C A1/E3 – 40, Wilhelm to Pratt (without number), 26 Dec. 1812, p. 2.

group cohesion for a decisive battle. It appears that such calls were frequently successful.

This being said, we should be careful not to overestimate the impact of such mobilisation attempts. As a strategy, they were an exception and not the rule. They normally represent an answer to existential external threats, threats that endangered the future of whole communities. To the contrary, under 'normal' circumstances individuals such as King Tom could claim to act as 'Temne', 'Mandingo' or 'Bullom', according to the situation and to their partners in the conversation. The prevailing multilingual environment of West African societies greatly facilitated such a flexible approach to group identity.

Africanist research will have to face the task of understanding why ethnic mobilisation as a reaction to extreme situations could become a tool under less outstanding circumstances. During the course of the twentieth century, emphasising ethnic group identity became increasingly a successful strategy in conflicts that did not concern the existence of a community, but resource distribution and relative power. Colonial manipulation must have played a role in this process, but it is challenging to understand up to which point the colonial experience only reshuffled the applicability of different parts of an existing repertoire. It is thus essential to trace the road from warfare in Wonkafong in the late eighteenth and early nineteenth century to the twentieth–century ethnic massacres during civil wars in West Africa and elsewhere on the African continent. Such a project would allow us to better analyse ethnic confrontation as a phenomenon with a sizeable power of destruction. Eventually, it can even furnish us with the means to formulate a strategy, with which political actors could attempt to find, under particular circumstances, the counter-measures to avoid seeing bloody inter-ethnic strife repeated, at least in war-torn Sierra Leone.

Bibliography

Abraham, Arthur, *An Introduction to the Pre-Colonial History of the Mende of Sierra Leone* (Lewiston – Queenston – Lampeter: Edwin Mellen Press, 2003).

Braidwood, Stephen J., *Black Poor and White Philanthropists* (Liverpool: Liverpool University Press, 1994).

Brooks, George E., *Eurafricans in Western Africa: Commerce, Social Status, Gender, and Religious Observance from the Sixteenth to the Eighteenth Century* (Athens/OH: Ohio University Press – London: James Currey, 2003).

Dorjahn, Vernon R., 'The Changing Political System of the Temne', *Africa (London)* 30(2), 1960, pp. 110–140.

Fyfe, Christopher, *A History of Sierra Leone* (London: Oxford University Press, 1962).

Goerg, Odile, 'Chefs de quartier et 'Tribal Headmen'. Deux visions des colonisés en ville', in Jean-Pierre Chrétien and Gérard Prunier (eds.), *Les ethnies ont une histoire* (Paris: 2nd edn Karthala, 2003), pp. 267–282.

Hair, P.E.H., 'Ethnolinguistic Continuity on the Guinea Coast', *Journal of African History* 8(2), 1967, pp. 247–268.

Harvey, M.E., 'Social Change and Ethnic Relocation in Developing Africa: The Sierra Leone Example', *Geografiska Annaler* 53B, 1971, pp. 94–106.

Hirsch, John L., *Sierra Leone: Diamonds and the Struggle for Democracy* (Boulder – London: Lynne Rienner, 2001).

Kandeh, Jimmy D., 'Politicization of Ethnic Identities in Sierra Leone', *African Studies Review* 35(1), 1992, pp. 81–99.

Kandeh, Jimmy D., 'In Search of Legitimacy: The 1996 Elections', in Ibrahim Abdullah (ed.), *Between Democracy and Terror: The Sierra Leone Civil War* (Dakar: CODESRIA, 2004), pp. 123–143.

Keen, David, *Conflict and Collusion in Sierra Leone* (Oxford: James Currey, 2005).

Lovejoy, Paul E. and Richardson, David, '"This Horrid Hole": Royal Authority, Commerce and Credit at Bonny, 1690–1840', *Journal of African History* 45(3), 2004, pp. 363–392.

Mouser, Bruce L., 'Trade, Coasters, and Conflict in the Rio Pongo from 1790 to 1808', *Journal of African History* 14(3), 1973, pp. 45–64.

Mouser, Bruce L., 'Landlords-Strangers: A Process of Accommodation and Assimilation', *International Journal of African Historical Studies* 8(2), 1975, pp. 425–440.

Mouser, Bruce L., 'The 1805 Forékariah Conference: A Case of Political Intrigue, Economic Advantage, Network Building', *History in Africa* 25, 1998, pp. 219–262.

Mouser, Bruce L., 'Rebellion, Marronage and Jihād: Strategies of Resistance to Slavery on the Sierra Leone Coast, c. 1783–1796', *Journal of African History* 48(1), 2007, pp. 27–44.

Richards, Paul, *Fighting for the Rain Forest: War, Youth and Resources in Sierra Leone* (Oxford: International African Institute in association with James Currey – Portsmouth/NH: Heinemann, 1996).

Skinner, David E., 'Mande Settlement and the Development of Islamic Institutions in Sierra Leone', *International Journal of African Historical Studies* 11(1), 1978, pp. 32–62.
Strickrodt, Silke, 'A Neglected Source for the History of Little Popo: The Thomas Miles Papers ca. 1789–1796', *History in Africa* 28, 2001, pp. 293–330.
Wylie, Kenneth C., *The Political Kingdoms of the Temne: Temne Government in Sierra Leone 1825–1910* (New York: Africana Publications, 1977).

Notes on Contributors

FELICITAS BECKER teaches African History with a focus on East Africa at Simon Fraser University, Vancouver. Her monograph *Becoming Muslim in Mainland Tanzania, 1890–2000*, was published in 2008 by Oxford University Press. Felicitas Becker's articles on colonial and post-colonial history and on the political evolution of Muslim communities in East Africa appeared, among others, in *Journal of African History*, *African Affairs* and *Africa: the Journal of the International African Institute*. She is the editor (with Wenzel Geissler) of *AIDS and Religious Practice in Africa* (Leiden: Brill, 2009). Her current research is on oral traditions on slavery in Tanzania and on the perspectives on history by Muslim preachers and their adherents.

JOSÉ CAPELA is the author of several studies and editor of collections of documents on Portuguese colonial history. He has been chief editor of the newspaper *Diário de Moçambique* and the hebdomadary journal *Voz Africana* from 1956 to 1968, has been attaché for cultural affairs at the Portuguese Embassy in Maputo (1978 to 1996), and is now researcher at the Centro de Estudos Africanos da Universidade do Porto.

PHILIP J. HAVIK is currently researcher at the Institute for Tropical Research (IICT) in Lisbon while also teaching at universities in Portugal and Brazil. His multidisciplinary research (political science, economics, anthropology and history) is centred upon the study of state formation, taxation, colonial administration, health services and female entrepreneurship, with a special emphasis on the Guinea Bissau region. His recent publications include 'Tributos e Impostos: a crise mundial, o Estado Novo e a politica fiscal na Guiné', *Economia e Sociologia* 85, 2008, pp. 29–55; Boticas e Beberragens: os serviços de saúde e a colonização da Guiné Portuguesa (séc. XIX/XX), *Africana Studia* 10, 2007, pp. 235–270; *Creole Societies in the Portuguese Colonial Empire* (ed., with Malyn Newitt) (Bristol: University of Bristol, 2007), and *Silences and Soundbytes: the gendered dynamics of trade and brokerage in the precolonial Guinea Bissau region* (Muenster – New Brunswick: LIT – Transaction Publishers, 2004).

ALEXANDER KEESE is Assistant Professor of African History at the Centro de Estudos Africanos of the University of Porto, financed through a Marie Curie Grant of the European Commission. He has published his monograph *Living with Ambiguity: Integrating an African Elite in French and Portuguese Africa* (Stuttgart: Steiner, 2007), and has currently completed a research project on group identity among the Ewe, Temne, and Wolof of West Africa, supported in different phases by the Deutscher Akademischer Auslandsdienst (DAAD) and by the Holcim Foundation, Holderbank, Switzerland.

EDUARDO MEDEIROS worked at Eduardo Mondlane University in Maputo, Mozambique, from 1976 to 1998. Since then, he has been a lecturer in the Departamento de Sociologia of the University of Evora, Portugal, where he also coordinates the Núcleo de Estudos Sobre África (NESA). Author of various books, journal articles, and book chapters on Mozambican History and Anthropology, his current scholarly work focuses on questions relating to ethnic identities and the presence of Chinese in Mozambique between 1885 and 1975.

MALYN NEWITT obtained a BA in Modern History at Oxford in 1961 and his PhD in London in 1967. He taught at the University of Rhodesia from 1962 to 1965, and at the University of Exeter from 1966 to 1998. At Exeter he served as Deputy Vice Chancellor from 1995 to 1998. In 1998 was appointed the first Charles Boxer Professor of History at King's College, London. He retired in 2005. Malyn Newitt is specialised in Portuguese colonial history and, in particular, in the history of Mozambique and of the Indian Ocean. He is the author of *Portuguese Settlement on the Zambesi* (1973), *The Comoro Islands* (1984), Portugal in *Africa: the Last Hundred Years* (1981), *São Tomé and Príncipe* (1988) with Tony Hodges, *History of Mozambique* (1995), *East Africa* (2002) (a collection of Portuguese documents in translation) and *A History of Portuguese Overseas Expansion* (2004).

PAUL NUGENT is Professor of Comparative African History and Director of the Centre of African Studies at the University of Edinburgh. He is the author of three monographs, most recently *Africa Since Independence* (2004), and has co-edited five other volumes. He is currently completing a comparative history of the Ghana-Togo and Senegal-Gambia borderlands, and is researching on the history of the Cape wine industry with funding from the Leverhulme Trust. He is the chair of the steering committee of the European Science Foundation network, which forms part of the African Borderlands Research Network (ABORNE), and is the current President of AEGIS.

CEAUP Studies on Africa

Vol. 1 Alexander Keese (ed.)
Ethnicity and the long-term perspective. The African experience.
ISBN 978-3-0343-0337-8. 2010.

FSC
www.fsc.org
MIX
Papier | Fördert gute Waldnutzung
FSC® C083411

Kolibri 360 GmbH
Ferdinand-Jühlke-Straße 7
99095 Erfurt, Deutschland
produktsicherheit@kolibri360.de